27.50

D1356502

Cambridge Studies in French

A QUESTION OF SYLLABLES
ESSAYS IN NINETEENTH-CENTURY FRENCH VERSE

Cambridge Studies in French

General editor: MALCOLM BOWIE

A QUESTION OF SYLLABLES

ESSAYS IN
NINETEENTH-CENTURY FRENCH VERSE

CLIVE SCOTT

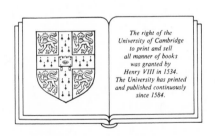

The right of the
University of Cambridge
to print and sell
all manner of books
was granted by
Henry VIII in 1534.
The University has printed
and published continuously
since 1584.

CAMBRIDGE UNIVERSITY PRESS

CAMBRIDGE

LONDON   NEW YORK   NEW ROCHELLE

MELBOURNE   SYDNEY

Published by the Press Syndicate of the University of Cambridge
The Pitt Building, Trumpington Street, Cambridge CB2 IRP
32 East 57th Street, New York NY 10022, USA
10 Stamford Road, Oakleigh, Melbourne 3166, Australia

First published 1986

Printed in Great Britain at
the University Press, Cambridge

British Library cataloguing in publication data
Scott, Clive
A question of syllables: essays in nineteenth-century French verse. –
(Cambridge studies in French)
1. French poetry – 19th century – History and criticism
I. Title
841'.7'09   PQ431

Library of Congress cataloguing in publication data
Scott, Clive, 1943–
A question of syllables.
(Cambridge studies in French)
Bibliography.
Includes index.
1. French poetry – 19th century – History and criticism.
2. French language – Versification.
I. Title.   II. Series.
PQ433.S36   1986   841'.7'09   86-6090
ISBN 0 521 32584 6

CE

CONTENTS

PREFATORY REMARKS

This book is a sequel to *French Verse-Art: A Study* (1980). Encouraged by its reviewers and anxious to pursue some of the issues which I could only treat there in a broad and cursory fashion, I return to that verse which has most preoccupied me, the verse of the nineteenth century. I have not scrupled to revisit the text of *French Verse-Art* and quote from it at some length where appropriate; this is certainly no attempt to confer upon my present opinions some specious authoritativeness, but rather a desire to establish my points of departure, so that the extensions and modifications of my views are more readily apparent. And, as in *French Verse-Art*, I have allowed myself to incorporate considerations of English verse, where comparison seemed enlightening (see particularly Chapters 3 and 5). But it has not been my intention to imply that a familiarity with *French Verse-Art* is in any way a necessary preamble to a reading of *A Question of Syllables*; and to facilitate the self-sufficiency of this set of essays, I provide as an appendix a summary of the chief principles and terminology of French versification, which may be referred to both as guide to my own scansional methods and as a glossary.

But this book has another source; it is partly motivated by a reading of Benoît de Cornulier's *Théorie du vers: Rimbaud, Verlaine, Mallarmé* (1982). Though I find myself frequently in disagreement with Cornulier, and though his text is often forbiddingly technical, he draws attention most rewardingly to two areas of French versification which have been too frequently ignored: the significance of syllabic position and the nature of the difference between metre[1] and rhythm in French verse. From time to time in his book, Cornulier dissociates himself from generative metrists, but syllabic position and the metre/rhythm relationship, in so far as they have been discussed at all, have been central to generative concerns (see, for example, Milner (1974), Lusson and Roubaud (1974)). It is not a generative treatment of these phenomena that I

vii

wish to pursue; I wish to demonstrate to the general reader of French verse how attention to such phenomena may extend our sense of the intricate, intimate life of the line of verse, and of the multitude of expressive pressures it is able to exert on language.

Syllabic position from the point of view from which I approach it, namely as a carrier of meaning through its grammatical, syntactic, rhythmic and intonational associations, is not equally significant in all types of line, but only in those with the strong internal articulation provided by a caesura, which allows them to operate as sensitive sliding scales of value. For this reason, I have limited my discussion of the positive role of syllabic positions to the alexandrine; my examination of the octosyllable, in Chapter 2, does something to reveal why this particular line deprives syllabic position of its power to mean.

One of the reasons why the metre/rhythm relationship in French verse has not perhaps received the attention due to it is its relative hiddenness. Whereas in English syllable-stress verse, rhythm is usually assumed to be the rhythm of 'normal' speech *set against* the abstract metrical pattern, in French verse rhythm is, as it were, contained *within* the metrical frame. Whereas in English syllable-stress verse, metre itself entails rhythmic presuppositions (patterns of stress and non-stress) of a thoroughgoing kind, French metrical descriptions define only syllabicity and accents at the principal prosodic boundaries (line-ending, caesura) and make no suppositions about rhythmic segmentation within the line (or hemistich). Thus, for example, the regular alexandrine can be described metrically as:

$$- - - - - \acute{-} \, || \, - - - - - \acute{-}$$

i.e. as a twelve-syllable line, with a caesura after the sixth syllable and accents at the sixth and twelfth syllables; the secondary accents (usually two in number, one within each hemistich) are not metrically determined, but rather are part of the individual line's rhythmic structure. The caesura in the alexandrine has both a metrical existence and a metrically determined position; in the decasyllable, on the other hand, the caesura may have a metrical existence, but its position is rhythmically determined – it may occur after the fourth, fifth or sixth syllable; if its position is to achieve any metrical form at all, it will be because the consistency of its position in a certain poem confers a conventional force upon it; otherwise its position will be defined by the rhythmic demands peculiar to each individual line. The authority of conventions and their bearing on metricity is itself a problematic issue. Can one argue that certain rhythmic configurations, by virtue of the frequency of their occurrence, achieve metrical status? Is it justified, for example, to claim that the *alexandrin tétramètre* (four-accent alexandrine) is a metrical norm? Obviously not, if agreeing involves branding three-accent or two-accent alexandrines as non-metrical. But if we underline 'norm' and treat three-accent and two-accent patterns simply as rarities (rather than as deviations) and if we do not lose from sight that a convention alone has created a metrical condition, then we can call the claim justified. Equally, in saying that the measures within a line or hemistich are properly rhythmical matters, we should remember that one measure necessarily predicts another inasmuch as the overall number of syllables in the line or hemistich is a known quantity, a goal of numerical combination. In Cornulier's (1982) view, any metric which engages with measures, with syntactic segmentation, inevitably means that prose does not exist, because it is verse, being equally segmentable (pp. 69–76). But quite apart from the fact that verse's condition as verse is indicated by other markers (principally lineation, but also, in regular verse, rhyme, and the pauses which accompany them), the nature of its measures and their possible combinations are controlled, where prose's are not. In fact, the metricity of French regular verse is perhaps best regarded as a metricity of combination, of permutation and equation within a fixed syllabic frame, and not as a metricity of aggregation (the serial addition of given units) as English syllable-stress metre is. It should be added, of course, that other English metres, pure-stress and syllabic, where number (whether of stresses or syllables) is metrically stipulated while measures are not, are closer to French kinds of metricity. It should also be added that concerns about the relative strength of accents and pauses, about speed and other paralinguistic features such as tone and emotional colouring, are obviously rhythm-related rather than metre-related, in both languages.

The essays which follow address themselves both to questions of syllabic position and to the relationship between rhythmicity and metricity. It was not intended that they should pursue a single consecutive argument or a homogeneous method; they are essentially separate essays loosely linked by common concerns. Chapter 1 investigates the pertinence of syllabic position to thematic studies; Chapter 2 asks whether syllabic position is of any significance in a line in which rhythmicity all but overwhelms metricity, the octosyllable; Chapter 3 explores the relationship between syllabic position and the way in which a figure of speech, simile, projects itself; Chapter 4 examines some of the workings of a syllable peculiarly privileged in French verse, the articulated e; Chapter 5 approaches issues of rhythmicity and metricity through 'difficult' poems which seem to locate rhythm beyond the text; and Chapter 6 addresses itself to the relationship between metricity and rhythmicity in free verse. The Conclusion reflects briefly on the notions of choice and authority in verse. All the chapters focus their enquiries on particular poems or collections of poems. While I hope that new light will be shed on the works in question, I have not undertaken systematic interpretations; rather it has been my purpose to offer methods of analysis which might be fruitfully applied to other material.

Many readers may be dissatisfied with my scansional methods. The plurality of scansions makes Cornulier (1982) despair – he counts about twenty possible readings of Racine's line 'Maître de mon destin, libre de mes soupirs' (pp. 121-4) – as does their apparent arbitrariness (pp. 124-6). But it would be disturbing if it were otherwise. We think about verse in the ways that our location in critical history and our mentalities as readers allow us to. Scansions are attempts to codify the givens of verse-construction, where those givens will themselves vary in relative importance with the passage of time and with the particular sensibility which undertakes their description. But while any scansional method should beware of trespassing on the freedom of each reader to realise any text (in recitation, etc.) as seems most fitting to him/her, and should thus content itself with a judiciously minimalist account, it should also be prepared to inspect its own implications; any scansion, after all, is susceptible of sophistication, especially in the methods and minutiae of its application to particular verse-instances. In the pages which follow, I have tried to refine the applications of traditional scansion, by exploring some of the functions of syllabic position and some of the interactions between metricity and rhythmicity. Every scansion is as much an act of interpretation as it is of description, covertly perhaps, but inescapably so; and the more comprehensive its ambitions, the more interpretative will be its nature. I must emphasise, therefore, that my own studies mark the point at which scansion crosses over into reading, with all its besetting subjectivities. What I offer is not so much the diversification of a scansion, that is, of a reliable source of knowledge about the mechanisms of verse, as the extension of scansion into the highly relativised responses of personal reading.

Many will doubtless find those responses uncongenial or questionable, but the plausibility of my responses is not quite so important as the plausibility of my approaches; if I have been able to demonstrate satisfactorily how fruitful the pursuit of certain scansional observations might be to an understanding of the reading experience, then I am content. And although I am, in one sense, trying to sophisticate scansional analysis, in another I am trying to convince the student and general reader that there is nothing arcane about scansion, that its insights are available to all.

Verse-analysis, over the last decades, has increasingly favoured a view of the poem as a spatial, synchronic structure whose parts are imagined as interacting simultaneously; this view proposes the poem as something readable or having been read, rather than as something being read. It has thus tended to gloss over the temporal dimension of reading, of finding one's way through a *sequence* of verbal signs, organised in a generically specific way, which act as a complex itinerary of stimulations, provocations, disorientations, tone-givers, mood-generators and much else besides. This view also implies that the attention one brings to the verbal surface is somehow uniformly spread, that all linguistic elements exist, as it were, with the same relief, with the same potential strength of impact; but verse, as much as any other discourse, is an intricate exercise in priority-giving, an intricate organisation of foregrounds and backgrounds and variations in modal colouring. It is the quick of the reading experience, that series of adjustments of perspective and ever-changing impulses, which this collection of essays seeks to reinstate.

And these essays *are* essays, in the strict sense of the term. They are try-outs of various scansional analyses, designed to be neither comprehensive nor conclusive, whose purpose is simply to prove their usefulness. They conduct themselves in an unashamedly digressive manner, trying to encompass ramifications, repercussions and more general reflections in their frequent detours, and thus to follow the meandering wilfulness of my own reactions. Sometimes my treatment is predominantly expatiatory and discursive (e.g. Chapter 2), sometimes more rigorous and clinical (e.g. Chapter 3), sometimes a blend of the two; I have not combated these variations in focus and pace, partly because the changing materials and issues seemed to compel them upon me, and partly because I felt that the reader would welcome respites from uniformity.

I am afraid that I have not always managed to avoid the

temptations of jargon, or at least of jargon's lexicon. I have not resisted coining substantival, adjectival and verbal forms, usually with a Gallic flavour – e.g. paratacticalise, desyntactify, similaic, hemistichiality, metricity, implicitate – which dictionaries do not acknowledge. But I trust that the meanings of these words are clear and would offer the following defence of my practice: these coinages allow processes and qualities to inhere in, to thoroughly inhabit, those words of which they are the agents or sites; to say, for example, 'make/render implicit' instead of 'implicitate', or 'quality as hemistich' instead of 'hemistichiality', is to make 'implicit' and 'hemistich' the servants of definition at their expense as moving forces. I might also be charged, at certain points in the text, with undue verbosity. Frequently, and particularly where intuition is the greater part of response, I have had to reach for a fitting formulation through a series of near-synonyms, or qualifications, or approximations. I hope that, far from weighing the text down, these instances of wordiness will provide the reader with more means of access to my examples.

Verse is a complex, unfolding structure of specific locations. Each prosodic location is charged with various kinds of motive and prejudice and tendentiousness, which interact with locations in the syntactic chain; each prosodic location releases particular semantic energies in particular words. In this sense, prosodic elements are semantic determinants, investing words with a certain aura of semantic activity. Indeed, some prosodic features – the *e atone*, verse-punctuation, for example – themselves constitute semantemes. While all this is evident, it is not easy to demonstrate, and insofar as I have succeeded, I am indebted to the sympathetic criticism and helpful suggestions of those close to me. I am grateful, too, to Michael Black for his steadying advice and encouragement, and to Dominique Hanley, who gave my *pattes de mouche* the surefootedness of a disciplined character with such skill and promptness.

I

THEME AND SYLLABIC POSITION

LAMARTINE'S *MÉDITATIONS POÉTIQUES*

Most thematic treatments of Lamartine's verse[1] have found beneath the intricate tissue of commonplace and allusion a real enough existential drama. But while thematic treatments uncover for us the concealed organisation of a poetic mentality, pick out those lexical items which have a peculiar loadedness in a poet's work and explore their relationships, they do not usually concern themselves with the more intimate lives of these items, the variations of emotional colouring, modality and projection which they undergo within a poetic corpus, thanks to their changing location in verse-structure. In this chapter, I would like to isolate a set of lexical items from a given Lamartinian corpus by undertaking my own brief thematic analysis, an analysis indebted to those works listed in the first note to this chapter, and select from this set of lexical items a small body of words upon which to practise a more thorough, prosodic analysis. From this analysis, which will concentrate on the syllabic position of words in the line, on their syllabic proportions, on the measures and combinations of measure they create, I wish to try and construct the range of activity of these words, the diversity of their moods, the tones that inform them. At the same time I wish to discover, through the study of these words, something more about the energies and the conditioning capacities inherent in the line of verse, and in particular, in the alexandrine. My corpus is the twenty-four poems[2] which constituted the first edition of the *Méditations poétiques*, published in March 1820. Although several of these poems are entirely in octosyllables or have octosyllabic passages or lines, my prosodic analysis will address itself to the alexandrines; the octosyllables will receive some attention in the second chapter.

What is the nature of Lamartine's existential struggle? It is primarily, I suppose, a struggle with time, with time's passage. It is easy to assimilate this to the great poetic commonplaces of man's mortality, the fleetingness of beauty, happiness and so on. But this

I

is to mask something unique about Lamartine. Lamartine is subject to time's cruelty *in the very fabric of his verse*: he experiences the passage of time directly, in the fluency of his own utterance, which carries him unrelentingly through and away from his experiences and memories. And this hand-to-hand struggle with time comes into its sharpest focus as a clash between 'encore' – the still there – and 'déjà' – the already gone:

> Au sommet de ces monts couronnés de bois sombres,
> Le crépuscule encor jette un dernier rayon;
> Et le char vaporeux de la reine des ombres
> Monte et blanchit déjà les bords de l'horizon. ('L'Isolement')

Lamartine's poetry is an attempt to prolong this slightest of moments between the still there and the already gone. But the suavity of his writing is his own worst enemy. And it would perhaps not be too fanciful to see the short last line of the stanza used, for example, in 'La Gloire' or 'Le Lac' as a form of exquisite self-torture:

> Eternité, néant, passé, sombres abîmes,
> Que faites-vous des jours que vous engloutissez?
> Parlez: nous rendrez-vous ces extases sublimes
> Que vous nous ravissez? ('Le Lac')

The abrupt finality of this last line is like time accelerated or abbreviated, like an exasperated reaching for an end that spells irrevocability. Ultimately the poet gives up trying to postpone the awful moment when all will be gone and, suicidally almost, accedes to time's consummation.[3]

Another factor which makes Lamartine's world peculiarly elusive, slipping through the poet's fingers, dissolving, is the lack of resistance in his landscapes. If we look at the opening of 'L'Isolement', we find the characteristic situation:

> Souvent sur la montagne, à l'ombre du vieux chêne,
> Au coucher du soleil, tristement je m'assieds;
> Je promène au hasard mes regards sur la plaine,
> Dont le tableau changeant se déroule à mes pieds.

Not only is the world itself in a state of constant change, but the poet looks at it in a gliding, glancing, drifting way. The passive randomness of his gaze echoes the passivity of his stance, seated as he is beneath a tree. 'Le Soir' opens in a similar fashion:

> Le soir ramène le silence.
> Assis sur ces rochers déserts,

Lamartine's Méditations poétiques

> Je suis dans le vague des airs
> Le char de la nuit qui s'avance.

The objects in Lamartine's world are not obstacles, do not detain the eye. They are, rather, transparent, or dissolved and rendered uniform by surrounding atmospheres, mists, twilight.

The instant, the precious moment between 'encore' and 'déjà' cannot, it seems, be arrested. But it is certainly not for want of trying. The poet's chief resources in this desperate attempt are rhetorical. By means of apostrophe, invocation, rhetorical question, he seeks to distract the elements of his environment from their single-minded preoccupation with moving on or moving away; he tries to engage them in his predicament, to create pauses in process, to find respite in the very request for answers, reasons, probabilities. These rhetorical devices usually have the ironic effect of further isolating the poet, leaving him to supply answers he has no access to, making his *recueillement* a *recueillement* of time-wasting speculation. But the poet frequently resorts to much more direct and unashamed methods, to the kind of plea that we find in 'Le Vallon':

> Prêtez-moi seulement, vallons de mon enfance,
> Un asile d'un jour pour attendre la mort.

What is noticeable about the plea is its eminent reasonableness; he wants the respite of only a day, where 'jour' is not to be understood strictly as twenty-four hours, but as a very limited period of time nonetheless. This is perhaps no more than a ploy to intensify the pathos of the situation and helps, of course, to emphasise time's intransigence. But the poet always makes apparently modest pleas like this – we have only to remind ourselves of the final line of the first stanza of 'Le Lac': 'Jeter l'ancre un seul jour'. 'Just one more moment, please' and after that 'Just one more moment, please'; Lamartine is the poet of patient prevarication.

But it is also true that no moment has any value for Lamartine unless it is, precisely, the last moment. The last moment is, of course, always the richest, because it is only when things threaten to leave us that we know how to treasure them, and this treasuring is imbued with the poignancy of its inevitably being too late. The last moment is the moment of the availability of all memories and the moment when the pressures of aspiration beyond the moment and beyond time are at their greatest. In 'L'Homme', the poet looks back to Elvire's passing away – and the notion of passage is certainly more suitable than that of death:

Je voulais retenir l'âme qui s'évapore,
Dans son dernier regard je la cherchais encore!
Ce soupir, ô mon Dieu! dans ton sein s'exhala;
Hors du monde avec lui mon espoir s'envola!

In true Lamartinian style, he has each day begged 'Soleil! encore un jour!', but to no avail. Elvire passes away, the last moment is lost and the world is of no more interest to the poet. Lamartine is a connoisseur in both the anticipation and enjoyment of last rites.

Some moments really are the final ones. But Lamartine also takes pleasure in savouring last moments which do not have the seal of finality, because they are part of the natural cycle, as in 'L'Automne':

J'aime à revoir encor, pour la dernière fois,
Ce soleil pâlissant, dont la faible lumière
Perce à peine à mes pieds l'obscurité des bois!

This is an enjoyment of the peculiar piquancy of last moments under false pretences, a vicarious last-moment experience. Lamartine cannot escape the paradoxical truth that things only really begin to exist when they are on the point of ceasing to exist; he has to push things to the very brink of their extinction before he can enter into a rich sensory relationship with them.

Lamartine clings to the light, but it fades from him; he tries to encompass the landscape, but his eye slips over it in such a way that the horizon seems to recede from him, to draw him away, annihilating objects as it goes; he follows without resistance towards a world that has a monotonous neutrality. This is a dismal picture, but one which has its brighter side. Built into Lamartine's understanding that he cannot arrest the world around him, cannot prevent the loved one and a topography slipping away from him, is a concomitant and conflicting understanding that this very process of effacement is the means by which access may be gained to the higher world. Lamartine is a transcendentalist; his desire is to rise above his surroundings, not to lose himself in them, however consoling nature manages to be for him.

With the instant gone, the last moment irrevocably taken from him, Lamartine must seek to preserve its vestige, its trace, its memory. How is he to do this? Simply by *recueillement*, by an ingathering of his intellectual and emotional impulses, by a quiet collection of his spiritual longing, by a special intimacy. As he puts it in 'Le Vallon':

Mon cœur est en repos, mon âme est en silence!
Le bruit lointain du monde expire en arrivant,
Comme un son éloigné qu'affaiblit la distance,
A l'oreille incertaine apporté par le vent.

D'ici je vois la vie, à travers un nuage,
S'évanouir pour moi dans l'ombre du passé;
L'amour seul est resté: comme une grande image
Survit seule au réveil dans un songe effacé.

The lure of surrounding space inviting the poet to try and make
sense of himself in relation to its diversity, is shown to be, precisely,
a *lure*, a dangerous seduction. The erasure of reality is not now seen
as a loss, but as a necessary process of spiritualisation and disembodiment. Lamartine has forsaken the commanding view which
led to such inner distress in 'L'Isolement', and taken up his position
in a valley, a locality that denies external space in favour of the
development of an inner space, a place of refuge, a womb at the
heart of the created world which promises a new kind of birth
(compare with the valley of 'Adieu' and the subterranean chapel of
'La Semaine Sainte'). Liberated from the interference of sense-
data, Lamartine can concentrate all his being on forcing a passage
into the super-terrestrial realm.

Hitherto Lamartine has used language to do battle against the
flowing, elusive world only to find that language itself is fluid, runs
away, confirms that which it sets out to gainsay. He has used
language to try to revive the past, to voice his sense of abandonment, only to find that language is not strong enough to
resurrect, is only a self-indulgent release of frustrations. But in the
valley, in his new realisation of redemption, isolation is beneficent
and language is no longer necessary. As the twilight creeps on, as
sounds die down and sights become obscured, with the elimination
of all distraction, Lamartine can cast off the exasperations that
language encourages, and communicate in a soundless spiritual
fashion, in prayerfulness, in fact. This is how he puts it in the last
stanza of 'Le Vallon':

Dieu, pour le concevoir, a fait l'intelligence:
Sous la nature enfin découvre son auteur!
Une voix à l'esprit parle dans son silence,
Qui n'a pas entendu cette voix dans son cœur?

and in 'La Prière':

Tout se tait: mon cœur seul parle dans ce silence.
La voix de l'univers, c'est mon intelligence.

Prayer is wordless communication with God. God was in Elvire, as Elvire is in God. In God are the poet's past, present and future, and in communicating with God the poet communicates with his own totality, he discovers his identity and essential continuity (see also 'Dieu').

How does this state of communication with the transcendental world manifest itself? It manifests itself in the 'rayon', the shaft of light which breaks through the clouds and acts as a corridor of release. Addressing the deceased Elvire in 'Le Soir', the poet describes the visitation of an Elvire-bearing light:

> Tout à coup, détaché des cieux,
> Un rayon de l'astre nocturne,
> Glissant sur mon front taciturne,
> Vient mollement toucher mes yeux.
>
> Doux reflet d'un globe de flamme,
> Charmant rayon, que me veux-tu?
> Viens-tu dans mon sein abattu
> Porter la lumière à mon âme?

It is perhaps worth noticing the gentle sensuality of this contact, expressed in 'mollement'; we shall have cause to return to this. It is worth noticing, too, not only that the poet is again absolutely silent – 'sur mon front taciturne' – but also that 'glisser' here has a positive charge: it does not describe that quicksilver quality of time, that awful, because imperceptible, leaking away of life into an anonymous void, which we find expressed at the beginning of 'Souvenir':

> En vain le jour succède au jour,
> Ils glissent sans laisser de trace

On the contrary, it is like a gesture of blessing, a soothing therapeutic caress of light, the holier, the more healing, for its being slight and insubstantial. This connection between the verb 'glisser' and the 'rayon' is to be found again in the penultimate stanza of 'Le Vallon':

> Avec le doux rayon de l'astre du mystère
> Glisse à travers les bois dans l'ombre du vallon.

As we have intimated, the movement through the 'rayon' is not exclusively a downward movement; the 'rayon' is something like a pneumatic chute for the poet, along which his yearning soul can thrust itself ('s'élancer', 's'élever', 's'envoler' are the characteristic verbs of this movement). The dawn, the rising sun offer the poet explicitly upward-thrusting rays:

> Que ne puis-je, porté sur le char de l'aurore,
> Vague objet de mes vœux, m'élancer jusqu'à toi!

('L'Isolement')

The word 'rayon' suggests a single, bright, focussed ray of light, cutting like a knife through the intervening space and alighting like a spotlight on the souls of the elect. One only has to change the noun 'rayon' to the verb 'rayonner' to multiply the rays and provide a more diffused kind of light: we find in 'Souvenir' for instance:

> Tes yeux, où s'éteignait la vie,
> Rayonnent d'immortalité!

The verbs which most typically describe this diffused light are 'inonder' and 'répandre'. The former appears, for example, in 'L'Immortalité', a poem once again addressed to Elvire:

> Tu viens d'un jour plus pur inonder ma paupière

and the latter in 'La Prière':

> Pour moi, c'est ton regard qui, du divin séjour,
> S'entr'ouvre sur le monde et lui répand le jour

In both cases the verb is not accompanied by 'rayon' at all, but by the generalised 'jour'. But it would be wrong to dissociate this more widespread light from the sharp light of 'rayon', for two reasons. First, because Lamartine does, in some images, attempt to reconcile the two, to use the 'rayon' idea to give light a direction, an urgency, an intensity, and to combine this with the process of diffusion, to convey the universal beneficence of an Elvire who has become something more than the poet's personal possession; thus the 'rayon' is endowed with a gentleness, a power of tender encompassment which generates a feeling of the warm solicitude of the divine, rather than of its authoritarian summariness. The unambiguous ray of light must somehow be allowed to invest the whole of existence. One of the examples of this effort towards combination concerns not a visual perception of light, but a visual perception which shades into an aural one; it is the image of the church in the fourth stanza of 'L'Isolement':

> Cependant, s'élançant de la flèche gothique
> Un son religieux se répand dans les airs

Here the spire stands in, as it were, for the upward ray of light, but the sharp thrust of the building disperses in a vague haze of sound;

the verticality of the spire is countered by the horizontality of the spreading religious note. In fact, there is a sense in which the image is quite literally a contradiction: how can 's'élancer' really be applied to a sound as diffuse as this? The image we are left with is as of a fountain, the jet of water breaking at its zenith and scattering in a fine mist of drops.

And this leads to our second reason for not dissociating diffused light from the concentrated light of the ray. What we find in the example from 'L'Isolement' is the association of two different sense-impressions, one visual, one aural, one specific, one generalised. The invasion of the poet's being by a vague, self-insinuating but balm-giving force involves other senses too, smell and touch, because Lamartine uses perfumes and light winds to fulfil the same function as diffused light. Here again are sensations which, at one and the same time, have a high degree of insubstantiality and a certain voluptuous charge. We find perfume and breeze fused in a single complex in a stanza added to 'Souvenir' in the second edition:

> Et si le souffle du zéphyre
> M'enivre du parfum des fleurs,
> Dans ses plus suaves odeurs
> C'est ton souffle que je respire.

Here is a much more pantheistic picture of Elvire's benign influence, coming from the immediate environment, which does much to restore the intimate and terrestrial side of the relationship, so necessary to the efficacy of the transcendental projection of it. And it does seem that the energy of Lamartine's spiritual longing depends on the impetus of a sensual experience, however masked this may be. We learn next to nothing about Elvire's physical appearance, it is true – apart from Ossianic commonplaces like her 'tresses d'ébène' – but the poetry exudes a kind of light-headed and pleasurable intoxication, conveyed in great part, perhaps, by the caressing melodiousness of the verse itself. Fine spiritual ecstasies often turn out to have solid physical sources, and Lamartine's are no exception; one of the stanzas excised from 'Le Lac' makes this abundantly clear:

> Nous ne pûmes parler: nos âmes affaiblies
> Succombaient sous le poids de leur félicité;
> Nos cœurs battaient ensemble, et nos bouches unies
> Disaient: Eternité.

The final word of this stanza, 'Eternité' looks like a last-ditch justification for, and rendering respectable of, an embrace so pleasurable as to need no moral support.

At all events, the benign light wind, the 'zéphyr', as opposed to the harsher 'aquilon', is like an exhalation, carrying the last breath, the perfume, of the dying beauty, rose or woman. The wind is also that part of the natural scene that can exist without the landscape, that profits by Lamartinian evanescence. Lamartine is no stranger to synaesthetic experience; we may have suspected this in the church spire example, we see it at the end of 'L'Automne', where while the flower expires in perfume, the poet expires in sound, the swan-song of his own verse. But more pertinently to our purpose, we might quote lines from 'La Prière':

> Sur les rayons du soir, sur les ailes du vent,
> Elle s'élève à Dieu comme un parfum vivant.

The 'elle' referred to here is the voice of the universe, the poet's 'intelligence'. Again we feel not only the will to fuse together different types of sensory perception, to create a spirituality which is connected with a total sentience, a total availability to the bodiless communications of a higher principle both beyond and within the natural world; we feel also the will to reconcile the 'rayon', now in a more amenable plural form, with more dispersive agents of communication.

There is one final form of contact between the terrestrial and transcendental worlds, which I would briefly mention, and that is reflection. This world reflects the other world. This is again an extremely vague and diffuse kind of contact, but unlike breeze and perfume it is utterly passive: it simply exists or does not exist, depending on symbolic atmospheric conditions. The advantage of the reflection system is obvious: reflections can multiply themselves, create a chorus of reflections, create a form of involvement, out of their very passivity, an involvement in which all contributors are put on an equal footing and thus more meaningfully conjoined; as Lamartine puts it in 'La Prière':

> L'univers tout entier réfléchit ton image,
> Et mon âme à son tour réfléchit l'univers.

where 'tu' is God.

The idea of reflection naturally suggests images of water, because it is the stretches of water which are the real mirrors of nature. Of course Lamartine's primary concern is whether the water is clear and smooth-surfaced or not, whether it is a good reflector or not, and this question naturally attaches to the concomitant emotional or temperamental condition of the poet. In 'Le Vallon', for instance, the poet has come in search of inner peace, to reconcile himself to his life of disappointment, to set his love in its right, celestial perspective. In the opening description of the valley, his eye alights on two streams:

> Là, deux ruisseaux cachés sous des ponts de verdure,
> Tracent en serpentant les contours du vallon;
> Ils mêlent un moment leur onde et leur murmure,
> Et non loin de leur source ils se perdent sans nom.

These lines would seem to allude to the poet's relationship with Elvire, its hiddenness, its gentle sensuality ('serpentant'), the moment of fulfilment and the subsequent return to oblivion. In the following stanza, the poet makes these streams explicitly significant to his own situation, but in another direction:

> Mais leur onde est limpide, et mon âme troublée
> N'aura pas réfléchi les clartés d'un beau jour.

The poet presents his doubts about his ultimate redemption as a fear that his soul, rendered turgid, no doubt by his hesitation and diffidence, will never have the ability to reflect the divine light. This contrast of limpidity or turgidity is to be found again, and perhaps more interestingly, in the second stanza of 'L'Isolement':

> Ici gronde le fleuve aux vagues écumantes,
> Il serpente, et s'enfonce en un lointain obscur;
> Là, le lac immobile étend ses eaux dormantes
> Où l'étoile du soir se lève dans l'azur.

Here the contrast is what one would expect: the flowing river is a destiny that cannot be guessed at, the troubled water of passing time, while the lake is the still, but not stagnant, surface, the achieved spiritual plateau and site of regeneration by reflection. Here, dramatically juxtaposed, are the two worlds of which we have been speaking all along, but we can begin to see how the one is a necessary condition or complement of the other. The lake is a kind of abstraction of the river, the river, like the disappearing landscape, a necessary preamble to spiritual quietude and self-realisation. Strangely perhaps the serpentine movement is here connected with the troubled water rather than the limpid. But we should recognise the essential ambiguity of much of Lamartine's

lexicon, or rather his own ambiguity and temperamental change-
ability. 'Serpenter' may in one context indicate elusiveness, even
deviousness, in another sensuality or integration, depending upon
what principle of the poet's existence it is applied to.

One of the other factors to which these last quotations draw
attention is the acoustic property of water. This is perhaps the more
necessary, since many Lamartinian events take place in the fading
light when water surfaces are difficult to make out. 'Le Lac' is
remarkable for its absence of visual impressions. The concord of
the lovers is answered by the regular, rhythmic striking of the oars,
and the sweet tones of Elvire's voice are answered by the echoes of
the spell-bound shore. Echoes like these might be considered as the
acoustic equivalent of reflections (see also 'Le Golfe de Baya').

These quotations point up the connection between the water and
the light. The still water not only reflects the diffused brightness of
the day, but also, by implication, the sharper, focussed image of the
moon. The water is also connected with light in a verb we have
already encountered in a line from 'L'Immortalité', namely
'inonder'. But most important of all, by way of rounding off this
brief thematic exploration, the ray of light itself, the nocturnal ray,
is equally a reflection, as a stanza from 'Le Soir', already quoted,
affirms: the rays of the moon are reflections of the sun:

> Doux reflet d'un globe de flamme,
> Charmant rayon, que me veux-tu?
> Viens-tu dans mon sein abattu
> Porter la lumière à mon âme?

This thematic outline is certainly far from comprehensive. There
is much, particularly relating to Lamartine's mystical experiences
and to the processes of memory, which is lacking. There are large
tracts of Lamartine's lexicon which are overlooked – one might, for
example, with equal profit study the lives of 'déserts', 'concerts',
'séjour', 'regard'; and the words/themes which have been selected
are by no means treated exhaustively. But we have sufficient
evidence to make some general observations about Lamartine's
lexicon, and sufficient material for a prosodic project.

Lamartine may have taken over a diction all but exhausted by the
eighteenth century; his poetry may have acquired the reputation of
being almost exclusively intertextual, with its sources in the Bible,
Milton, Ossian, Rousseau, Parny, Gray and Chateaubriand among
others. But in many instances, Lamartine may be as much quoting
himself as drawing on others, and besides, read as we have read it,

his verse gives no hint of its genealogy: refreshed by its immersion in an existential condition, his vocabulary acts as a gravitational centre for a multiplicity of private impulses; this vocabulary is as limited as it is apparently conventional, but its limitedness has the same kind of virtues as the limited vocabulary of Racine's theatre: that is to say an unflagging pertinence and an ability to encompass and highlight the changing and contradictory impulses of the speaker – hence the multiple value of so many of the words. Although critics may point to the heterogeneity of these twenty-four *Méditations*,[4] both in tone and form, they are all essentially about the same thing, but with so much variation in mood, emphasis and formal context, that there is no repetition, only an engrossing exploration.

Lamartine's landscapes do not belong to a specific time and specific place; they are accumulated landscapes, the products of superimposed images of the same thing ('Souvent sur la montagne . . .'), of superimposed images of different places, of superimposed literary topographies, all sifted through the colorations of interiority;[5] literarisation is indeed a cause or symptom of the general dematerialising tendency in Lamartine's work. All this produces a certain destabilisation of language. In Lamartine's poetry two worlds – a world of contingent existence, an uninhabited, purely natural, unregenerate world on the one hand, and, on the other, a world informed and visited by divinity, a world which may equally encompass the natural world – are served by the same vocabulary; as a result, the same word in different contexts may oscillate between opposing poles of value. Moreover, any word may flicker uncertainly between the literal and the figurative, for if God may inhabit anything at any time, then any object may at any time cease to be object and become a particular manifestation of His power, or solicitude, or mere presence. The evanescence of the landscape, encoding the passage of time, is a direct challenge to persistence and memory, a constant urge towards oblivion, a threat to all relationship, all sense of identity and purpose. At the same time, that same evanescence may be an exciting prelude to the fruitful hiatus between evening and morning, when the individual enters a purely spiritual space and establishes contact with a higher order of being; in these circumstances, evanescence becomes itself a form of concentration of the self in the self. Correspondingly, as we have seen, a verb like 'glisser' can belong to either world and derive from each a different emotional charge. Similarly, 's'envoler', which in relation to the spiritual world expresses release from mortality and flight to the stars, can, when used of the contingent world, just as well express a centrifugal movement of dispersal. 'Aurore' can refer either to the dawn that comes too soon and disturbs the quiet rapture of the poet communing with the night sky or indeed with the living Elvire ('Le Lac'), or, alternatively, to a mystic dawn, a dawn of birth to eternal life, a dawn of reunion with the deceased Elvire ('Souvenir', 'Le Soir'). It is with this sense of the mobility of Lamartine's language in mind, that we should approach the operations of his lexicon in verse-structure.

As a preface to observations about the way certain words operate in the Lamartinian line, I would like to reflect briefly on the general shape of the alexandrine, the line with which we shall be concerned, and more especially on the 'accent circonflexe' of its intonational outline:

$$\overline{}\Big\|\overline{}$$

The voice reaches a pitch-peak at the caesura and then gently descends as it moves towards the line-ending. This rough intonational shape is a function of the syntactical and rhythmic autonomy of the individual line, an autonomy which is, I hasten to add, relative; if accent in French is terminal and coincides with the terminus of a grammatical or syntactical group, then the accent at the end of the line will signal the closure of such a group, where that closure will be *more or less* syntactically significant.

This circumflex shape is, of course, by no means invariably present. It can be disturbed by end-of-line interrogation ($\diagup\!-\|\diagup$), by end-of-line enjambement ($\diagup\|\lor$), by enjambement at the caesura ($\diagup\|\diagdown$), by fragmented syntax within the line (e.g. $\diagup\diagup\|\diagup\diagdown$) or by the demands made by words themselves, as their meanings resist the circumflex's attempt to impose itself:

> Et prenant vers le jour || un *lumineux essor*
> ('L'Homme') ($\diagup\|\diagup\diagup$) (italics mine)

But it is sufficiently characteristic to provide a useful working base, particularly in Lamartine's verse, where the dominant tone is usually elegiac and where the forward flow is usually uninterruptedly smooth. Circumflexity suggests of itself certain movements of the spirit and emotions: the first hemistich is a movement of impulsion, aspiration, energy which subsides in the second hemistich; thus enthusiasm may be followed by discouragement, aspiration by a sense of futility, momentary happiness by a return to resignation or despondency. Equally, the growing pressure of an anger or an exasperation may yield to consolation or a restored equanimity. The possibilities are too manifold to enumerate. But it should be made clear that the circumflex may just as easily describe a *physical* movement:

> Une clarté d'en haut || dans mon sein descendit
>
> ('L'Homme')

though again we should qualify this assertion by remarking that movements of spirit may outweigh physical movements, or, in other words, that a downward physical movement may well signify an upward spiritual one:

> Un rayon descendra || dans l'ombre de ton âme?
>
> ('L'Homme')

(Here the interrogative construction also helps to sustain the pitch-level, supplying a new peak at the line-end.) We might also suggest that the circumflex shape is peculiarly adapted to a process we have already singled out from the *Méditations*, that of a focussed upward thrust ('s'élancer', 's'élever') which resolves itself into a horizontal and falling movement of diffusion and dispersal ('se répandre', 'inonder'):

> Cependant, s'élançant || de la flèche gothique,
> Un son religieux || se répand dans les airs   ('L'Isolement')

This particular configuration may be more generally expressed as a single-mindedness, a purposefulness, which broadcasts itself in a soothing, subdued emanation. But, in relation to Lamartine's verse, does this mean that 's'élancer' and 's'élever' will always appear in the first hemistich while 'se répandre' and 'inonder' occupy the second? This we will shortly discover. At all events, our quotations give some indication of how manifold the shape and significance of pitch outlines may be and how complex their determinants.

Although the circumflex pattern is not ubiquitous, it is a pattern of real pertinence to the Lamartinian alexandrine, e.g.:

> Lui seul est mon flambeau dans cette nuit profonde   ('Dieu')

> Peut-être de ce feu tu n'es qu'une étincelle   ('La Foi')

> Regarde! je viens seul m'asseoir sur cette pierre   ('Le Lac')

> Ici viennent mourir les derniers bruits du monde
>
> ('La Semaine Sainte')

and, even when not applicable, it does provide a structural norm against which to measure variations. I wish to concentrate my attention, to begin with, on some of the verbs that have figured in the thematic analysis and in the preceding discussion, namely 's'élancer', 's'élever', on the one hand, and 'se répandre' and 'inonder' on the other. In considering the way in which verbs operate in the verse line, we must bear in mind (a) what part of the verb they are, (b) their syllabic position, and (c) factors, syntactic and rhythmic, which may have played a part in determining that position, where (a) may also be a position-determining factor.

In the lines already quoted from 'L'Isolement' (see back, p. 14), the present participle of 's'élancer' finds itself at the caesura. This is perhaps the classic position for any non-adjectival present participle, whose durative nature is reinforced by its suspension at a major verse-juncture; in this example, the duration is further extended by the pre-echoes of the nasal vowels (ã) of 's'élançant' in 'cependant', and it is noticeable how the transition from upward thrust to diffusion is facilitated by this same vowel, 's'él*an*çant'→ 'se rép*an*d'. In fact we might argue that the upward thrust of 's'élancer' is inversely proportional to its duration, that in its participial form its thrust flattens out or does not reach the heights it might achieve in other forms. This surmise is endorsed, I think, by the only instance in the corpus of the present participial form of 's'élever', which obligingly occurs in the same position, at the caesura:

> Tandis que, s'élevant de distance en distance,
> Un faible bruit de vie interrompt ce silence   ('La Foi')

Once again, the present participle draws support and prolongation from the frequency of the nasal ã in its immediate linguistic environment ('tandis', 'distance' (twice), 'silence') and at the same time the phrase 'un faible bruit' indicates that the upward movement is of a very subdued and limited kind. The logical implication of these findings seems to me to be realised in lines from 'L'Immortalité':

> La lampe, répandant sa pieuse lumière,
> D'un jour plus recueilli remplit le sanctuaire.

Yet again, the participle has acoustic kinships with words around it – the nasal ã is to be found in 'lampe', 'remplit', 'sanctuaire' – but the repeated sound is not only an instrument of prolongation, it is also an enactment of the light's pervasiveness, enveloping objects with its beams; in other words, in this example, the source of the nasal ã is not so much 'répandant' as 'lampe', although 'répandant' is the perfect channel of the lamp's activity. But more important for our argument is that 'répandre' occupies a pre-caesural position. This should be explained partly by its present participial form; it should also be explained as the inverse of the trend we have just noticed: just as 's'élevant' and 's'élançant' gravitate towards 'répandre' by virtue of their suspension and protraction, so equally 'répandre' may move in the inverse direction, and by virtue of its participial form and its pre-caesural position, reach back towards a more generative and radiant role and have within it some of the spiritual 'lift' of 's'élancer' and 's'élever'.

The example from 'L'Immortalité' provides a negative answer to our earlier question: do 's'élancer' and 's'élever' always appear in the first hemistich, while 'se répandre' and 'inonder' occupy the second? The figures for 'répandre' and 'inonder', however, do seem to be significant; the figures concern only occurrences in the alexandrines of the corpus and are as follows: '(se) répandre' appears 8 times, three times in the first hemistich and five times in the second; 'inonder' appears 6 times, once only in the first hemistich and five times in the second. Thus, the tendency suggested earlier is borne out by the figures, but not as absolutely as the question would wish. Furthermore, the disproportion between the ratios – 3:5 ((se) répandre) as against 1:5 (inonder) – alerts us to the fact that 'répandre' and 'inonder' are far from having the same actional and affective tonality.

But before addressing ourselves to this difference, we should take a further caveat into account, which again relates position to verb-form:

> Quand mon oeil fatigué se ferme à la lumière,
> Tu viens d'un jour plus pur ‖ inonder ma paupière
> ('L'Immortalité')

'Inonder' appears in these lines in its infinitive form. It is characteristic for the infinitive to find itself in an immediately post-caesural position:

> Tu pouvais à longs flots ‖ répandre sans mesure
> Un bonheur absolu.   ('Le Désespoir')

The infinitive is the most neutral and inactive part of the verb; it is the part of the verb in which all the actional possibilities of the verb remain in a state of latency, or non-realisation, or suppression, depending on the modality of the specific instance. In the lines from 'L'Immortalité', the poet is addressing death and summoning its power to transfigure him; thus though the main verb ('viens') is in the present tense, its mood is optative, expressing wish, yearning; the present tense enacts a fulfilment which the poet knows to be premature. This optative mood finds a jussive formulation in lines textually very similar, at the end of 'La Foi':

> Viens donc la remplacer, ô céleste lumière!
> Viens d'un jour sans nuage || inonder ma paupière

'Inonder' in the infinitive form captures all the ambiguity of this situation. Activity is left in state of virtuality, is no more than a notion of activity. It enjoys some impulsion from its hemistich-initial position but because that hemistich is the second, the impulsion is already being let go of, the diffusion of light is under threat from potential evaporation. At the same time, we should recognise that the second hemistich, because of its quietening, withdrawing cadence, is the site of *recueillement*, of an ingathering of the self; while the first hemistich may frequently strike us as a movement of exteriorisation, the second may equally frequently suggest to us an intimacy, a descent into the self, which puts the poet's experience a little beyond our reach; the infinitive, because it defines no activity, leaves the perception of activity locked in the poet's head; or, put another way, *recueillement* involves a settling of consciousness to a zero-state of quietude, which is the ground from which a consciousness beyond words may expand. The lines from 'Le Désespoir' speak of an experience which is not denied to us by the poet, but rather denied to the poet by time, by God's unwillingness to do what he could have done, by the mystery of divine motive. And in the light of our findings about the pre-caesural present participle, it will perhaps come as little surprise to discover the infinitives of 's'élancer' and 's'élever' in the same post-caesural position:

> Que ne puis-je, porté sur le char de l'aurore,
> Vague objet de mes vœux, || m'élancer jusqu'à toi!
>
> ('L'Isolement')

> Je veux voir le soleil || s'élever lentement,
> Précipiter son char du haut de nos montagnes
>
> ('Hymne au Soleil')

These are the only occurrences of the infinitives of these verbs in the corpus, and they are again both governed by an optative mood. The infinitive form expresses, in the lines from 'L'Isolement', some of the exasperation of the poet's wish, in that it keeps the desired movement imprisoned in its mere possibility. In fact something of the confused frustration of the poet's yearning is conveyed by what seems to me a reversal of the natural order of hemistichs. If the second hemistich is more naturally the site of *recueillement*, of a meditative stillness, and of a dying fall, why not rather:

> Que ne puis-je, porté sur le char de l'aurore,
> M'élancer jusqu'à toi, || vague objet de mes vœux?

The ready answer, that considerations of rhyme do not allow it, is hardly sufficient. This 'alternative' version would maintain, with less interruption, the impulsiveness of the aspiration, it would endow the infinitive with more dynamic affirmativeness by locating it in a line-initial position, where it could be seen to generate the whole line, and it would make the 'vague objet de mes vœux' (the 'céleste patrie': manuscript variant) at one and the same time the goal of the 'élancement' and the achieved subject of fruitful interiorisation. Instead, the order of the true version bespeaks an admission of defeat even before the desired enterprise is undertaken; the onward movement from modal verb to infinitive is now doubly interrupted, so that by the time the infinitive arrives, it is no more than the recollected idea of an intention; in its first-hemistich location 'vague objet de mes vœux' acts as a distraction and a pretext for resignation: it is not a clearly-seen strength-giving objective, but an elusive, receding, disempowering source of dissatisfaction with the here and now; in its first-hemistich location, 'vague objet de mes vœux' is not so much a phrase in apposition to 'toi', a drawing of 'toi' inwards to make it a subject of contemplation and concentration, but something hanging awkwardly between the desired interiorisation of apposition and the desperate, exteriorised plea of invocation. The manuscript variant of this line is altogether less ambiguous:

> Que ne puis-je, porté sur le char de l'aurore,
> O céleste patrie, || arriver jusqu'à toi.

Not only is the first hemistich clearly an invocation, not only is it satisfyingly defined as vision, but the infinitive following it is less ambitious, more in keeping with a powerlessness that has come to terms with itself and with a falling cadence. Through the variant 'arriver', we can begin to see the bitter irony housed in the vaulting 'm'élancer'. The printed version has altogether more tonal and emotional complexity.

The infinitive 's'élever' from 'Hymne au Soleil' expresses not so much exasperation as impatience, made more apparent by the promotion of another infinitive to a line-initial position in the following line, by the acceleration from 's'élever lentement' to 'précipiter', and the abrupt inversion of upward movement into downward movement. But if the poet is impatient to see the splendours of the sun bursting out of these infinitives, he is equally anxious to enjoy the movement of anticipation. Here the infinitive's double-sidedness, its ability both to offer and to withhold, is paramount. The infinitive is perhaps one of the few linguistic forms which allow the poet momentarily to escape time. The present participle may seem to suspend time, but inevitably it suspends time *as process*, it gives, paradoxically, a kind of permanence to time's continuity. The infinitive is a time of dormancy, prior to the birth of action, a dead time which releases the poet from his subjection to the time-motivated world around him, and makes experience available to him without pressure. This alternative infinitive world is a world of pure imagination, where the poet's inner resources are no longer in competition with the incursions of reality, but are free to expand into their own space. The infinitive is thus related, in some of its manifestations, to *recueillement* and to prayer, where language's battle with external evidence is no longer necessary. This may seem a rather too heavy burden of significance to ask the lines from 'Hymne au Soleil' to carry; but qualities of this nature do colour 's'élever' here; and its occurrence in the second hemistich, with the concomitant damping down of activity and entry into a quietened intimacy, helps to release those qualities.

After this digression, we must return to the differentiation of 'se répandre' and 'inonder'. Of course their meanings are different: 'répandre' describes an act of dissemination, dispersal, distribution, discharging, while 'inonder' is an act of immersion, submersion, envelopment and invasion. In Lamartine's alexandrines, 'répandre' is connected with a variety of materials: sound, dust, light, happiness, soul, tears, prayer, while 'inonder' is always the activity of light, having persons or a metonymic stand-in ('ma paupière') as its object. Given that the process of 'inondation' is total and seemingly definitive, it is not surprising to find 'inonder' twice in the rhyme-position in 'L'Homme', and generally in the second hemistich: the subject (or, grammatically, the object) of the inundation, usually the lyric 'I', undergoes a transfiguration which is not only more soothing and consoling than firing or invigorating, but also essentially static, and stilled, like the lake's surface:

> Soit que, choisi par toi pour éclairer les mondes,
> Réfléchissant sur eux les feux dont tu m'inondes   ('L'Homme')

which is not to say that inundation may not be the ground-state from which energetic activity emerges, as the next line makes clear:

> Je m'élance entouré d'esclaves radieux

In the one line in which 'inonder' precedes the caesura:

> Quand l'astre à son midi, suspendant sa carrière,   2+4+3+3
> M'inonde de chaleur, de vie et de lumière   2+4+2+4
>
> ('La Prière', 73–4)

it also precedes the elements of inundation; in other words, the poet highlights not the fact of inundation but its wealth; 'm'inonde' is not itself rested in, as a voluptuous, beatific state, but is here the motor of its own attributes. Another factor which explains the position of 'inonder' here is the rhythmic context; the four lines preceding the couplet quoted have the following rhythmic patterns: 2+4+4+2 | 2+4+2+4 | 2+4+4+2 | 2+4+4+2. It is not necessary to say that this rhythmic context *determines* the position of 'm'inonde'; but 'm'inonde' does maintain the 2+4 pre-caesural hemistich and, in so doing, binds itself into an ongoing parallelistic pattern, in which natural terrestrial phenomena are interpreted as equivalents of divine actions. The syntactic skeleton of the whole sequence of lines (68–76) runs as follows:

> Là, quand l'aube . . .
> Entr'ouvre l'horizon . . .
> Et sème . . . les perles de l'aurore,
> Pour moi, c'est ton regard qui . . .
> S'entr'ouvre sur le monde et lui répand le jour:
> Quand l'astre . . .
> M'inonde de chaleur, . . .
> Dans ses puissants rayons, qui raniment mes sens,   4+2+3+3
> Seigneur, c'est ta vertu, ton souffle que je sens   2+4+2+4

Seen in this context it is clear that 'inonder' relates predominantly to the physical world and that it must consent to yield to, to be superseded by, the divine presence which informs it and makes it signify; that is, it cannot establish itself as an end-state, as something totally encompassing, it must give itself a peculiarly diversified activity. The end-state is a state of 'repeated' or 'completed'

2+4, the line of the Lord God; and the 4+2+3+3 which precedes this attainment of grace, throws the 2+4+2+4 into greater relief, gives it more finality, stands as an obstacle overcome in order to achieve it.

In these lines from 'La Prière', the location of 'inonder' in the first hemistich endows it, rather eccentrically, with a feeling of voluntariness; for it is in the nature of 'inonder', as it appears in Lamartine's verse, to operate as an involuntary act; light cannot control its capacity to inundate; the experience of inundation awaits whoever is able to communicate with, or surrender himself to, the light. 'Répandre', on the other hand, is usually a voluntary act, unless it is reflexive and/or relates to sound or light, in which case it will gravitate towards 'inonder'. Not surprisingly the two instances of first-hemistich 'répandre' not yet treated both have human agents:

> Je répandrai mon âme au seuil du sanctuaire!
>
> ('Chants lyriques de Saül')

> Il répand dans la nuit ses pleurs et sa prière
>
> ('La Poésie sacrée')

When it appears this early in the line, 'répandre' is not only more voluntary, but it may also carry with it overtones of effort; it is not a smooth diffusive action, an unforced emanation, as it so often is in the second hemistich. It is coloured now by strenuousness, by the sense of something adverse overcome. Thus while 'répandre' and 'inonder' certainly have a close thematic kinship, they do find characteristically different positions in the line, and their differences of placement point to differences of meaning and modality. And both words, considered individually, have within them a range of colourings which the poet plays upon by varying their position.

In turning back to 's'élancer' and 's'élever', I do not propose to undertake a similar exercise in differentiation. I would like, instead, to give some thought to syllabic proportion. Of the four verbs examined, all are trisyllabic in their present participial forms and three are trisyllabic as infinitives ('répandre' is the exception, though it would be trisyllabic in its pronominal form). The trisyllabic measure is, of course, of particular significance in the alexandrine; it is the only measure which can be successively repeated, it is the only measure which can create rhythmic regularity through the line at the same time as balance between its halves; what the 3+3 hemistich lacks is an ability, possessed by all other two-accent hemistich patterns (4+2, 2+4, 1+5, 5+1), to create effects of rhythmic chiasmus. One trisyllabic measure inevitably necessitates another, adjacent, a certain solidarity in the hemistich, equilibriating. Every word or word-group which constitutes a trisyllabic measure, imbues the line or hemistich, and indeed the verse-discourse, with a certain frictionlessness, smoothness of passage, evenness of relief. This should not be over-insisted upon, since it is more a potentiality of the trisyllabic measure than a necessary and invariable effect. But it may be of significance for Lamartine's verse, not only because any evenness of rhythm may embody the indiscriminate continuity of time's flow, and thus install at the very heart of the verse, as we have already intimated, the operation of that force which is, in so many respects, Lamartine's worst enemy; it may also, and conversely, be important as the opposite; namely the achievement of a kind of assurance which liberates the poet into a free-moving meditation outside time, as we suggested of the line:

> Je veux voir le soleil s'élever lentement
>
> ('Hymne au Soleil')

This apparent contradiction should not disturb us, since we have registered something of the same contradiction between a trisyllabic present participle which endows process with permanence and a trisyllabic infinitive which deadens time. And in our thematic treatment, we saw how the passage of time and the accompanying effacement of the physical world was a necessary prelude to the experience of *recueillement*. However, these remarks on the trisyllabic measure are intended only to highlight the nature of the uneven combinations of measure $(2+4, 4+2, 1+5, 5+1)$.

These latter combinations, by their very disproportionateness, encode the vicissitudinal, the engaged, the frictionful. If the trisyllabic measure can *register* the passage of time, the uneven combination suggests rather a hand-to-hand struggle with time. In dealing with trisyllabic measures, we were dealing with non-finite forms of the verb; it is perhaps no accident that uneven combinations are most frequently to be found with finite forms:

> Ainsi l'aigle superbe au séjour du tonnerre $3+3+3+3$
>
> S'élance; et, soutenant son vol audacieux $2+4+2+4$
>
> ('La Gloire')

The first line of this quotation has all the look of a conventionalised and totally generic description of the eagle; the recurrent trisyllabic measure makes a tableau of the depiction, installing it in a world of 'poetical' images, a world apart, self-sustaining and self-justifying. But the eagle leaves this world in the second line and launches itself into a world of conflict and contest, in which measures of different proportions rub against each other, where the peremptory and impatient force of the dissyllabic measures are given ballast and consistency by the tetrasyllabic ones. Here, balance is not ensured by the measure itself; it is won from a total arrangement of unequal parts: something achieved out of the threat of disorder. In these circumstances, the impulsiveness of 's'élancer' is potentially more anarchic than it is in trisyllabic units.

In the first three sections of 'La Prière', 's'élever' appears three times, twice in the present tense and once in the future:

C'est l'heure où la nature, un moment recueillie,	2+4+3+3
Entre la nuit qui tombe et le jour qui s'enfuit,	4+2+3+3
S'élève au Créateur du jour et de la nuit	2+4+2+4
	(lines 10–12)

Mais ce temple est sans voix. Où sont les saints concerts?	3+3+2+4
D'où s'élèvera l'hymne au roi de l'univers?	5+1+2+4
	(lines 27–8)

Sur les rayons du soir, sur les ailes du vent,	4+2+3+3
Elle s'élève à Dieu comme un parfum vivant	4+2+4+2
	(lines 31–2)

The first instance occurs in the context of the dying light, in the last convulsions of life before the darkness finally settles; the lines preceding line 10 are dominated by the clash of dissyllabic and tetrasyllabic measures, intermittently infiltrated by 3+3 hemistichs, which express the gradual invasion of the scene by the uniform, undifferentiated stillness of night. This invasion is finally accomplished in line 9:

Et le voile des nuits sur les monts se déplie	3+3+3+3

This is the moment of death, of existence at zero, but also the moment of *recueillement*, of the ingathering of energy prior to the assertion of life in another dimension. Lines 10 and 11 refer back to this moment, still bearing its traces in their post-caesural 3+3 hemistichs. How fitting that the 3+3 of line 10 should precisely refer to the moment of *recueillement*. How fitting, too, that these 3+3 hemistichs are second hemistichs, offering us movements of subsidence and muteness. But out of this zero state arises new life, the emerging 2's and 4's reintroduce emotional commitment,

23

unresolved aspiration, the changing fortunes of desire. It is only apt that in lines 13–14, which close the first section, there should be no further signs of 3+3:

> Et semble offrir à Dieu, dans son brillant langage,   4+2+4+2
> De la création le magnifique hommage.   6+4+2

In the third section of 'La Prière', the poet, surrounded now by silence, asks what voice will offer praise to God – the second instance of 's'élever' occurs in the second line of the section. The section begins with a 'zero-state' hemistich. The urgent question which follows disrupts that state. And, in the following line, urgency is intensified and focussed in the single-syllable measure of 'l'hymne'. The 5+1 pattern is rare because it involves the awkward need to accentuate two successive syllables; I have elsewhere described the consequences of this need:

... to facilitate reading and justify the immediately following accent, the voice tends to give more emphasis to the second accent than to the first, to slide up in crescendo; and the pause between 5 and 1 measures will be greater than the pause between 3+3 or 2+4, so that the voice can gather itself to attack another accentuated syllable immediately.   (1980, p. 27)

Thus, the 5+1 not only intensifies an urgency, it utters the very hymn whose origins it is seeking: the pause between 5 and 1 is a reverential moment which resolves itself into the higher, exalting peak of 'l'hymne'. And the extended syllabic proportions of 's'élevera', with support from 'D'où', encode the gradual accumulation of energy which explodes in hymn. In other words the tetrasyllabic proportions of 's'élever' here make it the verb not of a single abrupt action, but of a prolonged momentum-gathering *décollage*.

After the two questions asked in lines 27–8, a voice is identified, the poet's own inner voice:

> Tout se tait: mon cœur seul parle dans ce silence.   3+3+1+5
> (line 29)

The first hemistich harks back to line 27 and echoes its 3+3 structure, but this is interpreted by another highly disproportionate hemistich, 1+5, a reversal of the first hemistich of line 28 – utterance impinges on the surrounding expanse of silence, suddenly, peremptorily. And then in line 32, the voice rises to God, softened by the *e atone* of 'Elle' – 'Elle s'élève – and by its occupation of a 4-syllable measure. Again gradualism is the keynote, gradualism followed by triumphant attainment in the dissyllabic 'à Dieu'.

It might be argued that it is foolhardy, if not misleading, to try and attribute expressive capacities to different measures and combinations of measure. After all, the rhythmic structure of the alexandrine is inevitably and continuously diverse. It is in the nature of syntax to order itself in segments of different length; it is in the nature of the alexandrine to register and capitalise upon this variety, in purely rhythmic terms. But it would be equally foolhardy to propose that there is absolutely no connection between syllabic proportions and meaning. What I have tried to do in the preceding paragraphs is indicate some of the ways in which measures and their combinations might be significant in themselves, and how changing syllabic proportions can affect the manner in which verbs mean.

In continuing my itinerary through lexical items which are thematically central to Lamartine's verse, I want now to adopt another line of investigation: to examine how the position of a noun in the line of verse – in this case 'rayon' – conditions, or is conditioned by, its adjacent syntax. In the alexandrines of the corpus, there are twenty-three instances of 'rayon' (including the plural form), which are distributed as follows:

Syllabic position	1	2	3	4	5	6	7	8	9	10	11	12
Frequency	0	0	4	5	0	6	0	1	3	3	0	1

(These syllabic positions correspond to the positions of the second, accentuable syllable of 'rayon').

The following observations can be derived from Lamartine's usage of 'rayon':

(a)   When its accentuated syllable is at syllable 3, it is usually followed by a three-syllable past participial adjective of a negative or dispersive kind ('rayon éclipsé', 'rayons affaiblis', 'rayon égaré').

(b)   When its accentuated syllable is at either syllable 4 or syllable 10, it is usually followed by a two-syllable noun-complement ('rayon du jour', 'rayon d'espoir', 'rayons du soir' etc.).

(c)   When an adjective precedes 'rayon(s)', 'rayon' usually finds itself in a hemistich-terminal position (syllable 6 or 12).

(d)   At syllable 9, 'rayon(s)' is followed twice by noun-complements ('de sa gloire', 'd'un beau jour') and once by an adjective ('éclatants'); note the way in which, in this position, 'rayon' is intensified by what follows it.

Faced with these figures and these observations, it is difficult to tell whether we have evidence of almost automatic habits of composition or whether a deliberately significant pattern is intended. But we can discern certain large patterns which help to confirm assertions made earlier. The 'rayon' is a clearly defined, focussed beam of light; but this beam can either be sharp and penetrating or, on the contrary, soft and soothing. One might plausibly argue that it is sharper when accompanied by a noun-complement, which, as it were, leaves it single and unencumbered and reinforces it in its nominality, than it is when accompanied by an adjective which will tend to diffuse it in quality or effect, to envelop it in a particular atmosphere – it is not surprising that on the one occasion that 'rayon' yields up its accent, it yields it to an adjective:

> Seul, aux rayons pieux des lampes de la nuit   1+5+2+4
> ('Dieu')

This is one of the exceptions to observation (b). Another exception, of position this time, the occurrence of 'rayon' at syllable 8 in 'La Foi' –

> Pars du sein du Très-Haut, rayon consolateur   3+3+2+4

– has the same effect; although 'rayon' is accentuated, it is a dissyllabic measure which is overrun by the tetrasyllabic 'conso-lateur'. The two kinds of 'rayon' correspond roughly to the verbs 's'élancer' and 's'élever' on the one hand and 'répandre' and 'inonder' on the other hand, and, remembering the basic circum-flexity of the alexandrine, we might expect 'rayon' to be more thrustful when it appears in the first hemistich, more melting when it appears in the second. But just as the two pairs of verbs may mutually contaminate each other, so 'rayon' equally can find itself slung ambiguously between its two major types, as the remarks under (a) and (d) make clear. Thus the semantic operation of 'rayon' is a complicated affair, dependent upon which hemistich it occupies, what its position within the hemistich is, and what syntactical context it has (these latter two factors are interrelated). To these conditioners should be added the proportions of the measures in which it appears and what combinations of measures it creates (treated earlier, in connection with 's'élancer' and 's'élever').

The case of the adjective 'dernier' is altogether simpler. Because Lamartine always uses it in the sense of 'ultimate' (and never in the sense of 'previous'), it always precedes its noun. In the alexandrines of the corpus, 'dernier/dernière' occurs fourteen times, six times at syllable 4, five times at syllable 10, once at syllables 3, 5 and 9. This means that in the large majority of instances, 'dernier' is followed by a two-syllable noun (one-syllable if the noun is feminine and the *e atone* of 'dernière' is not elided), creating a 4+2 hemistich e.g.

> Près du dernier flambeau qui doive l'éclairer   4+2+2+4
> ('L'Homme')

> Et que des pleurs de joie à nos derniers adieux,   4+2+4+2
> A ton dernier regard brilleront dans mes yeux.   4+2+3+3
> ('L'Immortalité')

> Repose-toi, mon âme, en ce dernier asile   4+2+4+2
> ('Le Vallon')

In other words, the threat of loss implicit in 'dernier' is as it were carried out in the very abruptness of the following noun; a moment of poignant lastness, prolonged by its being tetrasyllabic, is cut short by the summary brevity of the dissyllable. And the process of prolongation is likely to be aided by the demand for an *accent oratoire* (or *accent d'intensité*) (see Appendix) on the first syllable of 'dernier', to underline the heavy-hearted pathos of its enunciation, thus:

> Repose-toi, mon âme, en ce *der*nier asile

The figures indicate no special leaning to either first or second hemistich, but one might wish to maintain that some expressive significance does attach to the choice made in each specific instance. In the lines quoted from 'L'Immortalité', for example, in which the poet draws positive strength from Elvire's death, from the idea that she is merely embarking on a new, divine, existence, the collisions between pain and pleasure are intricately mapped out, the position of 'dernier' being one important element. The 2 of the 4+2's is very much a last-minute perception, swiftly removed; in the first hemistich of the couplet, the dissyllabic measure is more like a last-minute adjustment of perception, with no guarantee of duration, as tears are hurried into joy; in the second hemistich, the disproportion between 4 and 2 helps to project 'adieux' forward into reality, as actually uttered words, and thus betrays a certain self-torment, while the falling intonation makes 'derniers' a 'dernier' of loss and morbid self-indulgence; furthermore, the overall rhythmic pattern of the line invites us, ironically, to equate 'adieux' with 'de joie'. The first hemistich of the second line tells a very different story. 'Dernier' now on a rising pitch-curve, is not a 'dernier' of loss but of shedding, of sloughing off, it is a 'dernier' which precedes a radiant 'enfin'; and the possessive adjective is of some importance here: whereas in 'à nos derniers adieux' the experience of lastness was shared, poignantly mixing two perceptions of 'last', the 'widowed' poet's, and the heaven-bound Elvire's, which might well be tragically different, in 'A ton dernier regard', the 'dernier' belongs peculiarly to Elvire; it is not the 'dernier' of one person's being abandoned by another, but the 'dernier' of a solitary experience of transcendence. And the dissyllabic 'regard' loses some of its abruptness by a surreptitious assimilation into the following verb, which, in strict grammatical terms, has nothing to do with it; because of the separation of 'brilleront' from its subject ('pleurs'), there is a temptation to see 'regard' as a substitute subject and to feel that the eyes of the poet will continue to reflect Elvire's last look indefinitely. At all events the sequence of 4+2 measures finally resolves itself into the equanimity of a 3+3.

The four instances of unaccentuated 'dernier', at syllables 3, 4, 5 and 9, need not detain us; without accent, 'dernier' is more a cool statement of fact rather than a wrenching experience:

> Ici viennent mourir les derniers bruits du monde   2+4+4+2
> ('La Semaine Sainte')
> Salut, derniers beaux jours! le deuil de la nature   2+4+2+4
> ('L'Automne')

Glided over like this, the sense of loss no longer competes with or heightens the physical sensation or phenomenon under threat; instead the experience hidden in 'dernier' remains unexpressed, subliminal even, and perception remains in the world of the purely sensory.

Finally, and briefly, I would like to give some consideration to two other words, thematically important, whose meaning oscillates between two poles, namely 'déjà' and 'seul'. 'Déjà' is either the 'already' of 'too late' or the 'already' of 'at last', the arrival of the ardently desired. Whether it has a negative or positive charge can easily be deduced from its context and has little to do with its position in the line. But its position does have significance of a modal kind. In the alexandrines of the corpus, 'déjà' always appears in the first hemistich, its accentuated syllable falling at position 2 or position 6 (there are two exceptions, but without consequence: 'Et déjà', where 'Et' acts as a kind of anacrusis, and 'Déjà, déjà', where the second 'déjà' merely reinforces the first).

> Et le char vaporeux de la reine des ombres   3+3+3+3
> Monte, et blanchit déjà les bords de l'horizon.   1+5+2+4
> ('L'Isolement')

At syllable 6, 'déjà' enacts a coming to consciousness; processes which are taking place imperceptibly, which threaten to catch the poet off guard, are registered on a time-scale and thus taken full cognisance of. This act of registration is, in the 'negative' case just quoted, an admission of powerlessness; the poet is doomed, it seems, to be overtaken by events, never to be properly prepared. In a 'positive' instance, the registration may encourage the consolidation of a state newly achieved:

> C'est par lui que déjà mon âme raffermie
> A pu voir sans effroi . . .   ('L'Immortalité')

At syllable 2, 'déjà' is almost in advance of the events which it marks; it bursts upon the line as a moment of transformation which events themselves have to catch up with; it may be a triumphant anticipation of a process which can then be more lingeringly enjoyed:

> Déjà mon front couvert d'une molle pâleur,
> Des teintes de la vie à ses yeux se colore
>   ('Hymne au Soleil')

What is perhaps most curious about 'déjà' is the way in which some of the sixth-syllable occurrences reach for second-syllable effects by virtue of their position not in the line, but in the syntax; though in a hemistich-terminal position, they are also in a syntax-initial position:

> Vous pleurez? et déjà || dans la coupe sacrée
>   ('Le Chrétien mourant')
> Et c'est l'heure où déjà || sur les gazons en fleurs
>   ('Hymne au Soleil')

This produces, naturally enough, some exchange of, or ambiguity between, second and sixth position effects.

Solitude is the bane and blessing of the poet. He may claim that without Elvire, 'tout est dépeuplé', but in truth Lamartine's world is never populated, or if it is, the other inhabitants are phantoms on the very margins of consciousness. Loneliness is part of the poet's sense of alienation from the world, of abandonment by God, of the impenetrability of the ultimate mysteries. But loneliness is equally part of the poet's sense of privilege, and an indispensable condition of *recueillement* and the mystical experiences it allows. Thus, loneliness and 'only-ness' are intimately linked, and 'seul' serves the interests of both. As one might expect, the 'seul' of solitude appears predominantly, accentuated, at the first syllable, not only for syntactic reasons, but because loneliness is, in many respects, the very origin of his utterance. The 'seul' of singleness has a much more variable position. Although it is easy enough to distinguish these two meanings, we cannot really avoid *hearing* the one in the other, and there are indeed textual moments when that distinction may slip from us:

> Entouré du chaos, de la mort, des ténèbres,
> Seul je serais debout: seul, malgré mon effroi,
> Etre infaillible et bon, j'espérerais en toi   ('L'Immortalité')

On reflection, we can see that on these two occasions 'seul' expresses 'only-ness', yet because of their positions, and because of the disjunction of the second 'seul' from its pronoun and verb, loneliness obtrudes through them; in fact, it only requires a comma after the first 'seul' to tip them both into solitude. To be one of God's elect is a solitary destiny.

In the preceding analyses, I have tried to suggest that thematically central words in Lamartine's lexicon have multifarious existences, and that this multifariousness has a prosodic foundation, in syllabic position, in syllabic proportion, in the size and combinations of measures. These analyses have been tentative and incomplete, and contain a large dose of intuition. But perhaps they have managed to demonstrate how diverse the modalities and affective charges of a single word can be, and how instrumental verse-structure is in releasing them. After including octosyllabic poems in my thematic treatment, I have expressly omitted them from my prosodic investigations. They are not forgotten. But the octosyllable is an animal so different from the alexandrine that it requires a chapter to itself. I shall approach the octosyllable through Gautier rather than Lamartine, and in particular through Gautier's almost exclusively octosyllabic *Emaux et camées*; but Lamartine will be returned to, after the detour.

2

THE OCTOSYLLABLE, RHYTHMICITY AND SYLLABIC POSITION

GAUTIER'S *EMAUX ET CAMEES*

The octosyllable has received, relatively speaking, as little attention as the poetry of Théophile Gautier.[1] This is partly because it has so consistently been overshadowed by the alexandrine, at least from the seventeenth century onwards, partly because it has been seen as the line peculiar to light verse.[2] As a point of departure for my discussion of the octosyllable, particularly as it appears in Gautier's *Emaux et camées*, I would like to refer to my summary in *French Verse-Art* (p. 42):

The octosyllable is perhaps the most mercurial and mobile of lines. Without the structural *point de repère* of a caesura, it situates itself uneasily between a two-accents-per-six-syllables norm on the one one hand, and a three-accents-per-decasyllable norm on the other. Of course the octosyllable has its own conventions: 3+5 and 5+3 are the classic divisions of the line, though 4+4 is probably as common. But measures of four and five syllables are already pushing towards the limit of tolerable accentlessness, particularly in a line whose brevity tends to encourage a more attentive reading, a reading that positively looks for accent. There may be some simplification in these assertions, but we can justifiably propose that recitational considerations interfere more continuously with the rhythmic structure of this line than with any other, and this characteristic, resulting from the line's instability, reinforces that instability.

When I suggest that 'recitational considerations interfere' more continuously with the octosyllable than with any other line, I have two considerations in mind. First, the prosodic or metrical substructure of the octosyllable is minimal: the only prosodic imperative that applies is that the line should have eight syllables, and an accent on the final syllable. There can be no further stipulations about accent, no stipulations about the degrees of rhythmic juncture, that is to say, no *coupe* is necessarily structurally pre-eminent within the line by virtue of position, nor, where there is more than one *coupe* within the line, can one be called major and the others

31

minor by reference to any metrical principle. Furthermore, it is extremely rare that sequences of octosyllables set up their own prosodic norms by installing a rhythmic regularity from line to line, partly because in units so small, and so recurrently rhyme-marked, regularity quickly becomes over-insistent, and partly because, as we shall see, the rhythmic segmentation of the octosyllable is extremely difficult to control. My second consideration is the octosyllable's lack of rhythmic parallels with other lines; it has no rhythmic relationship with any sub-group of longer lines – the hexasyllable, for example, can rhythmically refer itself to the alexandrine hemistich – it has no caesural relationship with longer lines (the nine-syllable line does have a caesura, however mobile) and it does not have the unequivocal two-accent constitutions of the lines immediately below it (the heptasyllable and the hexasyllable). In other words, the octosyllable is peculiarly without metrical anchorages either in itself or in its structural relationship with other lines. And one might add, or borrow, one further observation; Benoît de Cornulier (1982), on the basis of an experiment in which he asked readers and listeners to recognise syllabically false lines introduced into a doctored version of Hugo's 'Les Djinns', came to the conclusion that a sequence of eight syllables was the longest sequence which the French ear could encompass as a *numerical* entity and from which it could recognise one-syllable deviations; accordingly he could formulate the following 'law':

LIMITE DE LA CAPACITÉ MÉTRIQUE EN FRANÇAIS: en français, la reconnaissance instinctive et sûre de l'égalité exacte en nombre syllabique de segments voisins rythmiquement quelconques (c'est-à-dire égaux uniquement en nombre syllabique total) est limitée, selon les gens, à 8 syllabes, ou à moins. (p. 16)

Inasmuch as we rarely use instinctive or purely aural methods for ascertaining the number of syllables in a line, and inasmuch as we can safely assume that the incidence of *vers faux* in any sequence of lines governed by isometricity or strophic repetition will be exceptional, Cornulier's findings may seem to be of little direct relevance to verse-reading. But if, with the octosyllable, the reader is at the limit of his ability to register syllabic numericity, and if the octosyllable is devoid of any developed metrical system, to aid the process of orientation within the line, then we can assume that the reader will be more threatened by prosodic uncertainty than in other lines and that, consequently, he will be the more anxious to make the line manageable by segmentation, by creating or dis-covering accents as useful relays.

And this brings us back to 'recitational interference'. The reader asks, not 'How should it be read?' but 'How shall I read it?' It is this which produces the attentive, accent-seeking approach, which may pull against an equally strong desire to 'rationalise' the octosyllable into a binary structure (even though there may be three accentuable elements in the line). The truth of the matter is that, in one sense, all accents in the octosyllable are recitational, apart from the accent at the end of the line. If we call metrical accents those accents which indicate the line's rhythmic structure as system, as an inherent feature of its existence, and recitational or rhythmic accents those accents with which the voice (silent or otherwise) endows the line on an occasional basis, and which do not properly belong to a metrical description of the line, then it is difficult to see how the octosyllable's line-internal accents can be called 'metrical'. And if all this is so, can syllabic position be of any significance, given that it has virtually no structure to relate to?

But let us take a first step in scansion, and here again I would like to use a passage from *French Verse-Art*, as a point of departure. It analyses a stanza from Gautier's 'Symphonie en blanc majeur':

> Le marbre blanc, chair froide et pâle,
> Où vivent les divinités;
> L'argent mat, la laiteuse opale
> Qu'irisent de vagues clartés

the first line presents the noun + two adjectives problem again,[3] though with the accent on the fourth syllable and the brevity of the line, the question is no longer whether the accent should fall on the noun or the first adjective, but whether it should fall on either – if it did fall, the proximity of the fourth-syllable accent would naturally push it on to the first adjective. Do we then encapsulate the appositional group in a single measure – 4+4 – or do we give a physical immediacy to the metaphor by allowing 'froide' its resistance, its *noli me tangere* effect – 4+2+2? The second line is not ambiguous – 2+6 – but the third line allows us to treat its two constituents equally – 3+5 – in a conventional octosyllabic pattern, or to give relief to the preposed adjective of the second group, to give support to its opacity, to help it on its journey into the figurative, with a 3+3+2 distribution. The preposed adjective of the final line and the syllabically extended subject unit probably incline us towards 2+3+3 rather than towards 2+6.

(pp. 42–3)

What becomes apparent from this analysis is that the octosyllable frequently has two possible scansions operating within it at once, that is to say, that the octosyllable is, and almost inherently so, rhythmically ambivalent. And the two scansions which create its ambivalence both belong to rhythm rather than to metre, are both recitational rather than prosodic.[4] The prosody of the octosyllable, as we have seen, brings with it no segmentational imperatives. And so the reader finds himself in a somewhat paradoxical situation: the discovery of a scansion is peculiarly *his* responsibility, is already an interpretational act, an act of self-involvement in the line; but the search for a scansion reveals an essential ambiguity in the line which may be resolved by choice on any specific occasion, but cannot be removed from consciousness. As the reader therefore is invited to enter the poem, to create its rhythmic shapes, he is equally reminded of a rhythmic enigma at its heart which prevents him taking possession of it. With a line whose metrical structure is more developed, of course, a scansion is more or less imposed, and with it the ground-work of an interpretation; the reader 'reads' the scansional indications.

With this frequent double rhythmic perspective, the octosyllable retains a fluid, mobile, undefined surface which plants it squarely in the flux of relativity and change. For this reason it is impossible to agree with those who find in Gautier's octosyllables the deft, crisp outlines of the plastic model, who equate brevity with externality or who claim, like Claudine Gothot-Mersch (1981), that : 'La ré-gularité, la stabilité, la précision de l'articulation apparaissent donc comme les caractéristiques formelles les plus remarquables du recueil' (p. 17). Even within the restrictions of a consistently used form – almost all of Gautier's *Emaux et camées* are in octosyllabic quatrains, rhyming abab, with a as a feminine rhyme – the material maintains its suppleness, its lack of resolution; the external form may maintain a crispness of contour, a certain ideal plasticity, aided in Gautier's case by foregrounded, frequently rare rhymes; but the rhythmic structures which it contains have all the unpredictability, all the equivocality of that which has not found form. And this is one level, perhaps, at which Gautier is able to reconcile the complementary impulses which propel much of his work: the desire to idealise the real and at the same time to imbue the ideal with life.[5]

Gautier was well aware of the dangers which lay in the octo-syllable's lack of rhythmic definition; rhythmic ambivalence, unless made a positive feature of, unless pulling its expressive weight, easily degenerates into mere looseness, into mere arbitrary way-wardness. The octosyllable may, consequently, rely too heavily on rhyme to pull it into shape, with the further result that rhyme becomes over-obtrusive. In his chapter on Paul Scarron in *Les Grotesques* (1844), Gautier writes of the octosyllable:

Entre les mains d'un versificateur médiocre, il devient bientôt plus lâche et plus rampant que la prose négligée, et n'offre pour compensation à l'oreille qu'une rime fatigante par son rapprochement.

In order to give density to his line and to make the rhythmic ambiguity abundant in expressiveness, Gautier has recourse to four devices, which, as it were, hold the reader within the line.

The first of these devices is the preposing of the adjective. We have already encountered two examples in our stanza from 'Symphonie en blanc majeur'. This is by no means a ubiquitous procedure; if it were, it would soon lose all its power of arrest. But when it is used, it has an important involving function and compels a rhythmic reassessment of the line. The preposed adjective signals a moment of emotional commitment on the part of the enunciator, a desire to push the literal into the figurative, to expand the adjective's sensorial or spiritual associations; while the postposed adjective has a neutral, often purely physical quality and is an attribute applied to the noun on a specific occasion or is one of a number of possible attributes, the preposed adjective has an intrinsic, essential and thus permanent quality, which permeates the noun to the exclusion of other attributes, revealing its affective and spiritual core. It may be that *Emaux et camées* privilege the noun at the expense of the adjective, that Gautier's adjectives are frequently unassuming, even banal, in comparison, but prepositioning has the effect of revivifying the most unpromising attribute:

Voix de l'âme et de la nature,	3+5
J'écouterai vos purs sanglots	4+4 | 4+2+2

('Après le feuilleton')

'Pur' is the most convenient of clichés to express some undefined state of poetic elevation. Preposed, it recovers some of its expressive force; the poet bathes in its pervasiveness and the 'sanglots' are the very expression of that purity, deriving from it a certain melodiousness and ethereality. The voice is invited to insist on (accentuate) this adjective, and in the insistence we hear, too, the irony with which Gautier has also undoubtedly invested it. And prepositioning will be all the more significant for those adjectives which recur in *Emaux et camées*: 'blanc' is the adjective particularly associated with marble, with a lifeless, implacable and uncommunicative ideal; it has need of the leavening of 'rose', the colour of love, of mortality, of sensory reciprocity.[6] These colours are generally postposed as one might expect of colour adjectives. But when they are preposed, they are utterly transformed. 'Blanc', for example, keeps its distance and indifference when it appears after the noun; but preposed and attracting accent, it participates in life:

Par de lentes métamorphoses,	3+5
Les marbres blancs en blanches chairs,	4+4 | 4+2+2
Les fleurs roses en lèvres roses	3+5 | 3+3+2
Se refont dans des corps divers.	3+5 | 3+3+2
	('Affinités secrètes')
Vidant sa nacre, l'huître à perle	4+4
Constelle de son blanc trésor	2+6 | 2+4+2
Leur gorge, où le flot qui déferle	2+6 | 2+3+3
Suspend d'autres perles encor.	2+6 | 2+3+3
	('Les Néréides')

In the lines from 'Affinités secrètes', marble is transformed into flesh, and in the process a white of surface and neutrality is transformed into a whiteness of depth and involvement; the hard monosyllabic 'blancs' dissolves and softens into the dissyllabic 'blanches' whose linking *e atone* and alliterating *ch* melt it into 'chairs'. The prepositioning of 'blanches' endows it with an affective charge, a metaphorical colouring, an innateness in 'chairs', which pushes it in the direction of the life-giving 'rose'. In the lines from 'Les Néréides', the prepositioning of 'blanc' alerts us to the animating effect on the pearls of 'Leur gorge'; the pearls draw their rosy hues from the flesh reflected in them; but the 'blanc' is also deepened by a new figurative dimension, by a spiritual 'blancheur', which is transferred from pearls to nereids. A certain ironic light is cast on this vision retrospectively: the arriving steamer has little patience with mythology.

But the rhythmic consequences of prepositioning are equally important. It would be easy enough to justify a 3+5 | 4+4 | 3+5 | 3+5 reading of the lines from 'Affinités secrètes', on the grounds of general regularity, in order to maintain the completeness of the processes and their symmetry in lines 2–3, and to balance line 4 against line 1, introduction against conclusion. But our rhythmic uncertainty makes us feel our way into the line, feel for the richnesses of the preposed adjective, accentuate those richnesses, and in so doing delays us in the line and in the rhythmic tensions. Put simply, rhythmic uncertainty seduces us into the discovery of rhythmic ambivalence.

And this is the effect, too, of the second device, the *e atone*. We can hardly think of this as a device peculiar to Gautier, any more than we can think of the preposed adjective as an idiosyncratic resource. But we can argue that Gautier is peculiarly aware of the rhythmic usefulness of the *e atone*, particularly in the octosyllable. Claudine Gothot-Mersch (1981) draws attention to the frequency of, among other things, e mutes in *Emaux et camées*:

Un autre effet sonore contribue à la même impression de netteté: la fréquence de la diérèse (ainsi dans 'Le Poème de la femme': Itali-ens, musici-ens, ondulati-ons, Phidi-as, Gérogi-enne, di-amant, vi-olettes) et le nombre d'e "muets" qu'on est amené à articuler (dans le même poème: 'De grosses perles de Venise'). L'outil statistique nous manque pour apprécier l'importance de ce phénomène, mais il y a là un effet de martèlement très sensible: le vers s'égrène, les huit syllabes se détachent une à une. (p. 46)

Leaving aside, for the moment, the remark about diaeresis, and assuming that the second sentence of the quotation applies to both phenomena (diaeresis and e mute), I would like to take issue with the conclusions. The primary effect of the articulated e mute is its lengthening of the previous vowel; Lewis (1982, p. 31) adds the qualification that such lengthening occurs only when the syllable preceding the e mute is stressed (accentuated). I would hasten to add the corollary: since an increase in the duration of the vowel is usually a concomitant of its being accentuated, the lengthening of an accentuable vowel will usually lead to its accentuation. In other words, the e mute of 'blanches' is another factor which encourages us to accentuate it; just as, in the line quoted by Gothot-Mersch:

De grosses perles de Venise

the articulated e of 'grosses' will invite a 2+2+4 scansion to vie with a 4+4 one. The *e atone* thus produces a lingering effect in the reading, which may be described as an 'égrènement', but it is an 'égrènement' of rhythmic segments rather than of syllables: the articulated e does not engineer the disjunction of syllables, but, on the contrary, lilting transitions between them. And for this reason there is no 'effet de martèlement', but rather moments of accentuated perception followed by moments of reflective assimilation (the e mutes). The stanza announcing the arrival of the steamboat in 'Les Néréides' contains similarly significant e mutes:

Son pavillon est tricolore;	4+4
Son tuyau vomit la vapeur;	3+5 | 3+2+3
Ses aubes fouettent l'eau sonore,	4+4 | 2+2+4
Et les nymphes plongent de peur.	3+5 | 3+2+3

37

Here, not only do the articulated e's of the last two lines install alternative rhythms, not only do they parallel each other – the nymphs dive for safety in time, as it were, with the beating paddles – but they also have a repercussive effect: the e mutes are like a dying reverberation of the accentuated vowels which precede them. This not only imitates the general violent confusion of the scene, but once again the e's act as moments of absorption: the nouns ('aubes', 'nymphes') and verbs ('fouettent', 'plongent') have, in their second syllables, space for the reader to absorb the image, to internalise it, to make it part of his own imaginative play (the articulated e receives fuller attention in Chapter 4).

The third device has already been indicated in the quotation from Gothot-Mersch: diaeresis. Again it should be said that Gautier's diaereses have nothing unusual about them, but they do have two important functions in the octosyllable. First, they underline the fact that the reading of an octosyllable is a savouring process:

> Tous les vices avec leurs griffes
> Ont, dans les plis de cette peau,
> Tracé d'affreux hiéroglyphes,
> Lus couramment par le bourreau. ('Lacenaire')

The hieroglyphs on the hand of the murderer Lacenaire may be an open book to the executioner, but for the reader, as for the poet, the hand expresses paradox ('molle et féroce', 'criminelle aristocratie') and a life whose intimate secrets can only be guessed at; and the four-syllable 'hiéroglyphes', with the hiatus between its first two syllables, invites the reader to palpate it, to search among the labyrinth of its syllables, to practice a *sondage*. Diaeresis exerts a retarding influence, captivating the reader in vowel modulation and elusiveness. And this tasting of each syllable may make reading a sensual indulgence, a dalliance among pleasures only to be hinted at; Impéria's hand discloses:

> Impér*ia*les fantaisies,
> Amour des sompt*uo*sités;
> Volupt*ueu*ses frénésies,
> Rêves d'impossibilités. ('Impéria')

Secondly, and as can be seen from the above quotation, when the second vowel of an adjacent pair is accentuated, the diaeresis, or rather the hiatus associated with it, gives more lift to the accent by necessitating a more concerted thrust of the voice ('Impéri-áles', 'Volptu-éuses'). In both instances, in this example, the added insistence is further added to by the following articulated e's. So diaeresis involving an accentuated vowel intensifies the dwelling of the voice, the reaching into meaning and experience, which makes the octosyllable, and Gautier's octosyllable in particular, far from impassive, plastic or precise.

The final device I wish to consider, and which has as much significance for general readerly attitudes to the line as for the line's rhythmic structure, is Gautier's avoidance of enjambement in a line short enough to make enjambement seem probable. I have elsewhere (*French Verse-Art*, pp. 78–9) tried to show that the absence of punctuation is no necessary indicator of enjambement, that as long as the line's phrasal coherence is maintained, the line-ending produces no infraction of syntax. As one set of examples, I used the unpunctuated lines which occur in the three stanzas of the fourth part of Gautier's 'Fantaisies d'hiver':

> Sur la mode parisienne
> Le Nord pose ses manteaux lourds,
> Comme sur une Athénienne
> Un Scythe étendrait sa peau d'ours.
>
> Partout se mélange aux parures
> Dont Palmyre habille l'Hiver,
> Le faste russe des fourrures
> Que parfume le vétyver.
>
> Et le Plaisir rit dans l'alcôve
> Quand, au milieu des Amours nus,
> Des poils roux d'une bête fauve
> Sort le torse blanc de Vénus.

arguing that in two instances some form of punctuation mark could be easily imagined (lines 1, 7), that in two other instances inversion created a 'false' enjambement (3, 11), that one of the lines in question was in any case syntactically complete (9) and that, in the final case, though verb and subject were separated, they were not so much separated by the line-ending as by an extended parenthesis (5). The high incidence of non-enjambing lines, lines which are nonetheless no more than syntactical fragments, encloses the rhythmic ambivalence of the line in its own play and underlines the sense of enigma generated by the line's tantalising glimpse of a wholeness; it is the rhythmic ambivalence which interrogates that enigma. The fragmentariness of the line and the absence of the sense of sequence is reinforced by the discontinuous syntax so frequently employed by Gautier; his habits of inversion and parenthetic insertion (relative clauses, similes, etc.) drive the sentence apart and isolate its units. This means that temporary grammatical ambiguities are likely to endorse rhythmic ambiguities, though not necessarily in the same line. Thus:

Sur la mode parisienne   3+5

before being solved by 'pose', has musical overtones, the feminine gender being archaic (cf. Verlaine's 'sur le mode mineur'), and, equally, the 'des' of:

Des poils roux d'une bête fauve   3+5 | 3+3+2

is potentially a plural of the indefinite article before it is solved by 'sort'. Each line, then, exists as it were in its own atmosphere, is momentarily an object of reverie in its own right, susceptible of any number of syntactic resolutions. Even when the reader has at his disposal the completed syntax of the whole stanza, he may find that certain lines preserve a peculiar syntactic mobility: in the second stanza, for example, the final relative, 'Que parfume le vétyver', does not seem bound to 'fourrures' or 'faste', but reaches back across the whole stanza and is as much an emanation from 'parures' and 'l'Hiver'. Similarly in the first stanza, 'comme sur une Athénienne' achieves an autonomy by virtue of its being imaginable in almost any position in the syntactic chain. This autonomising of the line and the line's ambivalence is an important factor in the assessment of Gautier's place in the poetic trends of the late nineteenth and early twentieth centuries, and it is this I now wish briefly to reflect upon, as a way of re-angling my approach to the octosyllable.

One of Gautier's admirers was Wilde, and his lines on Gautier in *The Picture of Dorian Gray* are peculiarly illuminating. In Chapter 14, while waiting for the arrival of Alan Campbell, to dispose of Basil Hallward's body, Dorian idly flicks through his luxury edition of *Emaux et camées*. After comparing his hands to the hand of Lacenaire, he comes on to the second of the 'Variations sur le carnaval de Venise', 'Sur les lagunes', and selects for special praise its fourth, fifth and sixth stanzas:

How exquisitive they were! As one read them, one seemed to be floating down the green waterways of the pink and pearl city, seated in a black gondola with silver prow and trailing curtains.

But it is the sxith stanza which particularly holds his attention, and more particularly, the last two lines of that stanza:

L'esquif aborde et me dépose,	4+4 | 2+2+4
Jetant son amarre au pilier,	5+3 | 2+3+3
Devant une façade rose,	6+2
Sur le marbre d'un escalier.	3+5

The whole of Venice was in those two lines [cf. line 28: 'Tout Venise vit dans cet air']. He remembered the autumn that he had passed there, and a wonderful love that had stirred him to mad, delightful follies. There was romance in every place. But Venice, like Oxford, had kept the background for romance, and, to the true romantic, background was everything, or almost everything.

An ungenerous explanation of 'The whole of Venice was in those two lines' would be that Wilde has lazily adapted another of the poem's lines, to stand in for a response. A more generous explanation would be that these words are indeed a genuine response, but that it is manifestly not all Venice which is in these lines, but all Dorian's memories. Like a true decadent, Dorian treats Gautier's poem as a precious object, as a source of sensations which do not transform his experience into anything new, but merely enhance and refine what is already familiar in his experience; in fact the poem is merely an aesthetic and aestheticising mediator between Dorian and his accumulated biography. And one of the ways in which the poem mediates is by acting as a backdrop against which any sentimental adventure can be set and thus acquire an intensifying sheen, the patina of delicately moulded and culturally authenticated perception. It is not difficult to see other reasons why Gautier might have appealed to the decadent: his attempts to release art from morality and functionality through the 'l'art pour l'art' principle, his display of the butterfly perceptiveness of the inspired dilettante, of the connoisseur of sensations.

In Dorian's responses, then, we find no real evidence of the synthesising essentialism of Symbolism. The decadent is condemned to materialism and external appearances and denied the world of essences; however *recherché*, however intricate and rare, however carefully chosen, the language of the decadent can only describe, it cannot penetrate or evoke. His private experience remains private, its privacy can only be observed, from the outside, it cannot be shared. When the decadent does describe the effects created by an object or a sensation, these effects are by nature decorative rather than revelatory, and they each claim autonomy for themselves rather than being re-assimilated into the object as parts of its intimate meaning or essence (this is the principle that governs Wilde's 'impression', 'symphony', 'harmony', 'nocturne' poems). But if we can suppose that the reaction of Wilde's Dorian is decadent, in what direction does Gautier's poem point, what reaction does it *deserve*, decadent or symbolist? And how does this question relate to the octosyllable?

One critic sees Gautier's art as predominantly descriptive: 'L'objet est nommé, à la différence d'un Mallarmé et décrit plus ou moins tel que le poète le voit, sans être artificiellement transposé et embelli comme chez Baudelaire' (King, 1979, p. 85). Two objections to this view present themselves. The first is that the phrase 'plus ou moins tel que le poète le voit' has no sense; and, as the same critic points out (p. 88), even if the first person is present in *Emaux et camées*, it is peculiarly passive, anonymous even, the 'I' of a general observer. In other words, the object is not described as the poet sees it but rather as it is 'seeable', hence the frequency of impersonal constructions:

> On voit dans le musée antique ('Contralto')
> On dirait une rose blanche ('La Rose-Thé') etc.

or of formulations involving the first person, but underlining his substitute or representative function:

> En même temps molle et féroce,
> Sa forme a pour l'observateur
> Je ne sais quelle grâce atroce,
> La grâce du gladiateur! ('Lacenaire')

The reader is constantly invited into the poem, to see not so much what the poet sees as what the poet's description allows him to see or encourages him to see; the bareness or laconicness of the observations are precisely what creates around all objects an envelope of interpretative freedom and allows the infiltration of personal association.

And this brings us to the second objection: description is not so much a matter of manner as of function. Description needs to act as a given, locating 'truth' in the perceived, endowing itself with referential plausibility by its apparent non-selectiveness; description is a controlled, ordering activity in which what is described has already achieved significance, finality and hierarchy. Gautier presents us with something very different:

> Il me semble, quand on le joue,   3+5
> Voir glisser dans son bleu sillon   3+5 | 3+3+2
> Une gondole avec sa proue   4+4
> Faite en manche de violon.   3+5

Sur une gamme chromatique,	4+4
Le sein de perles ruisselant,	2+6 | 2+2+4
La Vénus de l'Adriatique	3+5
Sort de l'eau son corps rose et blanc.	3+5 | 3+2+3
Les dômes, sur l'azur des ondes,	2+6 | 2+4+2
Suivant la phrase au pur contour,	4+4 | 4+2+2
S'enflent comme des gorges rondes	1+7 | 1+5+2
Que soulève un soupir d'amour.	3+5 | 3+3+2

('Sur les lagunes' – stanzas 3–5)

Poetry, even in strictly third-person enunciations, implies or imposes a first person perspective, which may be the poet's, or the poet's and the reader's together, particularly if the poet lowers his own profile, or the reader's alone if the poet totally absents himself. In depictions like the one above, 'truth' is located in the solipsistic world of the perceiver (poet/reader), the distinction between background and foreground, décor and action is blurred (décor may itself be 'actional'), a selective and reactive process is evident, where reaction is the motivator of selection; in this kind of world, significance is not guaranteed, has to be implanted, hierarchies are not evident and finality is constantly dissolved under the flux of impressions. And the 'actional', experiential impulse of these 'descriptions' is made clear in the reflex of simile-making. Simile is important not only because it transforms object into impression, subjectivises object, but because simile is by nature partial and relative and thus invites other similes; simile, unlike metaphor, appeals to common knowledge, to our general familiarity with things, and thus is a sharing process; and what it shares, too, is the simile-making itself: the poet supplies a simile which may generate the reader's own similes. About simile we shall have more to say in the next chapter. Suffice it to say that Gautier's language is more figurative than it is often given credit for;[7] some poems depend entirely for their significance on the figurative parallel (e.g. 'Fumée').

And the part played by the octosyllable in all this is paramount, and not only for the reasons we have already proposed. The rhythmic ambivalence of the octosyllable denies periodicity, in the sense of *rhythmically organised* variations of measure. Periodicity implies the controlling impetus of voice, moulding language to the tempi of the poet's imaginative and affective impulses, and it implies, too, the presence of the rhetorician's art, an enchantment of the reader's critical faculties as he is borne along by a rhythmic design which has, as it were, already achieved its expressiveness, and is merely exercising its power to affect. Periodicity consolidates the unicity of the lyric voice and ensures its stamina. Although there are several of the *Emaux et camées* in which Gautier seeks to establish a consistency of voice, a lyric momentum which drives through the poem from one end to the other (e.g. 'Diamant du coeur', 'Premier Sourire du printemps', 'Dernier Vœu'), the octosyllable has a natural inclination, as we have seen, to interrogate, to encourage improvisation, certainly at the rhythmic level, and thus equally to encourage a diversification of tone. As Gautier says in his chapter on Scarron, already referred to: 'La vie est multiple, et beaucoup d'éléments hétérogènes entrent dans la composition des faits et des événements. La scène la plus touchante a son côté comique, et le rire s'épanouit souvent à travers les pleurs' (p. 353). But when we speak of tonal diversification in *Emaux et camées* we can rarely identify the actual tones involved; a first person is present in the poems, but so effaced by design, and by the mechanism of the octosyllable, that as readers we certainly do not feel manipulated, or toyed with, by an author whose intentions are inscrutable and whose sense of superiority wills that they be so. Rather the reader engages in a kind of tonal playfulness with the author in which motives may be suspected or suggested, but are never properly embodied. There is here none of the strenuous exertion of authorial personality, the scornful withdrawal into irony that one might associate with the dandy of decadence; there is rather a space of ambiguous play which the author and reader share, where they fence together, while both maintaining their interpretative rights. In the fifth stanza of 'Sur les lagunes', for example, do we ally ourselves with the aesthete's disingenuous matter-of-factness expressed by the binary readings? And if we follow this latter course, do we hear below the conniving sensualism, undertones of an equally knowing disabusedness:

Les dômes, sur l'az*ur* des ondes	2+4+2
Que soulève un soup*ir* d'amour	3+3+2

Are the waves of Venice that blue? Is this just a self-conscious licence? Do not the love-sighs strain a little too much for effect? Perhaps it is less sigh and more fatigue? And yet Gautier/poet knows no better than the reader where the truth lies; we are conscious of a tonal presence but it never seeks to interfere with our own tonal choices; and this is largely because the octosyllable is perhaps more author than Gautier; he is as much subject to its essentially ambiguous nature as we are to him. Or rather Gautier's own predilection for ambiguity, whether it be the ambiguity of paradox – as in the quotation from 'Lacenaire' above – sexual ambiguity ('Contralto') or ambiguity of colour (the blue-green of 'Caerulei oculi') predisposes him to the octosyllable. At all events, in their refusal of an informing, periodising, lyric voice, and in their creation of a multiple, but undefined, tonal play, Gautier's octosyllables come closer to Mallarmé – 'l'œuvre pure implique la disparition élocutoire du poète qui cède l'initiative aux mots ...' (*Crise de vers*) – and to the Imagists than to the Parnassians or Decadents.

If Gautier's octosyllables cannot be related to a principle of periodicity, they can perhaps be regarded as cinematic, as a passage between 'frames', where there is no guarantee of the continuity or consistency of that passage, where one may cut from one 'shot' to another, where there may be hiatus or interruption between frames. This cinematic effect may operate at any structural level of the poem: 'Variations sur le carnaval de Venise' and 'Fantaisies d'hiver' present different 'shots' in their different parts, 'Le Poème de la femme' and 'Les Joujoux de la morte' present a cinematic sequence from stanza to stanza; the non-enjambed nature of the Gautierian octosyllable creates, as we have seen, a framing effect for the line, and the discontinuity of his syntax separates one line from the next, so that the stanza is equally a series of shots, rather than an uninterrupted syntactic sequence; finally within the line, the rhythmic segments may have an almost cinematic relationship with each other, as the rhythmically uncertain reader separates out the different units. If we look again to the sixth stanza of 'Sur les lagunes', we can see these latter two levels of cinematic structure at work:

L'esquif aborde et me dépose,	4+4 | 2+2+4
Jetant son amarre au pilier,	5+3 | 2+3+3
Devant une façade rose,	6+2
Sur le marbre d'un escalier.	3+5

The syntax of this stanza – main clause: participial adjectival phrase: adverbial phrase: adverbial phrase – means that each line has a different point of focus: esquif/pilier/façade/escalier, each with a peculiar independence, each with its own atmosphere and associations and each suggesting its own set of possible syntactic contexts. And because of this cinematic dissociation of lines, one from the other, articles and possessive adjectives acquire a new diffused expressiveness. The definite article presupposes prior knowledge or determination, yet the 'esquif' has not been mentioned before; but even if this prior knowledge is not *explicit*, the definite article may be used to imply that we do in fact have such knowledge, or that we should have that knowledge, or that the poet at least has that knowledge; thus the definite article may imply an intimacy, a familiarity, with objects that the text gives no justification for. Equally the definite article may suggest that the 'esquif' is somehow predestined, specific in function, an inescapable part of the secret mythology of Venice. Or again, the definite article may be generical in nature, a blueprint for all 'esquifs', the kind of 'esquif' you would expect. Or again, the definite article may be the equivalent of a demonstrative adjective, that is, it may have a deictic role, pushing us beyond the world of the work of art to a reality, a piece of biography that can be directly referred to, increasing the visualness of the image. The indefinite article, for its part, is used of a specific item, before that item has been determined or taken up in a narrative. It endows the noun with a potentiality for all kinds of definition, it places the noun on the very brink of, makes it available to, the sudden direction of a destiny. The indefinite article of 'une façade rose', or of 'un escalier' signals a possibly deceptive randomness, signals that we may be entering a *terra nova* or *terra incognita*,[8] and until further help is given us to embed the noun in a pattern, we are peculiarly free to implant our own associations in it. Equally, of course, the indefinite article, like the definite article, may have a generic function. And because of the discontinuity of the octosyllable's linear series, the possessive adjective may become detached from a specific possessor and float free in a world of any number of possessors. This possibility is not as evident in the lines from 'Sur les lagunes', as it is, for example, in 'Carmen':

> Car sur sa nuque d'ambre fauve
> Se tord un énorme chignon

or

> Et, parmi sa pâleur, éclate
> Une bouche aux rires vainqueurs

If this suggestion seems a little far-fetched, then we should remember how natural it is for Gautier to superimpose one feminine image on another – a manifestation of his anamnesis[9] – Inès de las Sierras on Petra Camara ('Inès de las Sierras'), for instance, or a Greek Apollonie on a contemporary one (Mme Sabatier) ('Apollonie'). Be that as it may, the extended expressive range of articles and possessives in Gautier's *Emaux et camées* derives, it seems to me, from what I have called the cinematic effects of the octosyllable.

But we have not yet done with the syntactic dislocations and ambiguities of the sixth stanza of 'Sur les lagunes'. We have already had cause to suggest, in relation to a stanza from 'Fantaisies d'hiver', that a sense of the autonomy of the line results from its being imaginable in almost any position in the syntactic chain. The same holds true of this stanza from 'Sur les lagunes'. The interposition of the participial phrase at line 2 makes it unclear whether 'Devant une façade rose' belongs to line 2 or to line 1. If it belongs to line 2, then it produces a strange hiatus between lines 3 and 4 as agent and location change: instead of the steps being a projection from the façade, with the one as an extension of the other, there would be a spatial leap between 'devant une façade' and 'sur l'escalier'. If however lines 3 and 4 belong to line 1, then either it would be 'better' if their order were inverted, giving the stanza:

> Jetant son amarre au pilier,
> L'esquif aborde et me dépose,
> Sur le marbre d'un escalier,
> Devant une façade rose

(which would however break the sequence of feminine and masculine rhymes) or if their relationship were made clearer by the substitution of a definite article for an indefinite one, thus:

> Devant une façade rose,
> Sur le marbre de l'escalier.

A clearer re-lineation of our first option, maintaining the rhyme pattern, would give:

> Devant une façade rose,
> Jetant son amarre au pilier,
> L'esquif aborde et me dépose
> Sur le marbre d'un escalier.

These ambiguities, along with the postponement of the final line, seem to drive the adverbial phrases further into a space of their own and explain why Dorian finds it so easy to extrapolate and 'anthologise' them, and why they are so amenable as sites of his own fantasies and memories.

As far as the rhythmic segmentation of the individual line is

47

concerned, the *coupe* acts as the frame, making the line a series of punctualities. For all the displacements which occur in the syntax, Gautier's verse is very much located in time, in a chronometric progression of discontinuous moments. These moments are by no means temporally or experientially homogeneous, and their discontinuity does not disqualify linkages of various kinds (e.g. the frequent *coupes enjambantes*), but there is an overriding sense of movement from disembodied shot to disembodied shot, from object to agentless action, from object to self-sustaining quality or vice-versa. I am not of course trying to suggest that the octosyllable is by nature cinematic – it would be difficult to see why any other line should not equally be so; I merely wish to propose that the weight of contextual evidence indicates this cinematic propensity in Gautier and that the octosyllable is peculiarly suited to its realisation. Take, for example, the third line:

Devant une façade rose   6+2

Here the presence of the surrounding substantives, and the frequency of the two-nouns-per-line formula, tempts the reader, subliminally perhaps, to give substantival value to 'rose', so that the colour severs itself slightly from what it colours. And the brevity of the octosyllable, with its consequent intensification of rhyme-awareness and with the accent-seeking alertness which it stimulates, tends to give a peculiar relief to accentuated elements. The way that the brevity of the octosyllable makes it difficult to anticipate syntactic development is of particular importance here: because the reader cannot confidently make syntactic projections in the octosyllable, so he will tend to endow each octosyllable with an autotelic density.

It would not be difficult on the basis of the evidence so far encountered to argue that Symbolist murmurings are already audible in *Emaux et camées*. Gautier does envelop, by various ambiguity-creating mechanisms and isolating processes, his nouns in an aura of loaded understatement, does push objects into an imaginative space of their own. His cinematic technique produces a faceting effect, an intricate network of Mallarméan 'reflets réciproques', the sense of an experience or figure or object being turned through different angles and thus accumulating to itself a variety of images, responses, associations. And this relativising method is reinforced by the multiplicity of rhythmic realisations of the material. Within the apparent briskness of the octosyllabic quatrain, hesitations and protractions encourage moments of contemplative stillness.

But it might equally be argued that Gautier's metaphysical concerns are only intermittent, that because of the general absence of transitional devices in his work, that is to say, because his junctures are junctures of hiatus rather than fusion, synthesis never really takes place; rather, his images are driven apart into a sequence of privileged moments, a sequence of autonomies, discrete and self-seeking. In this light, Gautier does have real affinities with the Imagists. We may find it difficult to distinguish usefully between Pound's definition of the image as 'an intellectual and emotional complex in an instant of time' and the symbol; and Pound's assertion that 'the proper and perfect symbol is the natural object' seems to accept the symbolising function of verse and to wish, merely, that unnecessary abstractions be sheered away, so that the object can maintain its literalness along with its symbolic potential. The main differences between Symbolism and Imagism lie in emphasis and methods of approach, rather than in objectives; while Symbolism courts linguistic abundance, a wrought-up writtenness in its language, indirectness, allusiveness, conjuncture, musicality, a mediumic anonymity for the poet, the Imagist looks for linguistic bareness (no superfluous word, as few adjectives as possible), a conversational familiarity in language, directness, a presentational and isolational method, visuality, a hidden egoism. Part of Gautier's rejection of the alexandrine is motivated by a horror of the clichés, the linguistic redundancy and the rhetorical inflatedness enjoined upon the poet by the prosodic imperatives of the longer line:

[Le vers de huit syllabes] nous paraît plus propre que l'alexandrin, pompeux et redondant, aux familiarités du dialogue, à l'enjouement des détails, et nous aimerions à le voir en usage au théâtre. Il nous épargnerait beaucoup d'hémistiches stéréotypés, dont il est difficile aux meilleurs et aux plus soigneux poètes de se défendre, tant la nécessité des coupes et des rimes du vers hexamètre les ramène impérieusement.

('Paul Scarron', pp. 352–3)

But Pound's constant reference to Gautier's 'hardness' is not entirely justified. There is plenty of substantival presence in Gautier's verse, much that is laconic in its tone, and he does not achieve suggestiveness by a blurring of outline in abstraction or vagueness; but we have found much that is yieldingly affective in Gautier's verse, and much indeterminacy and fluidity in his rhythms. Nevertheless it is perhaps easier to align Gautier with the Imagists rather than the Symbolists, particularly bearing in mind Taupin's (1929) distinction between a symbolism in which the image is partial, a point of departure, a single element in a synthesis engineered by a language of dissolving effects and undertaken by the reader, and an imagism in which the image has a greater degree of punctuality, is itself a synthesis and point of attainment (p. 97–8). Other critics have dealt much more adequately with the relationship between Symbolism and Imagism than this cursory treatment can hope to do,[10] and, besides, differentiations are often difficult to maintain. What could be more imagist than Mallarmé's 'Chansons bas' or his 'Loisirs de la poste' or his 'Eventails'? It is my intention only to give some idea of how richly amenable to literary affiliation *Emaux et camées* are and what part the octosyllable and its associated syntax play in that amenability.

But the underlying question brooks no further postponement: can syllabic position be of any significance in the octosyllable, given that it has virtually no structure to relate to? The short answer to this is 'no'. But the converse positive formulation is perhaps more just: the octosyllable is anti-positional; in other words the octosyllable refuses the attribution to its contents of those colourings, modalities and implications which the operation of a scale of positional values would permit. Of course the final, rhyme position maintains its privileges, but these are conventional to rhyme as a whole, and not to octosyllabic rhyme in particular (though the rhyme of the short line may be said to have a function different from that of the alexandrine[11]), and, besides, the rhyme syllable has as much to do with the rhythm of stanzaic organisation and with other rhyme-words as with its own line. In refusing positional reference, the octosyllable equally refuses an authority to rhythmicity; the poem as a whole may exert a generical authority and indeed a formal authority, but the rhythms of individual lines are unauthorised. Of course the syntactical and grammatical make-up of the line authorises the rhythmic segmentation in a sense, but because of the syntactic incompleteness of the line, because one syntactic unit cannot easily be seen in relation to others, this authorisation is at best provisional and always questionable. What is important, however, is that the syntactic structure of the line cannot be rationalised in terms of metrical imperatives, cannot appeal to any principle of order beyond itself. Put another way, the meaning of a particular syntactic arrangement is not revealed by, or revelatory of, a poetic order embodied in it. The rhythmicity of any particular line is thus totally immanent to it, and the reading of any particular line a highly contingent experience. But is this to say that the reading of an octosyllable is an aspiration towards a transcendent validation, a yearning of the contingent to be transformed into the absolute, either by the rhythms created or by the octosyllabic quatrain's external form? Or is it something that delights in, benefits from, its very immanence and contingency, and from the absence of hierarchy and positional tendentiousness? Why indeed should it not be both?

Let us consider an example, the first two stanzas of 'La Rose-Thé':

La plus délicate des roses	5+3
Est, à coup sûr, la rose-thé.	4+4 | 4+2+2
Son bouton aux feuilles mi-closes	3+5 | 3+2+3
De carmin à peine est teinté.	3+5 | 3+2+3
On dirait une rose blanche	3+5 | 3+3+2
Qu'aurait fait rougir de pudeur,	5+3 | 3+2+3
En la lutinant sur la branche,	5+3
Un papillon trop plein d'ardeur.	4+4 | 4+2+2

With the octosyllable, we cannot, as we can with the alexandrine, think of a binary norm, susceptible to occasional ternary interference; there is no sense of some ground-segmentation occasionally syncopated by a cross-rhythm. Binary and ternary rhythms coexist, so that reading never settles, unless the poet expressly compels it to. In this sense we never really hear *the* rhythm, or the rhythmic substructure, of a group of octosyllables; we only hear the recurrence of the octosyllable's numericity and the rhythm of the stanza's rhymes. The line-internal rhythms float in an indeterminate and shifting mid-air; we may be sure of the rhythm of a line as we read it, but as that line recedes into its stanzaic group, its rhythm blurs and entangles itself. Thus, though cinematic effects can be achieved punctually or in terms of a step by step sequence, they are dissolved the moment we try and apprehend the steps all together; just as there is a paradoxical coexistence of framing and transition, so equally we find a paradoxical fusion of temporary focus and long-term indefiniteness. The presence of affective paradox, metamorphosis, superimposition of images in *Emaux et camées* is, one might argue, motivated by the octosyllable itself. In our example the pair 'à peine'/'trop plein' does not emerge as an engineered paradox, conceptually organised by rhythmic parallelism; rather the words form dissyllabic units with different rhythmic contexts which relate them more obliquely, more fluidly. Equally the potentially paradoxical juxtaposition of the intense red 'carmin' and 'à peine est teinté' is left more as modulation than collision by the wavering rhythm. And the elusiveness of the subject, presented as a sequence of partial glimpses, valuable in themselves, but adding up to a coherence with difficulty, is acted out in the rhythmic elusiveness. The rhythms of the octosyllable are in a state of constant change, not merely from line to line, but within individual lines as well.

And if the rhythms are in a state of constant change, so position too is governed by the principle of change. Lexical items cannot acquire a particular colouring, a particular kind of impulsiveness or relief, by virtue of the syllable(s) they occupy (except for the rhyme-position). The rhythms of the octosyllables do not provide sufficient positional stability, do not define degrees of juncture or accent sufficiently, for words to derive expressive leverage from their place in the line. Even if a reader chose a 3+5 reading for lines 3–5 of our quotation, he could not by that manœuvre allocate any special significance to position 3, simply because his reading would demonstrate that a 3+5 pattern was *repeatable* but would not establish that 3+5 was *repeated*, as a matter of prosodic fact. Nor can any case be made for particular parts of speech naturally gravitating towards certain positions, a case that certainly can be made in respect of the alexandrine. But the lack of significance in position does not mean that a lexical item's moveability is insignificant. Quite the contrary. In 'Symphonie en blanc majeur', 'blanc' appears in one grammatical guise or another – adjective: blanc/ blanche, noun: blanc, blancheur – at least once in every stanza; in fact there are twenty-one occurrences disposed thus:

Syllable	1	2	3	4	5	6	7	8
Frequency	1	2	4	5	2	0	0	7

In fact it appears in almost every position. Its absence at syllable 7 should not surprise us; since it is bound to seek accent, it is not likely to be adjacent to the necessary accent of the rhyme. And its absence at syllable 6 seems a matter of chance; it appears in that position in our earlier quotations apropos of 'blanc' from 'Affinités secrètes' and 'Les Néréides'. And its relative frequency at syllable 8 requires no explanation. Its mobility signals its protean nature, its refusal to search for a consistency, to attach to itself, or itself to, a system of values. And the octosyllable gives it this unanchorability, while accent and accentual pattern mould themselves to the word, pushing it through its metamorphoses, interrogating it. In each line in which it appears, it may be held for a moment, but it is held on sufferance, its accentuation authorised by nothing other than its accentuability, by the reader's desire to know it or see it in its variations, its position revealing nothing other than its being one (or two) syllable(s) located somewhere in an eight-syllable chain and promising no coded expressiveness. The octosyllable is antipositional; it does not interfere with the reader's bestowal of rhythms, but nor does it authorise a prosodic codification of the rhythms thus bestowed. If the achievedness of the octosyllabic poem's external form and the rich consummations of its rhymes are to vindicate themselves, then it will not be in terms of uncompromising brevity, neatness or clarity, but because they have been won from the invertebrate fluidity of its rhythms.

If position has any part to play in the octosyllable, then it will be at the level of the stanza rather than at the level of the line. The circumflex intonational shape of the alexandrine may arch across the octosyllabic stanza or each pair of lines within the quatrain, thus:

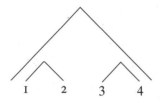

This diagram is something of a simplification. The circumflexes on the pairs of lines should look more like ∧ ∧, with line three beginning at a lower pitch point than line one, and line four ending at a lower pitch than line two. Equally the single circumflex spanning the whole stanza should look more like ⌒‿⌒ , with the intonational curves in lines two and three much flatter, with a slight dipping at the end of two and a slight rise at the end of three. Two stanzas from 'Les Joujoux de la morte' will serve to exemplify these two patterns:

Type 1: ∧∧   Sur le tapis et sur la table
                 Traîne l'héritage enfantin.
                 Les bras battants, l'air lamentable,
                 Tout affaissé, gît le pantin.

Type 2: ⌒‿⌒   Et des pleurs vous mouillent la joue
                 Quand *la Donna è mobile*,
                 Sur le rouleau qui tourne et joue,
                 Expire avec un son filé.

Any word which occurs in lines two and four of Type 1 and line four of Type 2 will thus attract to itself a dying coloration, whether of lethargy, resignation, despair, effacement. The Paris obelisk compares the Seine with the Nile in a stanza of Type 2:

> La Seine, noir égout des rues,
> Fleuve immonde, fait de ruisseaux,
> Salit mon pied, que dans ses crues
> Baisait le Nil, père des eaux
> ('Nostalgies d'obélisques I: L'obélisque de Paris')

and the Nile, because of its position in the final line, assumes a regretful coloration, an increasing and dispiriting remoteness in memory. But the very fact that it has come to mind is enough to revive memory, to provoke the obelisk to a defiance, to a reaffirmation of the Nile's value. And thus it appears in the first line of the following stanza, on a rising pitch-curve:

> Le Nil, géant à barbe blanche,
> Coiffé de lotus et de joncs

And so it is set directly against the Seine which had also appeared on a rising pitch-curve in the previous stanza, and in the same second position. But the Seine's rising pitch-curve is the thrust of anger and disgust, of exasperated impotence. Thus position may be of significance in the overall stanzaic shape, but it has no mapping function within the individual line.

Armed with these findings let us now briefly return to Lamartine, and in particular to two poems, 'Le Soir' and 'Souvenir', both written in octosyllabic quatrains with *rimes embrassées*. It is perhaps now clear what part the octosyllable has to play in the general, if unconscious, 'design' of the *Méditations poétiques*: the octosyllable acts as a melting-pot in which characteristic Lamartinian concerns can recover an unformedness, can express their essential ambivalence. Whereas in the alexandrines lexical items looked to hierarchise themselves in a prosodically motivated structure, to gauge their semantic and affective range, to define the gamut of their functions, by reference to a given, 'transcendent' system, these same lexical items more properly improvise themselves and constantly reassess themselves in the context of the octosyllable. Lamartine's octosyllables differ from Gautier's in that they are informed by a more consistent and explicit tone, in that their syntax does not have the same dislocations and discontinuity as his, in that substantives, with their focussing effects, do not have the same predominance. Nonetheless, the same thwarting of periodicity is to be found, the same undermining of rhetorical impulses, the same tendency towards punctuality, the same immanence and unauthorisedness of rhythm, the same, if more attenuated, cinematic effects.

The opening of 'Le Soir' depicts nightfall and the coming of silence. Suddenly a ray from the moon alights on the poet, and provokes a sequence of hopeful rhetorical questions about its nature. These questions change to imperatives as the poet asks the ray to realise what it seems to promise. Finally the moon is hidden from view. The questions and imperatives seem to be further examples of those delaying or distracting tactics so dear to Lamartine; it is as though he is attempting to prevent the circumflex shape of the octosyllabic stanza from asserting itself, by buoying up its closure with pitch-raising interrogatives and commands. Unfortunately, in the penultimate stanza, even though it, too, is governed by an imperative, signs of exhaustion and a desire for tranquillity at all costs allow for a lowering of defences, and the falling cadence is introduced:

Ramenez la paix et l'amour	5+3 | 3+2+3
Au sein de mon âme épuisée,	5+3 | 2+3+3
Comme la nocturne rosée	5+3
Qui tombe après les feux du jour.	2+6 | 2+4+2

After a final convulsion of the imperative at the beginning of the final stanza, the process of expiration and effacement are able to complete themselves:

Venez! ... Mais des vapeurs funèbres	2+6 | 2+4+2
Montent des bords de l'horizon.	4+4 | 1+3+4
Elles voilent le doux rayon,	3+5 | 3+3+2
Et tout rentre dans les ténèbres.	3+5

If time is present in the very fabric of Lamartine's verse, it is intensely so in the octosyllable. It is present as the principle of change which inhabits rhythm, it is present in the immanence of rhythms which function, and are perceptible, only in the experiential sequence of the reading act and are not able to abstract themselves from that flux, not able to establish themselves as prosodically authorised, as belonging to the timeless world of convention. It is present in the prohibition of periodicity.

Periodicity has two coextensive aspects, syntactical and tonal. In syntactical terms periodicity implies hypotaxis, discourse whose aesthetic and persuasive effects lie in the rhythm of its articulations and the intonational variations which those articulations engineer. If we look at the two stanzas from 'Le Soir' just quoted, we cannot but be struck by the predominantly paratactic structures that the octosyllabic stanza, by its very brevity, invites and the way in which it will tend to 'paratacticalise' any signs of hypotaxis. This is another way of expressing the cinematic phenomenon. Whatever devices may work to delay the reader within the line – rhythmic ambivalence, mute e's and so on – the octosyllable works to disarticulate, to force utterance into a series of declarative enunciations, in which new beginnings continuously produce new endings and in which the relation of an effect to a cause is constantly elided. The octosyllable does not permit processes of rationalisation and qualification, just as it discourages hierarchisation. As we read the final stanza, we read through a sequence of punctual events, of frames; no compromises or syntactic transactions can take place; and yet we know that this is not just a sequence of events; it is at the very least the workings of the divine mystery of the universe. And even where, as in the penultimate stanza, the syntax is more elaborate, our sense of each syntactical unit having a self-justifying declarative force is still very strong; clauses and phrases do not so much qualify each other and create their own extendable duration, as move out along their own radiuses, moments of perception caught out of the relentless movement of time, and juxtaposed. If the octosyllable's propensity for parataxis increases the inscrutability of its motivation and isolates perceptions in their own mystery, it also encodes the propulsiveness of temporality.

Periodicity's voice aspect we have already described (see above, pp. 43–4). The fact that the tone of Lamartine's verse is ostensibly more consistent and lyrical than Gautier's, and that his recourse to rhetorical devices is more overt, should not blind us to the octosyllable's obstructive power, its ability to take the rhetoric out of rhetoric. Six of the stanzas of 'Le Soir' carry rhetorical questions, as, for example, the eighth stanza:

Viens-tu dévoiler l'avenir	5+3 | 2+3+3
Au coeur fatigué qui l'implore?	5+3 | 2+3+3
Rayon divin, es-tu l'aurore	4+4 | 2+2+4
Du jour qui ne doit pas finir?	2+6

But the voice loses its authority when it does not speak in authorised rhythms. Whose voice do we hear when two scansions are available in a line? And how can a poet be said to be employing rhetorical strategies when no design can emerge, when the potential intention is scrambled by ambivalence? The moments of essayed rhetoric in Lamartine's octosyllables are indeed moments of peculiar poignancy: as we have seen, Lamartine's rhetorical strategies are already only too often strategies of desperation; but in the octosyllable, rhetoric cannot even sustain its own sense of purpose; if rhetoric is the exercising of an expressiveness already arrived at, we must accept that the octosyllable compels language to *search for* its expressiveness. How can Lamartine's poet persuade the moon, seduce the reader, if his language is rhythmically so malleable? Ultimately it is the reader's rhetoric, imprinting itself in a particular set of rhythmic choices or priorities, which is able to persuade the reader.

This eighth stanza contains a lexical item to which we have already paid some attention, namely the 'rayon'. It appears five times in this poem, its accentuable second syllable falling once at syllable 2, once at syllable 3, twice at syllable 4 and once at syllable 8. It has all the mobility of Gautier's 'blanc', the wealth of metamorphoses, which is precisely what necessitates the poet's questions about its nature. And yet this freedom of the 'rayon' to assume any of a number of roles, this refusal of definition, at once the source of multiple hope in the poet, is at the same time the threat of volatility, of a taunting unwillingness to be anything. Equally 'glisser' which in this poem, as already mentioned, has a benignly soothing, caressive quality, may, at the octosyllable's instigation, invert into negativity, into a process of unarrestable evaporation.

'Souvenir', which is a companion piece to 'Le Soir', written at the same place, the château d'Urcy, at about the same time (May–June 1819),[12] uses 'glisser' in this negative sense, as we have already noted. But the chief lexical protagonist in this poem is 'encore', appearing four times during the course of the poem; it is in fact the word on which the poem ends. The positions of its accentuable syllable are: once at syllable 4, once at syllable 5 and twice at syllable 8. In all instances bar the final one, 'encore' apparently has the positive value of the still there, the reassuringly persistent, the gloriously ineffaceable. But in the last two lines:

> Nos deux âmes ne forment plus
> Qu'une âme, et je soupire encore!

'encore' dips into a negative, a 'still' which has not yet become an 'enfin' or 'déjà' of new perception; the poet reproaches himself for hanging on to a regretful, yearning state when all the evidence of the poem points to a mystical union with Elvire having already been achieved. Letessier (1968) is of the opinion that despite this final expression of dissatisfaction, the conclusion is 'moins sombre que celle du *Soir*' (p. 534). I find this opinion difficult to agree with; it seems to me that Letessier has not taken full account of the ambiguating influence of the octosyllable.

This last line's tone is extremely difficult to catch. Is 'et je soupire encore' uttered in disbelief, with the exclamation mark also doing service as question mark, lifting the pitch? Or is 'et je soupire encore' an expression, perhaps painful to admit, perhaps simply matter-of-fact, of unfulfilled desire, of a yearning that will not be appeased by the fabrication of consoling images; and if this is so, is its pitch rising in aspiration and unfinishedness or falling in resigned determination and withdrawal into self? The rhythmic ambivalence of the last line only intensifies the problem:

> Qu'une âme, et je soupire encore!   2+6 | 2+4+2

One cannot say that the 2+6 reading belongs to the first interpretative option (disbelief) and the trimetric reading to the second (unfulfilled desire). But the trimetric reading with its protraction and its acknowledgement of the present experiential reality of 'soupire' is peculiarly apt to the second option. Accentuated, 'soupire' becomes the widowed echo of the 'soupirs' mentioned two lines earlier:

> Comme deux soupirs confondus!   5+3 | (1+4+3)

These 'soupirs' are not the convenient 'ideas', the almost allegorical images, that the 'rayons' of the stanza's first line are:

> Comme deux rayons de l'aurore

They are rather an only semi-sublimated erotic experience, whose wished-for persistence is indicated by a third and earlier occurrence of the 'sigh':

> Tandis que la terre sommeille,
> Si j'entends le vent soupirer,
> Je crois t'entendre murmurer
> Des mots sacrés à mon oreille.

In this, the twelfth stanza, one might argue that 'soupirer' and 'murmurer' are occupying each other's proper place and that the 'mots sacrés' are sacred to the poet, but have little to do with divine sacredness. And the infiltration of this erotic awareness is brought about not only by the positional versatility of the 'sigh' alone, but by less concealed moments of sensual indulgence:

> Du zéphyr l'amoureuse haleine
> Soulève encor tes longs cheveux;
> Sur ton sein leurs flots onduleux
> Retombent en tresses d'ébène.

And this stanza brings us back to 'encor' and ambiguates it. Perhaps the first three occurrences of 'encore' have more in common with the final one than we thought. This 'encor' is not the *reassuringly* persistent, but the provocatively, irritatingly, peace-denyingly persistent. This is the 'encor' which tells you not what you still have, but what you have and cannot enjoy. This is an 'encor' which will achieve neither the 'enfin' of consummation and satiety nor the 'enfin' of indifference or oblivion. The mystical union with Elvire is a consolation prize, an illusory consolation which does not dupe the poet. And even if it were not illusory, it would do nothing to quieten the yearnings of the flesh.

Such is the mercurial nature of the octosyllable. It is a web of ambiguities, dislocations, mobilities which provoke the reader to try and orientate himself, to plumb its enigmas without providing any guarantees of solutions. Its rhythms are without metrical authorisation, its syllabic positions without the value of a code. What may hold true for the expressive aura of lexical items within the alexandrine, will not do so if the same lexical items are put into an octosyllabic context. It is not difficult, on the strength of our evidence, to agree with David Scott's (1977) view of the octo-syllable: 'Sparkling enigmatically, it makes the twists and turns of its own internal processes the centre of attraction' (p. 161).

But I wish in the next chapter to turn back to the alexandrine, and to the Baudelairian alexandrine in particular. So far we have examined the relationship between syllabic position in the alexandrine and those 'loaded' lexical items revealed by a thematic analysis. This has led us to ask questions about the nature of the octosyllable in relation to the alexandrine and whether syllabic position has the same significance in the shorter line as it has in the longer one. In returning to the stabler and more codified world of the alexandrine, I wish now to consider syllabic position and its effect on the operation of a figure of speech, namely simile. In order to enlarge the scope of this analysis, I will compare the way 'comme' functions in Baudelaire's alexandrines with the way 'like' functions in the poetry of a writer whom Gautier's verse summoned, Oscar Wilde.

3
FIGURE AND SYLLABIC POSITION

SIMILE IN THE POETRY OF WILDE AND BAUDELAIRE

With recent concentration on the metaphor/metonymy polarity, comparatively little attention has been paid to the relationship between metaphor and simile. Criticism continues in the view that simile is essentially a metaphor that has come to consciousness, that metaphor is simply an elliptical form of simile; both figures are seen as figures of comparison, the difference between them being structural. Geoffrey Leech (1969), for example, says that 'metaphoric transference can only take place if some likeness is perceived between tenor and vehicle' (p. 151) and, further on, that 'simile is an overt, and metaphor a covert comparison' (p. 156). Where a distinction *is* made, the implications explored are not the expressive ones, but the different kinds of generical shadow that each figure casts; David Lodge (1977) concedes: 'Metaphor, it is sometimes said, asserts identity, simile merely likeness', but this challenging differentiation is absorbed into the generical remark: '... and perhaps on this account the former trope is usually considered the more "poetic"' (p. 112).

The assumption upon which my own exploration is based is that metaphor and simile, in their 'pure' state, are indeed radically different. Metaphor is an identification of one phenomenon with another, simile is a comparison. From this fundamental distinction follow distinctions of nature and function, which are perhaps best tabulated, thus:

Metaphor (identification)	*Simile* (comparison)
direct, immediate (speed)	discursive
urgent	leisured
absolute (essentialist)	partial, provisional (relativist)
permanent	temporary
committed	tentative, uncommitted
intuited	thought-up and rationalisable
functionless	explicative, illustrative
judgement-resistant	judgement-prone

inclusive   aspect-selective
toneless   toneful

These distinctions of nature and function can be summarised in this way: metaphor challenges the imagination to break new ground, while simile appeals to what we already know about things; metaphor reorganises the world and thus plays with chaos, while simile maintains the world order by keeping separate, as discrete phenomena, the items it compares; metaphor is a statement of fact, for better or worse, and we cannot, other than impertinently, bring our judgement to bear on it, while simile offers itself to us, expressly, for approval, and we would not be doing it justice if we did not give it the benefit of our full critical scrutiny.

The final distinction made in the table – toneless v. toneful – falls outside the summary and is particularly important for the present exploration. Simile belongs to voice, to poetic tone, in a way that metaphor does not. Simile is the positive assumption of a role by the poet, the determined inhabitation of the creative process, of the production of utterance. Metaphor, on the other hand, presents itself as a given, having its source not in the poet's embroidering rhetoric, but in a realm of truth beyond all control and all manipulation; metaphor tends always towards the mediumic communication. And it is this last factor that makes simile so necessary to one of the subjects of this essay, Baudelaire. For all his talk of the poet as translator, as decipherer, as mediator, Baudelaire finds it existentially impossible to relinquish his role as utterer, as acceptor of his own guilty condition. Simile, like allegory, may seem to indicate in Baudelaire's work a loss of faith, the failure of language; simile may seem to be a fall from the grace of metaphor, as allegory is a symbol fallen from grace. But may we not enjoy the poignancy and nobility of simile and allegory in *Les Fleurs du Mal*, the unevenness they admit, Baudelaire's obstinacy in accepting responsibility for his work, not moral responsibility merely, but the responsibility of sheer lyric production? At all events, simile is voice-derived, it projects tone and the presence of the poetic persona into the poetic texture, in a way that metaphor does not.

So far, I have spoken of metaphor and simile in a notional 'pure' state. Simile, in a pure state, offers the mirage of shared insight and refreshingly casual creativity. Metaphor, in a pure state, is beyond meaning: the points of contact between the identified phenomena are too manifold for us to be able to rationalise and interpret them. Metaphor is, thus, a linguistic structure, a category of substitution, which resists *lisibilité*. We might argue that the drift in metaphoric usage over the last century and a half has been in the direction of the pure-state metaphor: that is, the state in which metaphor ceases to be a figure of speech (i.e. a conventional licence, recognisable as an *accepted* mechanism of transference, to release connotation), ceases to be 'metaphor' in a sense, and becomes statement of personally revealed fact, recovers its literality and hence its total and final intractability. But we rarely meet these figures in their pure state. Metaphor and simile constantly contaminate each other. For example, much lyric poetry is in the present (and potentially omnipresent) tense, and thus aids the absoluteness and permanence of metaphor; but put a metaphor in a past-tense context, and already it has acquired some of simile's temporariness. The 'distance' between tenor and vehicle will also have its effect; a 'narrow-angled' metaphor will perhaps naturally slide towards similaic status, while a 'wide-angled' simile will do the reverse. Equally, a metaphor presented deictically will, insofar as it appeals to the evidence of the senses, have the feel of a simile, as in the sequence of metaphors which run through the octave of Hopkins's sonnet 'The Starlight Night':

> Look at the stars! look, look up at the skies!
> O look at all the fire-folk sitting in the air!
> The bright boroughs, the circle-citadels there!
> ... etc.

Here the sequence of metaphors built on stars – fire-folk, boroughs, citadels – falling within the sphere of influence of the deictic elements 'look at' and 'there', is presented in such a way that its visual aptness is thrown out as a challenge, and similarity is inevitably the paramount yardstick.

What governs the shifts of simile along the sliding-scale from 'pure' simile to 'pure' metaphor? We have already mentioned the importance of the 'width of angle' between tenor and vehicle. Syntax and prosodic juncture matter too of course. In Baudelaire's lines:

> Où l'Espérance, comme une chauve-souris,
> S'en va battant les murs de son aile timide
> > ('Spleen': 'Quand le ciel bas et lourd')

the first line presents a structure in which hope and bat are held momentarily in a relationship of totality, at the threshold of a multitude of possible verbs, in a conjunction where, for a moment, 'comme' might be the metaphoric copula.[1] If, on the other hand, we imagine the syntax 'où l'Espérance s'en va battant les murs comme une chauve-souris', then the simile explains and defuses the metaphor 's'en va battant les murs'. It is evident too that phonetic factors might have a part to play; in Wilde's poetry, which is the other subject of this essay, we find combinations such as 'Her neck is like white melilote', and 'And like bright sunbeams flitting through a glade', where the assonances between instrument of comparison and adjective – 'like white', 'like bright' – not only insinuate the appropriateness, necessariness even, of the comparison, but also absorb the similaic formula into the vehicle, so that the phrase has a more metaphorical insistence. It might equally be argued, as we shall see, that the similaic formula in these examples absorbs the vehicle.

But it is the prosodic context of simile upon which I wish to concentrate. And the question I want to ask is: how far is the way a simile projects itself dependent upon the position of the similaic formula in the line and in the line's pattern of accentuation, and upon the phonetic make-up of the similaic formula? I shall confine myself to a study of 'like' (in Wilde's poems) and 'comme' (in Baudelaire's alexandrines), leaving aside all other locutions that serve to signpost processes of simile.

'Like' and the poems of Oscar Wilde

Like 'comme', 'like' has some availability to stress (accentuation), which we will consider later. To begin with, however, let us examine 'like' as an unstressed element in predominantly iambic patterns.

When 'like' is followed by noun, or adjective+noun, without article, it presents no metrical problems; it is simply the first, unstressed syllable of an iambic foot – 'like burnt-out torches', 'like swarming flies', 'like silhouettes', 'like water bubbling' etc. When, however, 'like' is followed by the definite or indefinite article, the question arises: how can two consecutive unstressed syllables be accommodated in an alternating metre? The least problematic solution is to exploit the amenable first foot, which can either be inverted, giving, over the first four syllables, the choriambic pattern /xx/, or replaced by a pyrrhic foot and followed by a spondee, giving, over the first four syllables, the ionic pattern xx//. Neither of these variations produces any real disruption; the first foot is the expected, the accepted, site of metrical deviation. Of Wilde's 107^2 uses of 'like', 40 occupy the first syllable and 29 the second. Of the

40 first-syllable appearances, 16 involve 'like' + definite or indefinite article. Of the 29 second-syllable appearances, 24 involve 'like' + definite or indefinite article.

(i) First-syllable occurrences, with definite or indefinite article

Within a predominantly iambic metrical context, the appearance of 'like' in the first position, followed by an article, would lead the reader to suppose one of three possible explanations:

(a) The line is iambic, but with anapaestic intermixture.
(b) The unstressed syllable of 'like' is an anacrusis (i.e. an 'upbeat' or hypermetrical slack at the beginning of the line).
(c) There is pyrrhic substitution in the first foot.

The 16 instances we have under this heading are distributed among these three explanations as follows: (a) 5 (b) 5 (c) 6. Since in iambic/anapaestic mixtures, 'like the' and 'like a' are metrically unnoteworthy, let us turn to (b) and (c).

It should be suggested immediately that the two unstressed syllables of 'like a' or 'like the' throw the voice forward on to the image. Speed is a characteristic of metaphoric perception, whereas simile is discursively thought up; but here, metric structure endows simile with a peculiar urgency. The five examples of (b) occur, significantly, in a single poem, 'The Ballad of Reading Gaol', where urgency is not so much generated by the images themselves as by the mood of apprehension and anxiety which permeates the poem:

> At last I saw the shadowed bars,
>   Like a lattice wrought in lead,
> Move right across the whitewashed wall
>   That faced my three-plank bed,
> And I knew that somewhere in the world
>   God's dreadful dawn was red.   (stanza 57)

Iron bars = lead lattice is too 'narrow-angled' an image to function strongly *as image*; we would have to work at the leadenness of lead and the web-likeness of lattice to get our return. The real effect lies in the image-making process itself, in the inevitability of image-production for the confined prisoner, in the prisoner's subjection to image. Here, the alliterative l's make the glide from similaic formula to image smooth, relentlessly smooth, unavoidably smooth, helped as it is by vocalic modulation – long a and long i to short a and short i in a chiastic configuration: *like a lattice*. As in the examples of assonantal relationship between 'like' and adjective (white, bright) quoted earlier, the image is already installed in the image-making process, is anticipated by it.

But the anacrusis is equally important. In this dark world of stealthy, fearful men, living in half-knowledge of the world around them, themselves living through the condemned man's guilt, the heart intermittently quickens, yields to a weakness. This practice of anacrusis is not limited to the simile locution alone; in the stanza quoted, another line has the same initial extra slack syllable:

> And I knew that somewhere in the world

But it peculiarly suits the simile. At these points of momentary breathlessness, the mind is vulnerable to the incursions of hallucination and vision:

> With sudden shock the prison-clock
>   Smote on the shivering air,
> And from all the gaol rose up a wail
>   Of impotent despair,
> Like the sound that frightened marshes hear
>   From some leper in his lair.   (stanza 64)

Within the simile here, of course, is some metaphoric anthropomorphism. The anacruses in the two final lines remind us that the real vehicle is the sound of lepers and that the frightened marshes are dramatic decoration; we collide with the leper in the same rhythmic fashion, with the same irresistible immediacy, as we are invaded by the sound. And again the alliteration drives us through the similaic locution to the image of diseased pariah-dom (leper) and on to the image of a last retreat and regression to barbarism (lair) with the kind of intuited certainty characteristic of metaphor.

In the (c) explanation, the ionic pattern xx// over the first four syllables suggests, of itself, the sequence like+article+monosyllabic adjective+noun:

> The sky is laced with fitful red,
> The circling mists and shadows flee,
> The dawn is rising from the sea,
> Like a white lady from her bed.
>   ('Impression: Le Réveillon')

> And leapt upon a grassy knoll and ran
> Like a young fawn unto an olive wood   ('Charmides')

Again, the images are not striking in themselves. But their spondaic structure gives them a peculiar fullness, is an invitation to savour and dwell. Here the simile and the image it projects become a temporary terminus, an achievement of definition satisfied with itself. And to reinforce this sense, they call forth a following caesura. Though the similaic locution here also tends to efface itself, it does not generate a near-metaphoric charge in the way that the 'like' of anacrusis does. Simile is interested in making the unsuspected triumphantly self-evident. Metaphor, on the other hand, is not concerned about the degree of its persuasiveness. Wilde's spondaic images bask in *demonstrable* aptness and exude confident appeal. What is strange about the lines from 'Charmides' is that the way in which the image is metrically presented is not justified by the image. It has no need to convince, as the metrical structure implies that it has. At all events, though the similaic locution here becomes a kind of rhythmic assumption, the image it introduces is resplendent with uttered fittingness.

The similaic locution is, as we have said, the way the voice insinuates itself into the image-making process, is where the poet proposes himself as the visualising mediator. The nature of this mediation is determined by the simile's constitution. Poetry offers, as prose does not, a set of metrical alternatives which allow simile to explore its variability, to project its images with different focuses and functions. And these variations in focus and function are intimately connected with variations of voice-presence, of mood, urgent or complacent, controlled or anxious. It would be wrong to say that metaphor has no such modal value; but metaphor's modal value derives much more from the image itself, and from the general implications of metaphor as a figure (listed on pp. 61–2), than from the spirit which permeates its *presentation*.

(ii) Second-syllable occurrences

Let us now give some brief consideration to 'like' in the second-syllable position. Two broad possibilities obtain here:

(a)   That the first syllable is evidently stressed, so that a 'normal' first-foot inversion occurs in the iambic line.

(b)   That the first syllable is not evidently stressed, in which case either 'like' will tend to carry a stress or, in retrospect, the first syllable will be given a stress-value that it normally does not bear and a pause will be introduced after it to justify that new stress-value.

As far as (a) is concerned, verbs constitute the majority of stressed initial elements in Wilde's simile lines:

> The sea was sapphire coloured, and the sky
> Burned like a heated opal through the air
>
> ('Impression de voyage')

> The yellow fog came creeping down
> The bridges, till the houses' walls
> Seemed changed to shadows and St. Paul's
> Loomed like a bubble o'er the town.
>
> ('Impression du matin')

> And down the long and silent street,
> The dawn, with silver-haired feet,
> Crept like a frightened girl.   ('The Harlot's House')

In these examples, the suspensiveness of the preceding enjambement and the metrical inversion give the verb a surprising momentum, carry it through the whole line as an after-image. And so in these instances, the verb is not the bridge to the simile, the mystery that needs to be solved or the tired word that needs revivifying. Quite the reverse. The simile helps to support the verb, while gently pacifying it and bringing it under the poet's supervision. In the first two examples quoted – 'and the sky / Burned like a heated opal' and 'and St. Paul's / Loomed like a bubble' – the verbs have little obvious metaphorical charge. There is some transference from sun to sky in 'the sky / Burned' and 'Loomed' has a trace of movement and sinisterness which carries beyond the literal. But it is the prosody of these verbs which gives them an unexpected force. One would expect the similes, being of a more figurative nature than the verbs, to intensify them retrospectively, but this does not happen, simply because while the verbs are actional (dynamic), the similes are presentational (static) – 'heated' is already a past participle. So, far from taking the incipient figurativeness of the verbs further along the road to metaphor, simile acts as an agent of pacification, steadying the drive of the verb, dispersing its stress in two unstressed syllables. The unstressedness of the similaic locution facilitates the reaching for settledness. And, concomitantly, it is the poet reassuming a kind of creative responsibility, reaffirming his voice against the threatening autonomy of the image. The third example does involve the actual de-fusion (by explanation) of the metaphorical expression 'The dawn . . . / Crept'.

The examples of (b) usually involve lines beginning with 'And':

> And like a blossom blown before the breeze
> A white moon drifts across the shimmering sky
>
> ('The Burden of Itys')

And like a dipping swallow the stout ship dashed through the storm.

('Charmides')

> And like a withered leaf the moon
> Is blown across the stormy bay.   ('Les Silhouettes')

There are two obvious ways of reading the simile lines here: either as regularly iambic, in which case a stress, however light, will fall on 'like':

And like a withered leaf the moon

or one introduces a pause after 'And', suggesting the parenthetic nature of the simile and consequently leaning more heavily on 'And', creating an inverted first foot:

And | like a withered leaf the moon

The second option makes the simile excessively by the way to my hearing, even when framed by a pause after 'leaf'

And | like a withered leaf | the moon

It would not be difficult to argue that for Wilde simile is indeed something approaching a party trick, a little peace of interpolative verbal magic. But 'like' does have a density of its own: it constitutes a threshold of liberating invention, which makes the whole world available; or, alternatively, it is the fatal precipice of known and circumscribed possibilities. Simile is governed, as we have said, by the rational principle; 'like' is the sign for the exercise of reason; the charming thing about simile is that reason condones flights of fancy; the horrifying thing about simile is that reason necessitates the unavoidable choice of the apposite. After all there might be more poetry in the word 'like' than in the image it prefaces, and this can only be implied by an iambic reading:

And like a withered leaf the moon

Let us listen to two further examples:

And like a blossom blown before the breeze

and

And like a dipping swallow the stout ship dashed through the storm

I would want to suggest that the accentual 'lifting' of 'like' has a lightening, and of course lilting, effect on the image, creating a totally smooth rhythmic context. The ethereality of the second image is made obvious by contrast with the rhythmic fragmentation of the rest of the line, ionic run followed by choriambic run (or pyrrhic substitution in 4th foot, spondaic substitution in 5th foot, trochaic substitution in 6th foot). What makes this line so rich is precisely that the swallow image (graceful, effortless speed) does not fit the rest of the facts (strength, violence, struggle), is a kind of infra-image lodged not in the actual motion of the ship, but in its will or aspiration.

The choice of scansions presented here (inverted first foot or regularly iambic first foot) will frequently occur, and as much after a caesura as at the beginning of a line. Or, put more correctly, if read in a certain way (i.e. with 'like' unstressed, along with its following article), the similaic locution will require a pause before it and this pause may coincide with or create the caesura, as in the line from 'Panthea':

> Her warm soft body like the briar rose

It is virtually impossible to read an unstressed 'like' here, or rather the sequence of three unstressed syllables thus produced, without a caesural rest:

> Her warm soft bodý | lĩke thĕ briar róse

But we can let this warm, soft, body flow into the outlines of the Sleeping Beauty unhindered, we can enjoy it with the evenness of the caressing voice, only if we make a continuous, largely unpaused reading possible; and we can do this only by giving 'like' some accentual relief:

> Hĕr warm soft bódy líke thĕ briar róse

Let us close our treatment of Wilde with one last dilemma, a line from 'Charmides':

> And like bright sunbeams flitting through a glade
> Each startled Dryad sought some safe and leafy ambuscade.

Should we read the first line of this couplet as xx//x/x/x/ (i.e. with ionic opening) or more or less iambically x/x/x/x/x/. The ionic gives us a sudden flood of light. Iambic, on the other hand, provides smooth undramatic movement and asks us to use the assonance of 'like bright' to facilitate a retrospective transference of accentual force from adjective to similaic locution, or put another way, the assonance allows 'bright' to be absorbed, with a reduction of stress, by 'like'. In this latter reading 'like' is foregrounded both for its own sake and because it is half-performing the function of the accompanying adjective.

'Comme' and Baudelaire's 'Les Fleurs du Mal'

When we move to French verse, we must remember two things. 'Like' and 'comme' operate within different families of possible forms: 'like' may be an adjective, a conjunction, a noun, a verb, while 'comme' is not only a conjunction, with a variety of roles, but also an adverb, usually in exclamatory utterances; when 'like' and 'comme' are used as tools of comparison, these different grammatical associations may be present and colour our response to the words, either subliminally, or more explicitly if the poet cares to remind us of the affiliation, as Apollinaire does in 'Le Pont Mirabeau', for example:

> L'amour s'en va comme cette eau courante
> L'amour s'en va
> Comme la vie est lente
> Et comme l'Espérance est violente

Secondly, 'comme' differs from 'like' in that its phonetic substance is available to modification: its *e atone* may function as a full syllable or may be elided. It might also be proposed, as we shall see, that in French verse, 'comme' has a significant prosodic history of its own, in a way that 'like' has not in English verse.

In examining Wilde's poetry, we concentrated on 'like' in the first and second positions in the line. This was partly inevitable – about 65% of all Wilde's uses of 'like' occur in these positions – and partly because we can expect similaic locutions to fall, in the main, immediately after the principal junctures (line-ending, caesura) (although Wilde, in fact, makes little use of post-caesural simile); simile needs to lay itself out as a statement reflected upon, specially uttered, and its source in reason demands that it find a structurally stabilising position in the prosodic order. But whereas the basic rhythmic units in English verse, the feet, work in very much the same way whatever the length of the line, measures of equal length in the French line function in totally different ways depending on whether the line is, say, an alexandrine or an octosyllable, and they relate to measures of dissimilar length in totally different ways as well; in other words, whereas the relationship between line-length and rhythmic units (feet) is, in English, a distant one, the former being an almost accidental result of an accumulation of the latter, the relationship between line-length and measures in French verse is inextricable, the former determining the combinational possibilities, and thus the lengths, of the latter; in other words, the length of the line in which 'comme' appears and its position in that line are more crucial than the same factors in relation to 'like'. Since the alexandrine has a system of prosodic imperatives and defined expectations more developed than in any other French line, it is with this line that my investigation will be concerned.

The first step in this investigation is necessarily statistical. There are 343 instances of 'comme' in *Les Fleurs du Mal* (that is, including 'Les Epaves', the 'Nouvelles Fleurs du Mal', the poems added to the posthumous edition of 1868, but excluding the 'Juvenilia'). Of these 343 instances, 294 are properly analogical forms of 'comme', and again of these 294, 210 occur in alexandrines. The pattern created by these 210 'comme's' on the alexandrine scale is as follows:

Syllable	1	2	3	4	5	6	7	8	9	10	11	12	
Frequency	55	13	14	6	3	6	58	11	37	7	0	0	= 210

As one might expect, the figures at the beginning of each hemistich are high and nearly equal: 55 and 58. The figures which might cause some surprise are those at syllable 6, where zero would be more probable, at syllable 5, where zero is equally likely (as at syllables 11 and 12) and the high number at syllable 9.

In 'comme', we can detect two prosodically significant features:
(a)   An *e atone*
(b)   An availability to mild accentuation, which it shares with 'like'.

(a) With the frequency of the indefinite article in analogical formulations, the e of 'comme' often disappears. But when the e is not elided, it embeds 'comme' in the intonational suppleness of the line and gives the word a peculiar fullness. When accompanied by other sounded e's, 'comme' begins to assume an *imitative* function as well. 'Like' may also have some phonetic significance, but this is, as we have seen, limited to the processes of connection, transference and support allowed by alliteration and assonance. 'Comme' not only has alliterative and assonant capabilities,[3] but also an inbuilt rhythmicity; with its e, it can generate intonational curvature ('like' is a single syllable which can only have its rhythmic role conferred upon it). And because it has this marginally, but crucially, greater syllabic presence, 'comme' has the phonetic variation within itself necessary for primitive forms of imitation.

This rather nice distinction is best argued for by exemplification:

> La Haine est un ivrogne au fond d'une taverne,
> Qui sent toujours la soif naître de la liqueur
> Et se multiplier comme l'hydre de Lerne.
>
> ('Le Tonneau de la haine')

The simile is set within the second of the metaphorical identifications governing the poem: hatred is the jar of the Danaids, hatred is a drunkard. 'Comme' installs, *sotto voce*, the rhythmic shape that 'hydre' underlines by virtue of the *coupe enjambante* which occurs within it: com|me l'hy|dre. And on the basis of this progression, this repetition, with intensification, of an intonational shape, we can propose two closely related points: first, that 'comme' anticipates, insinuates, initiates the coiling, writhing movement of the hydra; and secondly, and consequently, that the shape of 'comme', of the similaic locution itself, somehow generates or imagines the image. As the poet reaches for the simile, so the similaic formula resolves *itself* into the fitting image. This is to say that the formulation of the similaic formula can itself be an imaging process. The same case could be argued, perhaps, about 'like bright sunbeams': the long i of 'like' produces 'bright' which produces 'sunbeams'. But absent here is any sense of *rhythmic* generation, and absent, too, is any real imitative reinforcement (unless one argues, unjustifiably, for the inherent brightness of long i).

The last stanza of 'Le Balcon' will perhaps provide a clinching example:

> Ces serments, ces parfums ces baisers infinis,
> Renaîtront-ils d'un gouffre interdit à nos sondes,
> Comme montent au ciel les soleils rajeunis.

As before, 'comme's' atonic e is taken up by 'mon|tent' and thrown into relief by the *coupe enjambante*. Here the pitch-changes in 'comme' and 'montent' enact the lilt, more spiritual than physical perhaps, in the ascensional movement; physically, the successive pitch-changes project the idea of an ascension by stages. It may be no accident that the 'comme' with *e atone* is connected with upward movement:

> Et promène ses yeux sur les visions blanches
> Qui montent dans l'azur comme des floraisons.   2+4+6 (1+5)
>
> ('Tristesses de la lune')

> Mais la tristesse en moi monte comme la mer   4+2+1+5
>
> ('Causerie')

In these two examples, 'comme' takes up the rhythmic suggestion supplied by the verb and dampens it down, reduces it, most aptly in the second example where we must find some way to reconcile 'tristesse' and 'monter'. Equally, though the visions rise in 'Tristesse de la lune', the woman likened to the moon is described as 'mourante'. In our example from 'Le Balcon', the disembodied sense of upward swinging produced by 'comme' is enjoyed before it is defined by the agent; the inversion allows the 'rajeunissement' to be a defined outcome of a dynamism already at work.

(b) Like 'like', 'comme' can, in certain circumstances, receive light accentuation. Whether 'like' receives accentuation or not depends on its position in a sequence of stressed and unstressed syllables; roughly speaking, it is possible for it to be stressed anywhere in the line, as long as it is an even syllable – supposing that we are speaking of 'like' in iambic pentameters. 'Comme' may receive accentuation:

(i) if it finds itself, idiosyncratically, at a syllable which demands accentuation (syllable 6 or syllable 12 in the alexandrine) and as long as there are no preferable alternative readings to circumvent it.

(ii) if it occurs within a hemistich where there are no other contenders for the second accent. In these circumstances, 'comme' may attract to itself a slight supportive accent. It is with this latter type that I wish to deal first.

For (ii) to apply, 'comme' has really to occur at the beginning of the hemistich and be followed by an article+polysyllabic noun (i.e. a 1+5 hemistich); the following selection of examples shows this supposition to be generally true, but not absolutely:

> Comme les mendiants nourrissent leur vermine
>
> ('Au lecteur')

> Comme des avirons traîner à côté d'eux
>
> ('L'Albatros')

> Celui dont les pensers, comme des alouettes
>
> ('Elévation')

> Comme des papillons, errent en flamboyant
>
> ('Les Phares')

> Comme dans un caveau dont la clef est perdue
>
> ('Châtiment de l'orgueil')

> Comme des exilés, s'en vont d'un pied traînard
>
> ('Réversibilité')

> Destructeur et gourmand comme la courtisane
> ('L'Irréparable')

> Et, comme le soleil dans son enfer polaire
> ('Chant d'automne')

> Grande et svelte en marchant comme une chasseresse
> ('A une dame créole')

> Qui montent dans l'azur comme des floraisons
> ('Tristesses de la lune')

> Qui bave des naseaux comme un épileptique
> ('Une Gravure fantastique')

> Grands bois, vous m'effrayez comme des cathédrales
> ('Obsession')

> Comme un vomissement, remonter vers mes dents
> ('Un Voyage à Cythère)

In the majority of these instances, 'comme' is given added substance by the non-elision of its e. But the accentuation of these
'comme' hemistichs is actually rather odd. In them there is usually
only one true prosodic accent, on the last syllable. But not only
does the 'comme' attract a weak accent, the long polysyllabic nouns
themselves attract support accents, countertonic accents, on their
antepenultimate syllables. Thus, instead of the two strong prosodic
accents of the normal regular hemistich, we have three, two of
which are weak. This creates a wonderful measuredness, even
sedateness, in these half-lines, often befitting the subject:

> Grands bois, vous m'effrayez || comme les cathédrales

or

> Qui montent dans l'azur || comme des floraisons.

And even where we imagine the line invested by a more aggressive,
more involved tone, as in:

> Destructeur et gourmand || comme la courtisane

the 'comme' hemistich provides the poet with a momentary
control, installs an ironic or disdainful distance between the poet
and his bitterness. The hemistich-initial 'comme' has a braking
effect, as the image breaks out of the turmoil of active, busy syntax
into an unencumbered and tonally equilibriated ether. Unless it is
line-initial, the English 'like' finds it difficult to establish itself in the

surrounding syntax, to locate itself in an order of tones and phrasal patterning, and thus to affirm its function. With the phrasal nature of French measures and their accompanying junctures, 'comme' can more easily provide itself with different degrees of impulse and relief.

In the seventh position, and with a slight accentuation and syllabic fullness, 'comme' proposes itself as a plateau in the line, and simile-making as a steadying, meditational process, with 'comme' acting as a kind of mantra. The moment of the beckoning forth of the image is certainly savoured, but here we would speak of neither threshold nor precipice (as we might of sixth-syllable occurrences, see below). 'Comme' is a point of anticipation, not the anticipation of something snatched gracefully from the air or horrifyingly self-imposing, but of something fully foreseen and almost already entered into. And so the accentuation of 'comme' acts as a confident herald, broadcasting poetic control, as the poet enters into possession of his own kingdom, feels and shares the experience of utterance or truth coming upon him. And this experience may well be signalled by acoustic relaying:

Destructeur et gourmand, comme la courtisane

In *Les Fleurs du Mal*, (i) exclusively concerns the six occurrences of 'comme' at syllable 6, and necessitates some preliminary remarks about the nature of the caesura. Because of the caesura's amenability in English verse, it is not easy to speak of internal enjambement in the English line. Even end-of-line enjambement in English verse, because of its frequency, because it can so easily be rationalised in metrical terms, that is, in terms of the very regularity and continuity of a metre, has difficulty in pulling its expressive weight, unless, precisely, it has strong caesural support, as in Milton's verse-paragraphs. In the French alexandrine, on the other hand, the stable location of the caesura, together with the phrasal nature of French rhythms, which tends to bestow a high degree of syntactic (and rhythmic) autonomy on the line and of grammatical autonomy on the measures within it, make all transgressions of prosodic juncture heavily loaded. If one wanted to distinguish between caesural effects in English and French, one might say that in English verse caesural significance is cumulative, that is, caesural expressiveness derives from caesural variations over a *sequence of lines*; but in the regular French alexandrine, because the medial caesura is built into the line's metrical structure, caesural significance can be generated by the single line, and not by variation with other lines, but by a tension, an active struggle even, between the reader's highly developed sense of a proper caesural position, and a need to efface or shift it.

And there is a sense in which, in the French alexandrine, the caesural juncture is more important than that at the end of the line. Looking cursorily through late nineteenth-century French verse, one might be led to suppose that because Baudelaire's syllables 11 and 12 stand at zero for 'comme' and because Rimbaud uses 'comme' twice in the rhyme position, in 'Mémoire' and perhaps more familiarly in 'Le Dormeur du val':

> Les pieds dans les glaïeuls, il dort. Souriant comme
> Sourirait un enfant malade ...

Rimbaud's verse has taken a notable step forward in prosodic daring or disregard. This case could be argued, and I am sure, at any rate, that the changing prosodic fortunes of 'comme' are a significant indicator of the general evolution of French versification. However, although I have not investigated the frequency of 'comme' at syllable 6 in the Rimbaldian line, its falling in *this* position seems to me prosodically more crucial than its occurrence at syllable 12, for two reasons. First, in the rhyme position, the accentuation of 'comme' is unproblematic; the last syllable of the line perforce attracts accent, however humble the word that receives it, and rhyme itself confirms this accentuation. Within the line, accentuation – and thus phrasal grouping – may be profoundly controversial and the line may thus become expressively ambiguous or multiform. And this leads to the second reason, namely that eccentricities at syllable 12 may create enjambements of varying audacity, but they affect only end-of-line and inter-line behaviour; they do not affect the whole rhythmic structure of the line in the way that eccentricities at syllable 6 do. Inter-line enjambement quickly becomes a known quantity for all the variety of its gradations; line-internal enjambement creates more marked turmoils, poses questions about rhythmic segmentation, degrees of accentuation, tone, and supplies no ready way of finding answers.

Les Fleurs du Mal contains six instances of 'comme' at syllable 6:

(a) Serré, fourmillant, comme un million d'helminthes,
Dans nos cerveaux ribote un peuple de Démons

('Au Lecteur')

(b) Bourreau plein de remords, je ferai sept Couteaux
Bien affilés, et, comme un jongleur insensible

('A une Madone')

(c)   Les jambes en l'air, comme une femme lubrique

                                          ('Une Charogne')

(d)   Quand la terre est changée en un cachot humide, $3+3+4+2$

       Où l'Espérance, comme une chauve-souris, $4+2\|3+3$ or

                                        $4+5+3$ or $4\|5+3$

       S'en va battant les murs de son aile timide $2+4+3+3$

       Et se cognant la tête à des plafonds pourris $4+2+4+2$

                     ('Spleen': 'Quand le ciel bas et lourd . . .')

(e)   Hélas! et j'avais, comme en un suaire épais,

       Le coeur enseveli dans cette allégorie

                              ('Un Voyage à Cythère')

(f)   J'ai peur du sommeil comme on a peur d'un grand trou

       Tout plein de vague horreur, menant on ne sait où

                                      ('Le Gouffre')

The following readings of the 'comme' lines in these examples seem to me to be possible:

(a) $2+3\|5+2$ or $5+5+2$

(b) $4+5+3$ or $4+2\|3+3$ or $4\|5+3$

(c) $2+3\|4+3$ or $5+4+3$

(d) $4\|5+3$ or $4+2\|3+3$ or $4+5+3$

(e) $2+3\|5+2$ or $5+5+2$

(f) $5+4+3$ or $2+3\|4+3$

In other words, 'comme' at syllable 6 presents the reader with three possible scansional strategies: the effacement of the caesura in a trimetric reading, the displacement of the caesura from post-6 to a post-5 or post-4 position, the maintenance of the medial caesura with enjambement over that caesura. All three possibilities are rarely available at the same time, a fact that can be explained by the following principle: when 'comme' at syllable 6 is immediately preceded by an accentuable syllable (as in instances (a), (c), (e), (f)), it cannot itself be accentuated and thus the medial caesura, with enjambement, cannot be maintained. In the other two cases – (b) and (d) – the threefoldness of the choice is only seeming; in fact the trimetric reading and the displaced caesura reading involve the same segmentation of the line, the only difference being that between *coupe* and caesura after the first unit. I would personally wish to disqualify the caesura from these trimetric readings, on the following grounds:

(i) In the alexandrine, the caesura is related to an underlying principle of binarity. This binarity may express itself (a) as a syllabic equality around a pivotal point i.e. 6+6 or (b) as an equality of accent around a pivotal point i.e. 1 accent + 1 accent or 2 accents + 2 accents. The 3-accent regular alexandrine (e.g.

6+4+2, 3+3+6 etc.) satisfies condition (a), while a two-accent (6+6) or four-accent alexandrine (*alexandrin tétramètre*: 4+2+3+3, 1+5+2+4 etc.) satisfies both (a) and (b). 4‖5+3 satisfies neither condition. The three-accent decasyllable is a completely different matter, and its caesura, as I have tried to argue in my Prefatory remarks (see p. viii), is essentially unlike that of the alexandrine.

(ii) The caesura in the alexandrine, again as I have already argued in the Prefatory remarks (see p. viii) has a metrical rather than rhythmic existence. In other words, it really has nothing to do with the nature or degree of syntactical junctures, nor with the length of pauses which may accompany them – pause itself is properly a recitational rather than a scansional concern. Prosodic junctures may override punctuational ones and punctuation has no necessary relationship with the nature or length of pause, since the reader is free to institute pauses wherever and of whatever duration he wishes. To use punctuational indications as a guide to the placement of the major prosodic 'break' (the caesura) is to misunderstand the mechanisms of verse.

What choices, then, are we to make for our six instances? Even if we take the most fruitful path and opt for unresolved, ambivalent readings, we must understand wherein the ambivalence lies. And unfortunately while the perception of ambivalence may be possible for the reader, and even for the listener, the reciter is obliged to choose. Let us then briefly consider the six examples in order:

(a) The trimetric reading (5+5+2) compacts the two adjectives, in a sense enacting the meaning of 'serré', and allowing the dynamism of 'fourmillant' to envelop the essentially static, positional description 'serré'; it also adds a certain urgency and relentlessness to the activity of the 'peuple de Démons'. The 2+3‖5+2 reading, on the other hand, separates out the adjectives and pairs them, respectively, with 'million' and 'helminthes'; this pairing is countered by another, syllabic, pairing: serré/helminthes (2 syllables); fourmillant/million (3 syllables); but pairing would not be one of the line's activities without the separation of the adjectives.

(b) When 'comme' at syllable 6 is not immediately preceded by an accentuable syllable, it has room to insinuate its own accent, indeed may be encouraged to do so by the transitional nature of the preceding word. Thus, although there is a good case for a trimetric reading of (b) – Bien affilés | et comme un jongleur | insensible (4+5+3) – largely because such a structure would echo the structure of the line immediately preceding those quoted:

Volupté noire! des sept Péchés capitaux   4+5+3

the transitional 'et' between 'affilés' and 'comme' makes it easy to envisage 'comme' as a reached-for *point de repère* and this makes a 'comme' suspended at the caesura much less improbable:

Bien affilés, et, comme || un jongleur insensible

But paradoxically, with this suspension, the reader is enticed into a moment of vertigo, a moment when all realisations seem possible. And how apt this feeling is, how aptly it is belied by 'insensible'. The poet plays with his reader as much as the 'jongleur' plays with his victim; simile is offered as an exercise in cool self-discipline, in impassive sadism. The suspension seems to turn the knife in the wound, enjoy a mastery. But we would not be wrong to find here, too, evidence of muted hysteria; the poet falls from the suspended 'comme' into the image in demented, jeering delight. If we read 4+2||3+3, we also maintain the syllabic balance of 'un jongleur | insensible' which helps the ironic effect.

(c) Here the trimetric reading (5+4+3) might have some claims to priority because, with its gradual reduction of measures by one syllable, it focusses dramatically down on 'lubrique', the word in which moral judgement comes to the surface, the word which alone justifies the simile. 2+3||4+3 seems to me to have slightly less point, though it does to my ear evoke a certain abandoned carelessness in the posture.

(d) This is even more probably an instance of accentuated 'comme' at a medial caesura: 4+2||3+3. There are prosodic arguments for this reading: the transitional *e atone* between 'Espéran|ce' and 'comme' and the dominant 4+2 pattern in the stanza as a whole. And by suspending 'comme' at a pitch-summit, by enforcing a hesitation, a groping on this word, the poet makes us fall more heavily on the 'chauve-souris' and its accentuation, so that the bat is all the more a grotesque bald mouse. The first line of the stanza installs the ground simile: the earth is like a damp dungeon. The physical turns into the abstract, Hope, in the next parallel, but the choice of the bat simile is already determined. What is not determined is the force, the anguish, with which it is apprehended. The suspension of 'comme' will lead us to suspect how great this anguish is and this suspicion finds confirmation in the linguistic deviation in the final line of the stanza: 'un cachot humide', 'les murs' (du cachot), but how do we arrive at 'des plafonds' rather than 'le plafond'? Either the bat has hit its head so often that it believes there must be many ceilings, or the poet's image has started extending itself on its own account, multiplying in its desperation. So the suspended, accentuated 'comme' foregrounds the simile-making process itself almost derisively. It is the manifest exercise of creative power and self-affirmation at the very point where these things are hardest to carry off and indeed under severe threat from a relentless chain of events in the imagination. What I would call the '*comme* of precipice' (in that the vehicle is, as it were, fallen into from a height of dawning apprehension) expresses the profound irony built into the figure itself, the myth of creative control, the agony which control is, when simultaneously achieved and relinquished. Simile, with accentuated 'comme', may be an exultant threshold, the key to a wonderfully available world, to a perception masterful in its fittingness; but it may equally be precipice, the slippery slope of a reverie of a very different kind, plunging into the black chasms of trauma, a deep nightmarish privacy forced to ape the public ritual of comparison.

(e) The choice here between 2+3||5+2 and 5+5+2 is simply a choice between an overtly rhetorical, emotionally more inflated reading and one which mutes, or half-suppresses, the line's personal desolation. But a more general observation should be made. When 'comme' occurs at syllable 6 and is immediately preceded by an accentuable syllable, it will disrupt the line at the expense of its own claims to accent. But although 'comme' is effaced as accent, it may be *perceived*, because of its occupying the sixth position, as aspiring to accent, and, indeed, its presence may be all the more acutely felt for the way it unbalances the line and has to be prosodically circumvented. In other words, in these circumstances, 'comme' is, as it were, negatively accentuated, and its being skated over, by displacement of caesura or *coupe*, serves only to underline the strategy of evasion. If the poet is avoiding a suspension of the voice on 'comme', it may be because he is equally avoiding the 'comme' of precipice, the 'comme' which is a painful confrontation with the only possible and the only really intolerable image. In the fourteenth stanza of 'Un Voyage à Cythère', we can see why such an evasion should be necessary:

Le ciel était charmant, la mer était unie; .	2+4+2+4
Pour moi tout était noir et sanglant désormais,	2+4+3+3
Hélas! et j'avais, comme en un suaire épais,	2+3+5+2 or 5+5+2
Le coeur enseveli dans cette allégorie.	2+4+6

This is the point at which the poet is extricating himself from involvement in a scene, to interpret and order it. This is no place for vertiginous experience, no place for the suggestion that simile-making, that index of poetic control, may draw one into an image, only apparently public and in reality full of private shock. And although the suspended, accentuated 'comme' is avoided, note how it is implied, even argued for, not only by the underlying structure of the regular alexandrine, but also by the fact that the first hemistichs of the other three lines in the stanza are all 2+4 in pattern.

(f) Here, as in (a), but rather more obviously, the choice of reading depends on whether one wishes to emphasise a pattern of pairs or not. 2+3‖4+3 carefully aligns 'peur' with 'peur' and 'sommeil' with 'trou'. This reading certainly conveys the feeling of a controlled demonstration. But does it take the fear out of fear? Not only does the trimetric 5+4+3 reading have the advantage that it has in (c), funnelling attention on to the 'grand trou' by the progressive syllabic reduction of its measures, it also highlights the second 'peur', makes it more real and compelling than the first, by absorbing the first into a ready-made and, by implication, well-known condition, 'la peur du sommeil', totally unlike his own experience in which fear juts out in an altogether less assimilable way.

Our three fifth-syllable 'comme's' are not as unnerving as the sixth-syllable ones:

(i)   Exaspéré comme un ivrogne qui voit double   4+4+4
                                                  ('Les Sept Vieillards')
(ii)   Chacun plantant, comme un outil, son bec impur
                              4+4+4 ('Un Voyage à Cythère')
(iii) Qu'il s'infiltre comme une extase dans tous ceux   3+5+4
      Dont elle chante les louanges.   ('L'Imprévu')

In these examples, 'comme' signals trimetric structures, and with this sudden syncopation of the verse, it is the simile which centres the line, rather than a caesura. But this has more radical implications. Let us replace our second example within its stanza:

      De féroces oiseaux perchés sur leur pâture   3+3+2+4
      Détruisaient avec rage un pendu déjà mûr,   3+3+3+3
      Chacun plantant, comme un outil, son bec impur   4+4+4
      Dans tous les coins saignants de cette pourriture

                                              4+2+6

The homophony of the four rhymes alerts us to the obsessive nature of the stanza and to the fixatedness of the poet. But within the monotony of the dissection work, the poet's rage and disgust and the jealousies of the birds emerge, in the third line's erasure of the caesura. The caesural boundary is something like a safety valve, inasmuch as it enjoins upon the poet a conventional segmentation of speech and a balanced rhythmic periodicity; it ensures a kind of rhetorical recognisability in utterance. By this, I mean that the caesura allows us to see the uttered unit as a unit in an anterior, preordained pattern. Simile, too, is a signal of ordered utterance, but there are times when it may wish to break free from the bondage of rhetorical imprinting. And it is not the force of the image itself which produces this liberation – the comparison of a bird's beak with a tool will not unsettle the universe. It is the de-structuring and re-structuring of the binary (tetrametric) organisation which does. In trimetric simile, where simile is the central unit, I hear a change of voice, an inwardness of voice, quiet, unadorned. Certainly this third line has none of the colour and drama evident in the other lines, and in the exclusively tetrametric following stanza. In the trimetric line, simile, however modest the image it brings, finds a deep-seatedness within the uttering voice, an intimacy, which, in other circumstances, it does not have. And if this proposal has any truth in it, then we must equally claim that the English 'like' does not enjoy the same capacity to relate itself to, or to dissociate itself from, the rhetorical suppositions upon which the verse-structure rests.

Finally, I would like, very briefly, to consider occurrences of 'comme' at syllable 9, principally to demonstrate again how position suggests, if not dictates, the syntactic structure governing simile and the relief of the image. 'Comme' at syllable 9, i.e. two syllables from the caesura on one side and three from the line-ending on the other, leads one to expect the following sequence: adjective or verb (the *ground* of the comparison) + comme + noun (the *vehicle*). This is not the only syntactic possibility, but it turns out to be the dominant one, e.g.

> Ce qu'il faut à ce coeur profond comme un abîme
>
> ('L'Idéal')
>
> Bizarre déité, brune comme les nuits
>
> ('Sed Non Satiata')
>
> Tout cela descendait, montait comme la mer
>
> ('Une Charogne')
>
> Son fantôme dans l'air danse comme un flambeau
>
> ('Que diras-tu ce soir')
>
> Avec tes yeux de feu, brillants comme des fêtes
>
> ('Causerie')

Here we know that 'comme' will not receive any accentuation or foregrounding; 'comme' is the word which surreptitiously reminds us that the vehicle has not become the tenor, that it exists on sufferance, as a privileged, perhaps fragile, glimpse into universal analogy. Ninth-syllable 'comme' gives some relief to the ground, allowing quality or activity to exist disembodied for a moment, in their own pure air, before attention, inquisitive in a more vulgar way, is fixed on the vehicle-noun, the conventional site of the poetic miracle of simile. The adjective or verb of the ground may be banal ('brillant', 'profond', 'monter', 'danser'), but they are points of radiation into totalities of quality and movement, they are the keys to association, conjunction, integration.

The versification of 'like' and 'comme' reveals several things:
(i) That versification is one way among others (e.g. syntax) in which simile can explore the gamut between 'pure' simile and 'pure' metaphor.
(ii) If simile signals the presence of voice, is a special movement of utterance, then versification can determine its tonality, the quality of its impulse and the degree of its urgency.
(iii) 'Like' and 'comme' have different grammatical associations, but more important for our study is the difference in their phonetic constitutions. 'Comme' has greater syllabic versatility which endows it with greater expressive potential. The difference in versatility can be summarised thus: the relationship of 'like' with its linguistic environment is limited to mechanisms of alliteration and assonance; 'comme' can also have alliterative and assonant relationships with its linguistic environment, but it can also generate expressive patterns through its rhythmic constitution. In fact, it can be inherently imitative of movements, both spiritual and physical, in a way that 'like' cannot.
(iv) Both 'like' and 'comme' are to a certain extent accentuable. The accentuation of 'comme' has more far-reaching implications for the prosody of the French line than the accentuation of 'like' has for the prosody of the English line. Which is to say that, for the French poet, the making of simile can be an act of prosodic disorientation in a way that it cannot be for the English poet.
(v) It would seem that the French alexandrine works with a much greater awareness than the English iambic pentameter of the significance of positions on its own scale, this largely because of the syntactic self-sufficiency of the alexandrine and the fixedness of its caesura. This means that a knowledge of the syllabic position of

'comme' automatically arouses certain expectations and produces certain prosodic repercussions; in the alexandrine, in effect, the tonal and modal accompaniments of simile can almost be predicted by observation of position alone.

An ultimate question is left: is there an inherent and fundamental difference between French and English simile? An answer would require a thorough investigation of both languages in their totality. But there are, I think, demonstrable differences in the way that simile can present itself in the verse of the two languages and these should be taken into account when we attempt to describe the poetic effects of simile.

The *e atone*, or articulated e, has played some part in our consideration of the octosyllable and has been a significant element in our treatment of 'comme'. It is now time to pay more undivided attention to this syllable, which has an existence peculiar to verse. I want to examine some aspects of its expressive resourcefulness and to suggest some of the ways in which a particular poet, again Baudelaire, may bend this resourcefulness to his own imaginative concerns.

4

A PRIVILEGED SYLLABLE

THE ARTICULATED E IN *LES FLEURS DU MAL*

The *e atone* is, as Morier (1975) calls it, 'une voyelle fragile' (p. 378), an *e instable*, and views about its phonetic status and its expressive functions vary a great deal. No one would deny that in regular French verse, the unelided e has the status of a syllable, except when it occurs at the end of the line as a marker of a feminine rhyme. But does its syllabic status justify its phonetic realisation, as a definite enunciation? My view is still (*French Verse-Art*, p. 20) the same as that expressed by Theodor Elwert (1965): 'Si on veut lire correctement les vers français et leur garder leur caractère de vers, il faut sans aucun doute prononcer l'*e caduc* à l'intérieur du vers' (p. 56). But if this is so, how pronounced is its pronunciation? And here Guiraud (1970) seems to me to have the right answer: 'Enfin, la diction poétique en prononçant l'*e* sourd admet des variations de durée qui vont du simple soupir à une articulation pleine' (p. 102). There seems little point in trying to categorise, and locate the contexts of, these variations; the articulated e is such a special and controversial case and for that reason so vulnerable to recitational/readerly contingencies, to paralinguistic features, that any attempts to define its pronunciation must remain pure speculation; we may admire Morier's effort to fix the degrees of the articulated e's duration and intensity on a scale from 6 to 0 in relation to specific contexts, but his own conclusion is the only tenable one:

Le lecteur voudra bien considérer les données de cette classification comme purement relatives; elles dépendent de multiples facteurs: variations du débit, fluctuation du temps, jeu des compensations, charge phonétique. (1975, p. 385)

In my own treatment of the articulated e, I have left the degree of its enunciation as an open question, assuming only that its enunciation is a real phonetic fact.

Against those who would argue for a muting of the e, so that it becomes as it were an empty syllabic space, a pause, these counter-arguments suggest themselves: the line would lose its continuity and suppleness in favour of a staccato and unmodulated fragmentariness; the reader's desire to rationalise the syllabic status of the e by realising its presence in enunciation produces a range of expressive effects unavailable to prose and demonstrably capitalised upon by poets; the conventionalised nature of regular verse presupposes a diction peculiar to it and the articulation of the e affirms that diction and in some senses may be said to establish a rhythmicity peculiar to verse; the articulated e is a crucial element in liaison – 'La poésie impliquant une diction soignée, la liaison doit être faite dans tous les cas où elle est possible' (Delas, 1977, p. 79). Guiraud's (1970) position in relation to the phonetic status of the e is much more ambiguous (pp. 102–6) than the previous quotation from his work implies. Much of the ambiguity is terminological in origin: he moves between 'e sourd', 'e muet', and 'e "muet"' in a rather confusing manner and when he refers to 'le français moderne' it is not clear what he means historically by this term and whether what he says about it applies to verse-language or not. He does not differentiate between elided and unelided e's and his distinction between the *coupe lyrique* and the *coupe enjambante* –

On a donné le nom de *coupe lyrique* à cette division de la mesure qui tombe après l'*e*; par opposition à la "coupe enjambante" dans laquelle l'*e* s'amenuit, escamoté par l'intégration du paroxyton dans un syntagme lié.

(p. 105)

– removes, it seems to me, all traces of enjambement from the *coupe enjambante*, as indeed it removes paroxytonality itself. And his scansion, with *coupes enjambantes*, of a line from Verlaine:

L'ómbr | (e) des árbr | (es) dans la rivièr(e) embrumé(e)

strikes me as barbaric, not only because consonantal clusters suffocate the tonic vowel, but because the articulated e is denied in precisely one of those contexts that seem to make it imperative, when a liaison needs to be made between two or more preceding consonants and a following one: om*br→d*, ar*br→d*. A conventional scansion of this line makes much better sense of the line's syllabification and the principle of liaison:

L'óm | bre des ár | bres dans la riviè: | r(e) embrumée

Morier (1975) has plenty of suggestions to make about the expressive values attributable to the articulated e, in all its guises; of the e of a *coupe lyrique*, for instance, he writes:

A privileged syllable

Par la coupe lyrique, l'*e* atone exprime ... la discontinuité syntaxique, la discontinuité de fait, l'énumération pédante ou rigoureuse, l'opposition de deux idées, la ligne brisée, la violence, l'éclat; la hauteur, l'action de lever ou de monter; la durée, l'étendue, la majesté; la chute, la tristesse.

(p. 386)

Here is an embarrassingly rich range of options, many of which will depend on the indications of the particular semantic contexts in which the *coupe lyrique* finds itself. During the course of the previous chapters, we have already encountered some of the e's expressive diversity: we have seen some of the effects which derive from its lengthening of the vowel preceding it, we have suggested that it creates moments of contemplative inwardness, we have examined its influence on the role of 'comme'. In pursuing this investigation, using *Les Fleurs du Mal* as material, I wish to look for categories that might be described as underlying, that is to say 'ground' activities of the articulated e upon which any number of specific modal and expressive variations can be constructed, consistent with any given verse-context. For the purposes of my enquiry, I am not going to deal with all instances of articulated e with an ə (phonetic) transcription; I am concerned only with those e's whose enunciation is actually created by verse-convention (that is, I leave aside the e's of pronouns (se, me, te, etc.) and other particles (le, de, etc.)) and which occur as word-terminal syllables (that is, I pay no attention to internal e's, as in 'lent*e*ment', 'seul*e*ment', even though, equally, their enunciation relates to verse-convention).

What the articulated e does, above all else perhaps, is to give the French line its peculiar suppleness, by introducing modulation or a lilting effect into pitch-curve, and its fluid continuity, by facilitating transition and liaison. It is with these qualities of suppleness and fluidity that I wish to begin, using as my point of departure an analysis of the articulated e in Baudelaire's 'Avec ses vêtements ondoyants et nacrés':

> Avec ses vêtements ondoyants et nacrés,
> Même quand elle marche on croirait qu'elle danse,
> Comme ces longs serpents que les jongleurs sacrés
> Au bout de leurs bâtons agitent en cadence.
>
> Comme le sable morne et l'azur de déserts,
> Insensibles tous deux à l'humaine souffrance,
> Comme les long réseaux de la houle des mers,
> Elle se développe avec indifférence.

The articulated e in Les Fleurs du Mal

Ses yeux polis sont faits de minéraux charmants,
Et dans cette nature étrange et symbolique
Où l'ange inviolé se mêle au sphinx antique,

Où tout n'est qu'or, acier, lumière et diamants,
Resplendit à jamais, comme un astre inutile,
La froide majesté de la femme stérile.

This poem is broadly speaking the confrontation of two views of
a woman, the one a vision of elasticity and elegance (stanza one),
the other of unyielding, metallic impenetrability (the sestet). The
word 'confrontation' is perhaps a little too abrupt, since the second
stanza acts as a bridge-passage between the two. It is hardly
surprising to find a high incidence of the articulated 'e' in the first
stanza, where the willowy, undulating quality of the subject is
paramount. There are, in effect, five instances ('mêm*e*', 'ell*e*',
'ell*e*', 'comm*e*', 'agitent'). What is perhaps rather more puzzling is
the even higher incidence in the following stanza (namely 'comm*e*',
'sabl*e*', 'insensibl*e*s', 'humain*e*', 'comm*e*', 'houl*e*', 'ell*e*'), where the
emphasis of the images is on flatness and uniformity, an emphasis
borne out by the 6+6 segmentation of the final line of the quatrain,
stretching out its measures across a spiritual emptiness. The admi-
rative *e* of the first stanza has, it seems, become an ironic one; the
sinuous multiformity of the dance figure has become a movement of
repetition; the self-surrender of the 'prostitute' (see below), spon-
taneously generating analogy and participating in the universal
context, radiating outwards, has become the self-absorption of the
(female) dandy, for whom the poet, in exercises of his own
imagination, must create access-seeking similes. The articulated 'e'
has become part of a taunting, but unfruitful seductiveness. As we
move into the first tercet, e's are not so much offered as deleted,
actively so ('natur¢', 'étrang¢', 'ang¢', 'mêl¢') and the only one left,
that of 'cett*e*', is part of the mesmerised state of the poet, willing a
relentingness, making an abortive grasp at inwardness. And this
process of the cancellation of the e continues in the second tercet
('lumièr¢', 'comm¢', 'astr¢') until the final line of the poem, where
the e recovers its articulation ('froid*e*', 'femm*e*'). Is this a recurrence of the ironic e of the second stanza? Or is it, rather, a
nostalgic e, reaching behind the resistant exterior towards an
unselfconscious primitiveness, an innocence which is only a
memory, buried deep within artifice?
    Several inferences are to be drawn from this brief analysis. The
first is that the articulated e is a tonal instrument, but of an

essentially covert kind. A more acceptably cautious formulation would be: the articulated e *can be* tone-carrying, but the tone is not so much heard as guessed at. In this sense the articulated e is the underside of the word it completes, and precisely the enunciatory aspect. What I mean by 'enunciatory aspect' is this: the peculiar property of the e mute in verse is that it is the point at which enunciation exists in its purely enunciatory state; in a sense the articulated e is *no more than* an enunciation, a moment in the syllabic chain which is pure vocalisation, the anomaly of paroxytonality; if I say 'mêm∉' then I have conveyed the adequate information about grammatical and semantic function; if I say 'mêm*e*', then I add voice, a moment of voice's presence. This is not to say that in some circumstances, the articulated e *may* not be a morphological marker, of the present tense, or the feminine, but this is not a necessary function, and even as it acts as such a marker, it may equally bear a tonal colouring.

To say that the peculiar property of the articulated e in verse is to act as a purely enunciatory event is also to imply that the articulated e in verse is the marker of verse enunciation, or that it marks the presence of verse and the processes of imagination peculiar to verse. We have already indicated in the previous chapter, as in this one, some of the properties of the e in relation to rhythmicity. But I would also like to suggest that the articulated e actually sustains imagination. Again, in the chapter on Gautier, I proposed that the articulated e is a moment of contemplative interiority, a moment when words are able to achieve their fullness of effect and expand in the consciousness. But further than that, the articulated e might be envisaged as the very force of imagination; it is a moment of enunciation in a pure state, outside the flow of information-giving, outside the temporality of utterance; it is a moment of imaginative involvement which is also a 'standing outside', a moment of creative ecstasy, a moment of what Baudelaire would have called 'ivresse'. It is significant that in 'Avec ses vêtements', the similes of the first two stanzas stretch over two lines (3–4, 5–6) or one (7), and that the 'comme' is endowed with its e, summoning others, while in the second tercet the simile ('comme un astre inutile') occupies only a hemistich and the e of 'comme' is cancelled. While in the first two stanzas imagination has the freedom to develop itself, to fill out verse space, in the second tercet the imagination is as it were disempowered, unable to sustain itself, to generate a full movement of the verse; furthermore the simile occurs in the second hemistich, on a falling intonation of afterthought or dispiritedness or bitterness in undertone; and its e is cancelled, as if by the woman herself, an emasculation of the imagination, a denial of the poet's poeticity. The woman of the sestet has none of the amenability to voyages into the imaginary that she has in 'Parfum exotique' or 'La Chevelure', or indeed in the first two stanzas of this poem; on the contrary, she closes off that possibility. And the articulated e's of the final line:

> La froide majesté de la femme stérile

are perhaps, besides being ironic or nostalgic, a repossession, or attempted repossession, of a poetic ascendancy and re-liberation of imaginative faculties.

It would be only logical, on the basis of these suggestions, to propose that the articulated 'e' has a privileged relationship with that pole of Baudelairian dualism which belongs to 'prostitution' and 'surnaturalisme'.[1] The dualism can be expressed schematically thus:

Dandy/femme fatale	Prostitute
Irony	Surnaturalisme/Universal analogy
Self-condensation (i.e. cult of personality)	Self-vaporisation/self-expansion (i.e. achievement of anonymity)
Paris/ici	Exotic landscape/là-bas
Angularity, abruptness	Supple, undulating elasticity
Lethargy of ennui	Lethargy of sensuous abundance
Escape from remorse – memory as corrosive process.	Pursuit of nostalgia – memory as 'un retour vers l'Eden perdu'

'Prostitution' is here not to be understood in either professional or social terms but as a principle of being:

Ce que les hommes nomment amour est bien petit, bien restreint et bien faible, comparé à cette ineffable orgie, à cette sainte prostitution de l'âme qui se donne tout entière, poésie et charité, à l'imprévu qui se montre, à l'inconnu qui passe.   ('Les Foules')

Il n'est même pas de plaisir noble qui ne puisse être ramené à la prostitution.   ('Fusées')

Prostitution is a movement of generosity, of self-surrender, of self-forgetfulness, for the benefit of the first passer-by. Love itself partakes, of course, of this noble form of prostitution, but it is likely to be disfigured by sexual conflict, by the need to dominate and possess; love resolves itself into the contradiction 'charité et férocité'. But prostitution does not limit itself to a sense of confraternity or empathy with one's fellows; it is the capacity to participate in experiences of 'surnaturalisme', in that expansion of consciousness, in that complete sensory and spiritual *disponibilité* which permits, on the one hand, the infinite interpenetration of the senses and thus the achievement of total sentience (so-called horizontal 'correspondances'), being present to the world at all points of one's being at any given moment, and on the other, penetration to realities beyond reality, to the pure world of spirit (so-called vertical 'correspondances'):

Le surnaturel comprend la couleur générale et l'accent, c'est-à-dire intensité, sonorité, limpidité, vibrativité, profondeur et retentissement dans l'espace et dans le temps. Il y a des moments de l'existence où le temps et l'étendue sont plus profonds, et le sens de l'existence immensément augmenté. ('Fusées')

Dans certains états de l'âme presque surnaturels, la profondeur de la vie se révèle tout entière dans le spectacle, si ordinaire qu'il soit, qu'on a sous les yeux. Il en devient le symbole. ('Fusées')

In this beatific state of 'surnaturalisme', the limits of the soul are infinitely extended. The intensity with which one's feeling of existence is imbued is directly proportional to the enlargement that reality seems to undergo. Put in a converse form, the expansion and extension of time and space indicate the increase in the spirit's ability to embrace existence. These states of heightened consciousness are accompanied by an opening up of perspectives, by an acute sense of reality's third dimension; objects acquire an amazing relief, space is focussed into experiences of its depth, the past superimposes itself on the present as all time becomes simultaneous. The self is thus liberated into the universe, and the universe is liberated across its own endless spaces: sounds begin to resonate and vibrate, as do colours, in an unconfined fashion, making contact with other sensory experiences across great imaginative distances. And if this kind of perceptual state is rich in symbols, it is because sensations from the world become figurative of themselves; that is to say, phenomena become their own ideas, ideas of their most intimate selves; appearance extends without interruption into essence; to perceive a phenomenon, in this state, is simultaneously to perceive it as meaningful, in the design of the universe. The words which Baudelaire most frequently uses to describe the experience of 'surnaturalisme' are 'ivresse' and 'extase' and the vocabulary through which the 'surnaturel' most characteristically manifests itself is a vocabulary close to that used in the definitions above: 'profond', 'frémir', 'retentir', 'vibrer', 'vaste', 'sonore', 'immense', 'éblouissant', etc.:

> Un port *retentissant* où mon âme peut boire
> A grands flots le parfum, le son et la couleur;
> Où les vaisseaux, glissant dans l'or et dans la moire,
> Ouvrent leurs *vastes* bras pour embrasser la gloire
> D'un ciel pur où *frémit* l'éternelle chaleur.
>
> ('La Chevelure' – italics mine)

Closely associated with the 'prostitutional' pole of Baudelaire's poetic mentality, is what might be called the 'distributive' articulated e. In the chapter on Gautier we have already mentioned the 'repercussive' effect of the articulated e: the preceding syllable (accentuated or not) reverberates through it. In the context of 'surnaturalisme', the articulated e carries forward the reverberations of the word to which it belongs both on to the following word and out into the surrounding atmosphere. In his description of perfumes in the sestet of 'Correspondances', Baudelaire speaks of some:

> Ayant l'expansion des choses infinies

The articulated e of 'choses' and the liaison of the 's' with 'infinies', enacts the expansion and and dissemination of 'choses' across infinities of time and space. Richard (1955) attributes this vaporising and broadcasting capacity to the Baudelairian adjective:

Ce sens [of the noun], l'adjectif le vaporise et le fait rayonner. Il dispose tout autour du nom un halo de vibrations immobiles. Il humanise encore la transcendance et la concentration substantives en les diluant en *qualités* idéales. Ces qualités s'étalent alors de mot en mot, glissent les uns dans les autres et tendent d'objet à objet un *vernis*, une nappe, une continuité sensibles qui permettent l'établissement horizontal des correspondances.

(p. 161)

Richard uses as his illustrative example the ninth line of 'Correspondances':

> Il est des parfums frais comme des chairs d'enfants

and might have added the tenth:

A privileged syllable

Doux comme les hautbois, verts comme les prairies

Richard's argument is persuasive, but I would wish to add that the articulated e has a crucial part to play in the pervasiveness and dilation of quality. None of the adjectives in the two lines have an e, still less an articulated one, but it seems to me that they 'borrow' the 'e' of comme (articulated in all three cases) as their instrument of 'glissement' and distribution.

This distributive capacity of the articulated e is perhaps at its most effective when the e follows an accentuated syllable and thus creates a *coupe enjambante*. Some commentators believe that the *coupe enjambante* is a falsehood created by scansion, which misrepresents the facts of reading; S. W. Taylor (1983), for example, remarks:

Since the French sense-group ends with the stressed vowel the *mute e* that follows it cannot be counted in that group; on the other hand it is certainly not pronounced as part of the following group, but is in fact indicated by a slight pause. The above way of recording it schematically [i.e. by bracketing it and thus throwing into question its status as syllable: e.g. 3[e]2.4.2], proposed by Guiraud, comes nearer to representing the realities of spoken verse than the traditional solution of counting such mute e's as though they were fully pronounced members of the following group.   (p. xxvi)

Leaving aside my misgivings about Guiraud's treatment of the *coupe enjambante* mentioned earlier (see above, p. 87), I would object to Taylor's view on several counts. First there are as many realities of spoken verse as there are speakers of it, and those realities cannot be represented, since they cannot be imagined. Secondly, *coupes* are themselves the fictions of scansion; they are governed by the accents in the line and segment the verse in relation to those accents. Segmentation is a convenience of rhythmic identification; it defines units of the line without having any designs on the line's continuity. And even given these qualifications, the argument of Morier (1975), taking into proper account the intensification of liaison that occurs in verse, is more compelling:

La *coupe enjambante* est une coupe rhythmique qui tombe droit après la voyelle accentuée, entre cette voyelle et l'*e* atone qu'elle précède. Elle est conforme à la chaîne parlée du français qui est continu. Toute consonne finale de mot, à l'intérieur d'une mesure, se rattache à la voyelle suivante, et devient une consonne croissante:

Le linceul mê | m(e) est tiè || d(e) au cœu: | r enseveli
(Lamartine)

94

Il devient alors évident que l'*e* atone final de mot doit couler dans la mesure suivante:

Aux fê: | t*es* du combat, || aux lu: | tt*es* du savoir   (p. 404)

The articulated e of the *coupe enjambante* is thus both a dying reverberation of the word it ends and the initial impetus of the measure it begins; it is the point at which the suggestivity of a word is absorbed and then cast up again as the force which informs, expands into, that which follows it. In the first tercet of 'Une nuit que j'étais près d'une affreuse Juive':

Car j'eusse avec ferveur baisé ton noble corps,	2+4+2+4
Et depuis tes pieds frais jusqu'à tes noires tresses	3+3+4+2
Deroulé le trésor des profondes caresses	3+3+3+3

the articulated e works with a powerful insistence in the second hemistichs, at first as an adumbration in the unaccentuated 'noble' and then fully realised as part of the *coupes enjambantes* of 'noi:|res' and 'profon:|des'. What we witness here is in fact the 'prostitution' of two words: 'noires' and 'profondes' surrender themselves, yield up all their tonalities, so that they can become centres of imaginative diffusion. 'Noires' expands into a whole gamut of peculiarly transparent multi-nuanced blacks, so that the 'tresses' are, like those of 'La Chevelure':

Cheveux bleus, pavillon de ténèbres tendues

And, as in 'La Chevelure', 'noires' is much more than a colour; it is a point of access to the very things it hides, it is the darkness of intimacy, it is the place where 'volupté' is transformed into 'connaissance', where sensual pleasure gives way to spiritual apprehension; thus, as in 'La Chevelure', the 'tresses' are 'ce noir océan où l'autre est enfermé'. And, equally, 'profondes' is the site of a 'trésor', an almost vertiginous depth into which the imagination reaches in order to wrest a spiritual fertility, an intensity of experience which will relieve the poet of the curse of self-consciousness and integrate him into the harmony of a being which itself integrates all.

As a corollary to these remarks, one might wonder whether those words peculiarly attached to the experience of 'surnaturalisme' have a privileged relationship with the articulated e. Of the sixteen occurrences of 'vaste(s)'[2] in *Les Fleurs du Mal* (including annexes), for example, twelve have an articulated e. Of the eighteen occurrences of 'immense(s)',[3] eleven have an articulated e, and four are denied their e for prosodic reasons, because they occur at the

caesura. Most of the instances of 'profonde(s)' occur at the rhyme-
position, but of the four that do not, three retain their e. These
statistics are eloquent enough; and we should remember that even
where the e is elided Baudelaire still has the device of prepositioning at his disposal, to give his adjectives more depth, and open
up their figurative and affective dimensions; most frequently
perhaps, Baudelaire combines prepositioning with the articulation
of the e, as we have seen in our example from 'Une nuit que j'étais
près d'une affreuse Juive'.

But if we are right to suppose that the articulated e, and
particularly the articulated e of the *coupe enjambante*, has special
affinities with the principle of prostitution, and if we are to suppose,
on the evidence of 'Avec ses vêtements ondoyants et nacrés', that
the elision of the e is a dandyish gesture, what are we to make of the
articulated e of 'affreuse' in the line just quoted? Before we can
answer that question we need to stand a little further back.

In distinguishing between the unregenerate and exhausted world
of Paris, and the primordial and vivifying exotic landscape, we may
feel occasionally that we have good lexical reasons for doing so. In
the exotic landscape we find:

> Des hommes dont le corps est *mince* et vigoureux
> ('Parfum exotique')
> (italics mine, as in following examples)

and we can confidently set this supple, sappy slenderness against
the kind of life-deprived emaciation we find in Parisian contexts:

> Je pense à la négresse, *amaigrie* et phtisique ('Le Cygne')

> Les pauvresses, traînant leurs seins *maigres* et froids
> ('Le Crépuscule du matin')

And when we find the 'passante' in the Parisian crowd described as

> Longue, *mince*, en grand deuil, douleur majestueuse
> ('A une passante')

our expectations of an image of exotic, undulating gracefulness are
not disappointed ('. . . d'une main fastueuse | Soulevant, balançant
le feston et l'ourlet'). It is precisely her power to recall a lost
harmony, a 'vie antérieure' of unalienated sensuousness which, we
suspect, draws the poet to her in the first place, causes his feeling of
rebirth, and impels him to locate their next possible encounter in a
'là-bas' ('Ailleurs, bien loin d'ici'), an encounter, however, already
too late. 'Mince' and 'maigre' sustain their differentiability, so that

even when they are applied to the same figure in the same poem, as to the female skeleton of 'Danse macabre', we can distinguish between a threatening cadaverous thinness ('maigre') and an attractive slenderness which is part of the skeleton's fine, if illusory, garb, and part of 'L'Elégance sans nom de l'humaine armature' ('mince').

But, like Lamartine, Baudelaire often uses the same lexical item to evoke very different sensations and associations. The trees of the exotic island of 'Parfum exotique' are described as 'singuliers', presumably by virtue of their extravagant and vivid novelty, their power to fascinate. The old women of Paris and the blind men are equally fascinating, and yet 'singuliers', in their connection, has very different overtones:

> Des êtres singuliers, décrépits et charmants
> > ('Les Petites Vieilles')

> Terribles, singuliers comme les somnambules
> > ('Les Aveugles')

Here the sense of the outlandish (rather than exotic), of the grotesque and ill-adapted predominates. And the apparently privileged vocabulary of 'surnaturalisme' is equally prone to negativisation, and its articulated e's with it:

> Quand la pluie étalant ses *immenses* traînées
> D'une *vaste* prison imite les barreaux,
> Et qu'un peuple muet d'infâmes araignées
> Vient tendre ses filets au fond de nos cerveaux
> > ('Spleen': 'Quand le ciel bas et lourd . . .')
> > (my italics)

The state of 'surnaturalisme' is as likely to be an experience of horror as of ecstasy, if what the extra-vulnerable sensibility, the hyperaesthesia, of the 'surnaturaliste' is subjected to has its origins in a splenetic condition, in an acute awareness of man's fallen state, rather than of his integratedness. In this state, blackness has a suffocating opacity and density, 'immenses' does not open up space to exploration but offers only an unencompassable sameness, is a belittling and derisive gigantism, as is 'vaste', measuring out the acreage of despair. The articulated e's and *coupes enjambantes* still pursue their distributive and dilationary activities, but these are not activities which support, carry forward and disseminate the imagination; rather they outstrip the imagination, circumscribe an impotence by their very expansiveness. Tonally speaking, this kind of articulated e therefore is an enunciation shot through with exasperated rage, irony and dispiritedness; there is nothing in it of the 'émerveillement' and intoxicated identification with sensation that we find in the articulated e's of the exotic landscape. And if we try to apply to the city-scape the ideas of 'retentissement' or 'vibrativité', we find them manifesting themselves in equally sinister fashion; the images of anguish that the poet sees before him reverberate not in ramification and diversification, but rather in self-parodying repetition: one old man finds his echo in six others ('Les Sept Vieillards'), one little lady becomes a group ('Les Petites Vieilles'), one blind man begets a string of blind men ('Les Aveugles'). The 'ivresse' or 'enivrement' of a paradisal 'surnaturalisme' is degraded to 'ivrognerie':

> Exaspéré comme un ivrogne qui voit double,
> Je rentrai, je fermai ma porte, épouvanté,
> Malade et morfondu, l'esprit fiévreux et trouble,
> Blessé par le mystère et par l'absurdité!
>
> ('Les Sept Vieillards')

In our quotation from 'Spleen': 'Quand le ciel bas et lourd', 'immenses' and 'vaste' rub shoulders with 'infâmes', an adjective of an apparently very different water. For many, these swingeing adjectives like 'infâme', 'atroce', 'affreux', 'horrible', 'terrible', 'effroyable' are a peculiar weakness in Baudelaire, unsubtle, over-rhetorical, gratuitously melodramatic. But these words are more self-expressive than descriptive; they have a stridency, almost an hysterical quality, which we might read as attempts to extirpate an evil *from oneself*. That is to say that these words are as much admissions of association as they are disclaimers of association. Baudelaire speaks of his 'besoin d'oublier son *moi* dans la chair extérieure, que l'homme appelle noblement besoin d'aimer' ('Mon Cœur mis à nu'), and yet reality is in the habit of returning to the poet mirror-images of his own abject condition, so that escape itself turns into imprisonment. And thus, frequently, we find combined in Baudelaire's work fascination and disgust, tacit confession and overt dissociation; the 'Juive' is somehow 'affreuse' as an extension of the poet.

Adjectives like these are expressions of negative 'surnaturalisme', and as such are also expressions of linguistic defeat. The hyperbolism of negative 'surnaturalisme' has no outlet, does not open on to a diversification of language and image, produces no liberation of the imagination into self-renewing lexical fields.

Instead the hyperactive sensibility hammers away at abstraction and phantasmal forms of reality, and produces personifications and blanket-effect attributions, until it finally consumes itself in nervous exhaustion. But the energy generated by these signs of linguistic frustration is real enough and the energy owes much to the articulated e, in two respects.

We have already had cause to mention, on several occasions, that the articulated e protracts the syllable preceding it, particularly when that syllable is accentuated. Many of these adjectives – e.g. 'infâme', 'atroce', 'affreuse', 'horrible', 'hideuse' – have a purely vocalic first syllable,[4] their first consonants operating as part of the second, accentuated (accentuable) syllable. Now these are words which, because of their extravagant expressiveness, might be expected to attract an *accent oratoire* or *accent d'intensité*. Let us just remind ourselves of what the *accent oratoire* is:

> This ... is a recitational accent and only in the rarest instances can it be considered to be rhythmically determining. This accent attacks the first consonant of the word concerned and reverberates through the following vowel, so that it is, properly speaking, a syllabic accent.
>
> (*French Verse-Art*, p. 53)[5]

The *accent oratoire* is an accent of emotional emphasis which is supplied by the voice of the reader, not by the verse-structure itself. But with the adjectives we are considering, given their phonemic make-up, any *accent oratoire* applied to them would coincide with the prosodic accent; or put another way, the prosodic accent calls forth an *accent oratoire*, demands to be intensified expressively. Thus what would normally be a secondary accent, within the hemistich, lower in degree than either the accent at the line-ending or at the caesura – the normal scale of accentual degree in the alexandrine can be represented thus:

$$\underline{}\underline{}\overset{(\prime)}{\underline{}}\underline{}\underline{}\overset{\prime\prime}{\underline{}}\underline{}\underline{}\overset{(\prime)}{\underline{}}\underline{}\underline{}\overset{\prime\prime\prime}{\underline{}}$$

– achieves an unusual prominence, surpassing both caesural and, on occasion, line-terminal accents:

> ... l'Espoir
> Vaincu, pleure, et l'Angoisse at*roce*, despotique   3+3+2+4
> ('Spleen': 'Quand le ciel bas et lourd ...')

> Et les vagues terreurs de ces a*ffreu*ses nuits
>   3+3+4+2
> ('Réversibilité')

A privileged syllable

Le gouffre de tes yeux, plein d'ho*rr*ibles pensées

2+4+3+3
('Danse macabre')

And it is precisely the coincidence of *accent oratoire* and prosodic accent which removes some of the dangers of gratuitous melodrama from these adjectives; because it is as much the prosodic structure of the line and the presence of the articulated e which produces the *accent oratoire* as the emotional indulgence of the speaker's/reader's voice, so the responsibility for, and authorisation of, the affective hyperbolism lies with the imperatives of convention, and the hyperbolism is thus endowed with a strange impersonality, escapes the purely partisan, while retaining all its energy.

But the articulated e's of these adjectives, whose affectivity is further increased by their being either preposed (quotations 2 and 3 above) or dislocated from the noun by the caesura (quotation 1), also energise them by allowing them to envelop what follows them. In the examples from 'Réversibilité' and 'Danse macabre', the adjectives so thoroughly infiltrate the nouns, as worms the carcase, that the nouns have peculiarly little existence of their own. The adjectives do not really determine the nouns; rather the nouns are merely locations where the adjectives, and the all-encompassing and unutterable nightmares which they are, can be embodied or pin-pointed. But even as the process of location takes place, so the locations themselves are eroded, cannot contain their charges. The articulated e still has its distributive function, but it distributes the adjective like a pernicious and insidious influence. In the first example, from 'Spleen', the postpositioning and the intervention of the caesural break already make 'atroce' an instrument of 'Angoisse' rather than a description of it; and the articulated e of 'atroce' further distributes (it seems to me) the adjective's grammatical function, that is to say, the 'e' of 'atroce' spreads, enlarges its field of grammatical activity, so that not only does one feel that it has an adverbial role in relation to 'plante' in the following line:

Sur mon crâne incliné plante son drapeau noir

a relationship reinforced by the articulated e in 'plante', but that it is a substantivalised adjective, itself determined by 'despotique'. About the grammatically distributive function of the articulated e we shall have a little more to say in a moment, and our suggestions of such a function here must be of a most tentative kind. But one of the most precious resources of the *coupe enjambante* is precisely its ability to reach across barriers of punctuation and syntactic grouping, and when it does this, it inevitably blurs the outlines of syntactical and grammatical categories. It is true that it needs a fairly special context in which to exploit this potentiality, but the line we have before us:

> Vaincu, pleure, et l'Angoisse atroce, despotique

by virtue of its syntactical fragmentariness and the punctuational and prosodic junctures which, cutting across each other, produce an even greater syntactical disarray, provides just such a context. I should just add that my reading of the first hemistich as 3+3 (rather than 2+1+3), a reading whose principle I have tried to justify elsewhere (*French Verse-Art*, pp. 43–8), equally pushes the adjective 'vaincu' in an adverbial direction.

In taking our leave of negative 'surnaturalisme', we should just remind ourselves that no Baudelairian state is stable and the most abrupt oscillations or inversions are possible. Paris is one of those 'vieilles capitales,| Où tout, même l'horreur, tourne aux enchantements' ('Les Petites Vieilles'). In 'Les Petites Vieilles', in fact, the poet achieves a 'prostituted' state against all the evidence:

> Mon coeur multiplié jouit de tous vos vices!
> Mon âme resplendit de toutes vos vertus!

But better not to rely on chance as way of avoiding 'horreur'. Dandyism is the programme of behaviour by which the poet seeks to insure himself against the invasions of negative vision and self-immolation. Dandyism combats nightmare with irony, the cold, relentless state of the disabused, looks to the individual will to assert itself in a campaign of the perverse, the arbitrary, the shocking, looks to outwit lethargy and the feeling of impotence with a rigorous ethic of self-discipline and work, and to outwit remorse in a moment-by-moment existence, in which self-creation is continually available. Dandyism is many things beside, but above all it is a recipe for self-help in the 'ici' of the Parisian environment.

Before leaving this discussion of the distributive 'e' and 'surnaturalisme', I would like to return to the exotic world and to a fine example of the processes of expansion, dispersal, metamorphosis in action, the opening lines of 'La Chevelure':

> O toison, moutonnant jusque sur l'encolure!
> O boucles! O parfum chargé de nonchaloir!
> Extase! Pour peupler ce soir l'alcôve obscure

Des souvenirs dormant dans cette chevelure,
Je la veux agiter dans l'air comme un mouchoir!

'Toison' is already a metaphor for hair, on the move towards the animal, towards sheep, a move confirmed by 'moutonnant' which in its turn transforms 'fleece' towards foam. 'Encolure' reinstalls an animal image, a neck powerful with muscle. 'O boucles' returns to base, to hair, but sees it now as multiform, as a plurality hard to enclose. Perception then takes an abrupt leap; it is no longer sight that is involved, but scent. The multiform has become intangible, evanescent, and the image it creates is no longer concrete, but abstract, the leisure or indolence of 'nonchaloir'. But this phrase does not merely open out in terms of sensory involvement and meaning; it opens out in terms of time as well; 'nonchaloir' is an archaic word, overtaken after the sixteenth century by the modern form 'nonchalance'. It is only fitting, therefore, that as a climax of this series of images, which gradually spread and become diffused over an ever-wider area, should come 'Extase', the word that expresses achieved expansion of consciousness. But these brief remarks are only a necessary preamble to our real concern: the articulated e's in 'boucles' and 'Extase', and whether they create *coupes enjambantes* or *coupes lyriques*.

We have so far connected the articulated e of the *coupe enjambante* with processes of dissemination, infiltration, metamorphosis. In the treatment of the *coupe lyrique* in *French Verse-Art* (pp. 57–61), particular reference was made to its frequency in connection with address, exclamation, imperative; its effect is disjunctive and therefore it accompanies, is accompanied by, breaks in syntactic continuity, changes of direction. There seems little doubt that we should practise a *coupe lyrique* after the exclamation 'Extase!'; the line continues with a new departure, a shift from reaction to intention. Is this to say that, at this culminating point, the e loses its disseminating capacity? The answer is 'no'. The e of the *coupe lyrique* disseminates the word into its own space; that is to say that its action is retrospective rather than projective, and it is precisely this characteristic which makes it so disjunctive; the e is not an enunciated pause, but an articulation willing regression. Ecstasy is constantly to be reinhabited, its intoxication summons one back; the articulated e seals it in its own circularity. It is thus also the e which privatises the experience of ecstasy, since it is the agent of closure and withdrawal. Words, like 'extase', which might seem no more than rhetorical assertions of an experience beyond speech, are thus able to actualise their unspeakability by being returned to themselves. But can we be so confident in our scansion of the apostrophe 'O boucles!'? There is some case for encapsulating it in itself with a *coupe lyrique*, as an apostrophe summarising the effects of the first line, as a breathtaking arrestation in a polysemic abundance. But this would be to dissociate its perfume from it, locate the perfume elsewhere, when it is precisely the plurality of the hair which engenders sensory metamorphosis; thus the *coupe enjambante* is more persuasive:

O bou: | cles! O parfum || chargé | de nonchaloir

The exclamation mark should not be allowed to mislead us; if anything, it marks the hyperbolism of the experience, not the strength of a stop or the loudness of the voice. Punctuation in poetry is only too often a redundant, mechanically applied convention, demanded by syntactical forms rather than interpreting their relationship. All poetry is in a deep sense unpunctuated, or punctuated only by the junctures and segmentations of prosody. Thus the articulated e of 'boucles' crosses the syntactical boundary to modulate and evanesce into perfume.

The grammatically distributive function of the articulated e, its ability to cross syntactic boundaries in the *coupe enjambante* has more significance for twentieth-century poetry, for a poetry without punctuation and with more syntactic disjunction and elisions, than for the poetry of the nineteenth century. If we look forward to Eluard, to his 'Le guerrier et la coquille', for example, we find the articulated e redistributing adjectives and appositional phrases:

La coquille fusion des angles le poisson
Dans l'eau libre enfermé comme un coeur dans sa gangue
La poterie émue et fraîche l'écriture
Sont des baisers forgés pour calmer le guerrier

Our natural response would be to assign the adjectives 'émue et fraîche' to 'poterie', and indeed, we could 'impose' this assignment by practising a *coupe lyrique* after 'fraîche', thus ensuring that 'l'écriture' is treated as a new departure. If however we practise a *coupe enjambante* at 'fraîche' (thus 4+4+4), we ambiguate the links of the adjectival pair, which belong to 'poterie' by virtue of 'normal' word-order, but which the articulated e associates with 'écriture'. Equally of course, we might adopt a tetrametric, rather than trimetric, reading of the line – 4+2+2+4 – in which case 'émue' would belong to 'poterie' and 'fraîche' to 'écriture'. An equally complex question is posed by the appositional phrase 'fusion des angles' in the first line. Does it belong with 'la coquille' or with 'le poisson'? If we practise a *coupe enjambante* at 'coquille' and a *coupe lyrique* at 'angles', then it gravitates towards 'coquille'. If we reverse that pattern, then 'le poisson' will seem to have the greater claims. If, on the other hand, we practise *coupes enjambantes* at both 'coquille' and 'angles' (or indeed, *coupes lyriques*) then the ambivalence is complete. These two lines, the first and the third, seem to me to be trimetric and should be set against the tetrametric lines 2(3+3+3+3) and 4(4+2+3+3); if the tetrametric lines deal in paradox – libre/enfermé; baisers/forgés; calmer/ guerrier – then the trimetric ones indeed give hint of that fusion, that ambivalence of bothness, which takes away from paradox what is problematic in it and releases the warrior from his inherent need of opposition.

In the analysis of 'Avec ses vêtements', we saw how the articulated e can act as a covert tonal commentary on the declarations made by the poem. But this kind of sub-voice need not simply provide an accompaniment; it can install counter-currents, indeed even deny the evidence of the ostensible meaning. In 'A une passante', for example, the poet insists at certain points on the momentariness of the encounter:

> Un éclair . . . puis la nuit! . . . Fugitive beauté

But the *erzählte Zeit* (*temps de l'histoire*) does not necessarily correspond to the *Erzählzeit* (*temps du récit*) or rather to the time of poetic imagining. Where, in the two lines:

> Une femme passa, d'une main fastueuse
> Soulevant, balançant le feston et l'ourlet

the past historic supplies information about the speed and finality of the woman's passing, the articulated e's which surround that tense create a temporality of another order, slow-motion, durative, interiorised, a temporality whose self-sufficiency is borne out by the non-tense-related present participles of the second line. With these articulated e's we enter the poet's imaginative space, we espouse a perception in which the woman's movements are stayed, enjoyed, fixed to the pace of *rêverie*. Just as the first line of the poem:

> La rue assourdissante autour de moi hurlait

introduces the din of the Parisian street only to blot it out in the following line, so the rapidity of the woman's passing is noted only to be denied by poetry's own digressive and protractable temporality, of which the articulated e is a principal generator.

The counter-currents provided by the articulated e in 'L'Albatros' are somewhat different. The albatross's elastic and effortlessly soaring flight is established by the articulated e early in the poem:

> Souvent, pour s'amuser, les hommes d'équipage
> Prennent des albatros, vastes oiseaux des mers
> Qui suivent, indolents compagnons de voyage,
> Le navire glissant sur les gouffres amers.

But as the poem proceeds and the albatross is subjected to the derision of the crew, articulable e's are noticeably elided, particularly in the third stanza, and particularly in a construction – adjective with e+et+adjective – to whose significance we shall return later:

> Ce voyageur ailé, comme il est gauche et veule!
> Lui, naguère si beau, qu'il est comique et laid!
> L'un agace son bec avec un brûle-gueule,
> L'autre mime, en boitant, l'infirme qui volait!

But even here the articulated e hangs on to a tenuous existence; its real potency may seem to be denied by the word it is attached to (e.g. 'naguère', 'infirme'), but this can be conversely expressed: the articulated e denies the very words that deny it. It is a dormant, latent element which can at any moment be fully revived. Paradoxically, the more a creature is put into a context alien to it, the more it becomes itself – in the very moment of its torment (agace, brûle-gueule), an ineffaceable capability is affirmed. And in the final line of the poem, fittingly, the articulated e comes back into its own:

> Ses ailes de géant l'empêchent de marcher.

The wings that prevent the bird from walking enable him to fly; the very prevention of walking is the imperative to fly; prevention, in short, has flight locked within it.

If the articulated e is a real event in regular French verse, its cancelling by elision, as we have already intimated in our treatment of 'Avec ses vêtements', is no less so. The elided e is not an enunciation which never existed in our consciousness, but rather an enunciation which we thrust away, which is swallowed into the following vowel. The very fact that we are aware of the same word having its e articulated in one context and elided in another confirms that the elided e is a potential enunciation cancelled rather than a zero, like other letters which are the unpronounced, purely orthographic relics of an etymology (ryt*h*me, ba*p*tisme, fasciner, etc.). The elision of the e will naturally lead to a certain compacting of elements within the line, thanks to the persistent pressure of liaison, and certain syntactic configurations will necessitate elision. It is this relationship between the life and death of the e and syntactic formulae that I wish now briefly to explore.

Perhaps the most obvious instance in which an articulable e will be elided is when it occurs at the end of the first element of a pair coordinated by 'et', and it is coordinated adjectives that I wish to settle upon. It is precisely their formulaic nature which marks coordinated adjectives off from adjectives merely juxtaposed, in enumerative sequence. 'Je t'adore à l'égal' ends with the couplet:

> Et je chéris, o bête implacable et cruelle!
> Jusqu'à cette froideur par où tu m'es plus belle!

which might be re-imagined as:

> Et je chéris, o bête implacable, cruelle,
> Jusqu'à cette froideur par où tu m'es plus belle!

The effect of the intervening 'et' is to suggest a ready-made pairing of attributes whose justness has been arrived at prior to writing; this construction gives the impression of being a *total* description, in which the first adjective naturally calls forth the second and in which the force of the attribution lies in the complete, compound, formula. In other words, the 'et' signals a construction whose drive is rhetorical rather than perceptual, which seeks its effect through its structure, rather than through the compellingness of its constituent items. The enumerative sequence, on the other hand, seems to be created in the very act of writing, spontaneously, and to derive from direct perception, putting together its findings in the temporal sequence of their occurrence – this *temporal* feature is totally absent from adjectives coordinated by 'et' – findings which are relativised, provisional, capable of infinite multiplication. For this reason the enumerative sequence has something impressionistic about it, while the adjective+et+adjective formula is magisterial and final and beyond adjustment. Thus, while the articulated e of the enumerative sequence 'implacabl*e*, cruelle' with the accompanying *coupe enjambante*, acts as a *trigger* for the next perception, is as it were the incitement to find another adjective, to look again and not be satisfied by unequivocal singleness, the elided e of 'implacable' in 'implacable et cruelle' ('implaca:|bl(e) et cruelle') is a submission to the coordinating device; 'implacable' yields itself up to a compound, formulaic existence, agrees to serve rhetoric and the closed totality of the pair. The elision of the e, by driving 'implacable' on to the coordinating element and second adjective, also expresses a peremptory impatience, connected with the poet's clarity of mind and his refusal to be duped any further by alternative illusions. In other words the elided e in these co-ordinated adjectives helps to reinforce the construction's function as instrument of domination, as a means whereby the poet can retreat into the masterfulness of his own language.

These remarks seem to be borne out by the overall structure of 'Je t'adore à l'égal', whose first six-line section of caressingly ironic tribute, in which the articulated e has a large part to play, gives way to a four-line section of brutal exposure, in which articulable e's are systematically elided, apart from the second e of 'cette', comparable in its function to the 'cette' of the first tercet of 'Avec ses vêtements . . .', already discussed (see above, p. 89); the poet throws off the playfulness of the first section's mystificatory conceits to traffic only in denuded home truths.

Where the presiding tonality is very different, ecstatic rather than dismissive, as in 'La Chevelure':

> Cheveux bleus, pavillon de ténèbres tendues,
> Vous me rendez l'azur du ciel immense et rond

the compacting and encapsulating effect of the elided e before 'et' has a rather different application; the forward momentum expresses now the urgency of aspiration, the magisterial quality of the formula belong now not to the poet's voice, but to the object to which the adjectives are attached, the sky; and the sense of closure and finality is connected with encompassment *of* the poet *by* the object rather than *by* the poet *of* the object. With the achievement of self-prostitution, the perspective on the adjective+et+adjective construction changes, wheeling round from the self-surrendering poet to those phenomena to which he is surrendered. Each verse-context gives its own slant to this syntactic configuration and its own modality to the elided e; but the underlying tonality remains fairly stable.

One other consequence of the elided e which has specific grammatical connections, is its disaccentuation of the potentially accentuable third person singular present indicative of a monosyllabic verb. The play of such present indicative forms seems to me particularly rich in Lamartine's verse, and we should return to 'L'Isolement' and to the line:

Le crépuscule encor ‖ jette un dernier rayon

If asked whether we would read this line as 4+2+1+5 or
4+2+4+2, both theoretically possible, then our answer would, I
think, be the latter. Because it is monosyllabic, because it has no
articulated e to shore it up and give more duration to its vowel, so
'jette' yields up its potential accent which slides forward to an
alternative placement on 'dernier'. This slippage of accent, of
course, suits the sense of the line very well: the twilight can no
longer hold its own against the relentless oncoming of the night,
'encor' is on the point of being overtaken by a 'déjà', and thus the
ventured thrustfulness of the hemistich-initial 'jette' is, as it were,
confiscated or suppressed, and instead it is the pathos of finality
that finds a voice. That 'jette' is robbed of its self-assertiveness need
not, however, have implications of defeat; in 'La Foi', for example,
we encounter the couplet:

> La foi, se réveillant, comme un doux souvenir,   2+4+3+3
> Jette un rayon d'espoir sur mon pâle avenir   4+2+3+3

Here, a too prominent verb would disrupt the 'douceur' of memory
and, besides, the verb seeks the haven of its object, looks to rest in
the substantiality of the divine light. It might be argued indeed that
the 1+5 hemistich is by nature alien to Lamartine's poetry; we have
already seen that this particular pattern is peculiar to expressions of
solitude:

> Seul, invoquant ici son regard paternel   1+5+3+3
>
> Seul, au sein du désert, et de l'obscurité   1+5+6
> ('La Prière')

Solitude may be a state of privilege, but loneliness can trust in this
privilege only if it is guaranteed by the achievement of 'only-ness'.
It threatens, otherwise, to be ostracisation and abandonment; it is a
critical moment for the poet's self-confidence, which the 1+5
pattern throws into relief. There is certainly drama in Lamartine's
verse, but it is a drama which seeks a quietude, as isolation seeks
integration; the smoothness of time's flow, though it calls for
interruption, has a gently sedating effect of its own, as it breaks
down resistance; and the escape from time is an escape from one
smoothness into another, into a smoothness of exchange with the
divine world beyond the grave and with the natural environment
seen as a reflection of that divine world.

If the elided e of the third-person present-tense verb is to have
this disaccentuating effect, then, as has become apparent, two

conditions are necessary: the verb must be hemistich-initial and the hemistich must contain two other accentuable elements. I do not want to suggest that if these conditions obtain, the verb will *always* yield its accent; if the verb is followed by punctuation or syntactical pause, then it will naturally tend to attract accent to underline its status as the *rejet* of an enjambement. The lines that follow our quotation from 'L'Isolement', for example, run:

> Et le char vaporeux de la reine des ombres
> Monte, et blanchit déjà les bords de l'horizon.

In Chapter I, we suggested a $1+5+2+4$ reading of the second of these lines; to read it as $4+2+2+4$ would be to make the whole hemistich the *rejet* and to tend to assign 'déjà' as an adverb to 'monte' as well as to 'blanchit'. But certainly there is nothing intrinsically faulty with a $4+2+2+4$ reading; indeed, much is to be said for encapsulating the two verbs, to increase the speed of events, to ensure that the two verbs are not read as separate events but as concomitant ones, and to give 'déjà' dominion over them both. The rhythm of this first hemistich is altogether more ambiguous than it might appear at first sight. And even when the hemistich-initial verb may seem to claim an accent in the absence of other *obvious* contenders for the secondary accent, there seems to me to be a case for arguing for some slippage. The line:

> Que mon encens souillé || monte avec votre encens

from 'La Semaine Sainte' seems to propose a $4+2+1+5$ reading; but 'avec' is phonetically more able to bear accent than its humble grammatical status might lead one to believe,[6] and the general emphasis of the stanza in which this line appears is on the idea of fusion, of blending – in both the first and fourth lines of the stanza, 'mêler' is used. In other words, there seem to me to be reasons for looking upon 'monte avec' as a kind of compound verb, and it further seems to me that the elision of the e in 'monte' facilitates this compounding. I would not like to insist on this point, but would offer for the reader's further reflection two other examples: another line from 'La Semaine Sainte':

> Souffrez qu'un étranger || veille auprès de leur cendre
> $$2+4+1+5/2+4+(3+3)$$

and a line from 'Le Vallon':

> Glisse à travers les bois || dans l'ombre du vallon.
> $$1+5+2+4/(4+2)+2+4$$

The elision of the e of monosyllabic present-tense verbs is frequent enough to be a feature of the *Méditations poétiques*; it signals a certain avoidance of rhythmic abruptness and the absorption of the verb's activity into the syntactical flow. Odd examples of the monosyllabic verb with articulated e are to be found, but have specific contextual justifications. In this couplet from 'La Prière', for instance:

> Et quand la nuit, guidant son cortège d'étoiles,   4+2+3+3
> Sur le monde endormi, jette ses sombres voiles   3+3+*1*+5

the rhythm of the final hemistich finds its explanation in the line which follows, quoted earlier, and which has the same 1+5 pattern in its first hemistich:

> Seul, au sein du désert, et de l'obscurité   *1*+5+6

The challenge to faith offered by the all-obliterating night, acting with peremptory suddenness, is answered by the poet; at first that same movement which casts darkness over the earth, equally casts the poet into isolation, an isolation exacerbated by the expanding measures of a featureless landscape and the enveloping gloom; but by consolidating his inwardness in meditation and silence, the poet is able to find his way back to the light, now interior, and to contact with a world beyond darkness:

> D'un jour intérieur je me sens éclairer,
> Et j'entends une voix qui me dit d'espérer.

The aggressive violence of the night lies in the very 'verbality' of its activity; the articulated e of 'jette', creating a *coupe enjambante*, certainly has a dispersive or diffusive effect, but the attack on the verb is not diminished by that, and the poet's solitude is seen as the direct result of the force of the verb, a solitude made of disempowerment and defiance.

Baudelaire does not make as much use of the hemistich-initial present-tense verb, and when he does place monosyllabic verbs in this position, they are more frequently accompanied by an articulated e. In the last line of 'Spleen': 'Quand le ciel bas et lourd', for example:

> Sur mon crâne incliné plante son drapeau noir   3+3+1+5

which echoes the rhythmic pattern of the first line of the poem:

> Quand le ciel bas et lourd pèse comme un couvercle   3+3+1+5

there is no suggestion of slippage of accent; however much the poet may rebel, by irony or vituperation, the overpowering actional insistence of 'L'Angoisse' cannot be side-stepped or parried; and that insistence is supported by the articulated e. It is in the fourth stanza that the poet's raging against the depressive downward pressure of his splenetic condition finds its most unequivocal expression:

> Des cloches tout à coup sautent avec furie
> Et lancent vers le ciel un affreux hurlement,
> Ainsi que des esprits errants et sans patrie
> Qui se mettent à geindre opiniâtrement.

His revolt assumes the same 1+5 pattern, in the second hemistich of the stanza's first line, as his oppression, where the articulated e is like an attempt to make the verb count, to consolidate it. But the defiance is no more than a gesture and quickly evaporates: the noise-level falls abruptly from the clanging bells to the derisory 'geindre opiniâtrement', and the verbs increasingly surrender their assertiveness, by falling back from the hemistich-initial position:

> | sautent avec furie | 1+5 |
> |---|---|
> | Et lancent vers le ciel ... | 2+4 |
> | ... | |
> | Qui se mettent à geindre opiniâtrement. | 3+3+6 |

And this final 6-measure embodies the loss of will in apparent wilfulness, a zero of activity in apparent persistence. Of course this particular pattern – monosyllabic verb+articulated e as initial element in a 1+5 hemistich – offers its positive side, even though, as in 'Un Voyage à Cythère' the promise of richness may turn out to be illusory:

> De l'antique Vénus le superbe fantôme
> Au-dessus de tes mers ‖ plane comme un arôme,
> Et charge les esprits d'amour et de langueur.

'Elévation' celebrates the gravity-less and penetrative freedom of 'planer', which gives access to the secrets of things and allows the unhindered achievement of self-prostitution. In the lines of our quotation, Venus enjoys the same expansion of self and distribution of self through her 'planing'. But even here, the 1+5 pattern has a certain darkness. In the opening stanza of the poem, it was the poet's own heart which was hovering around the rigging of the ship; this activity is now taken possession of by Venus, and the poet, no longer acting, is acted upon; the poet's loss of individual identity is borne out by the progression 'Mon coeur'→ 'nous'→ 'les esprits' (does he in fact now cast himself as one of the 'vieux garçons' for whom Cythera is an 'Eldorado banal'?). Furthermore,

Venus's distributive munificence is expressed by 'charge', a verb with an apparently very different function in 'Elévation':

> Derrière les ennuis et les vastes[7] chagrins
> Qui chargent de leur poids l'existence brumeuse

Thus 'plane comme un arôme' has within it, more covertly perhaps, much of the tyranny of the 1+5 pattern of 'Quand le ciel . . .'; here it is the tyranny of a chimaera of promised bliss which paradoxically weighs on the human spirit, with its burden of non-fulfilment.

Another of the 'Spleen' poems, 'Pluviôse, irrité contre la ville entière', provides one of the rare examples in *Les Fleurs du Mal* of a monosyllabic present-tense verb with its e elided:

> Pluviôse, irrité contre la ville entière,   3+3+4+2
> De son urne à grands flots verse un froid ténébreux 3+3+3+3

The personified fifth month of the Revolutionary calendar (20/21 Jan – 18/19 Feb) vents its spleen on the city with cold, gloomy rain. Here one might have expected, in the second hemistich of the second line, the 1+5 pattern we have just explored: the conditions, the downward inhibiting pressure and actional insistence, seem to authorise it. But instead the verb is disaccentuated by the elision and by the availability of 'froid' to accent. One might simply argue, of course, that the inverted 'à grands flots' makes 'verse' as good as redundant and that it is for this reason that we pass glancingly over the verb; but it could equally be argued that if Baudelaire had it in mind to underline the unremittingly torrential nature of the downpour, then an accent at either side of the caesura and the protractiveness of an articulated e on 'verse' would have suited his purposes very well. But the disaccentuation of 'verse' seems to me to have a structural rather than expressive purpose; the caesura of the second line is a kind of cross-over point, where the grandiose classicising paraphernalia of personification and the consistency of a classical language give way to an inconsistent (or incongruous) language and the specific locations of the contemporary townscape. The progressively self-confirming sequence which would be provided by, for instance, 'Pluviôse . . . de son urne à grands flots verse la pluie' (liquid) is in fact broken by the arrival of 'un froid' (temperature) as object; and it is not, say, 'un froid pénétrant', but, further surprise, 'un froid ténébreux'. By backgrounding 'verse', Baudelaire withdraws semantic continuity the better to favour the metaphoric juxtaposition of 'à grands flots' and 'un froid' and to engineer a seamless transition from the generalised classical

figure to the localised and concrete, from a self-consistent imagery
to the life-in-death and death-in-life paradoxes of the final lines of
the stanza:

> Aux pâles habitants du voisin cimetière
> Et la mortalité sur les faubourgs brumeux.

If a structural significance outweighs an expressive one in the
above example, it is the phonetic structure of the stanzaic context
which supplies our final instance of the monosyllabic verb with
elided e with its expressive power; in 'Le Vin du solitaire', the poet
compares the spiritual rewards offered by the looks and kisses of
women, the money of the gambler, and provocative music with
those offered by wine, and finds them wanting:

> Tout cela ne vaut pas, ô bouteille profonde   3+3+3+3
> Les baumes pénétrants que ta panse féconde   2+4+3+3
> Garde au coeur altéré du poète pieux   3+3+3+3

Acoustically, this first tercet is striking in its self-indulgence; the
recurrent articulated e's (bouteill*e*, baum*e*s, pans*e*, poèt*e*), the
careful diaereses (po|ète, pi|eux), the insistence of the twice
repeated é (pénétrants, altéré) and the p's, and the predominance
of the 3+3 hemistich, all create an atmosphere of easeful and
unhurried harmony. But we are aware that the spiritual 'ivresse' is
directly proportional to a physical one, and that the harmony is
more the harmony of complacent, mindless equanimity than of
achieved spiritual self-integration. The irony of the final line is only
too apparent: the thirst of the poet hardly has any figurative
dimension, and the devotion expressed by 'pieux' does not go
beyond the bottle. And this undermines our response to the
acoustic texture: we see there evidence of the obsessive repeti-
tiveness and enunciatory difficulties of the befuddled head as much
as signs of rich inner experience. The elision of the e of 'Garde'
seems to me to be a moment of disabusement, the point at which
the lulling securities of the articulated e are refused and the poet
pushes us impatiently on to the realities beneath the dream, on to
the paralleled pairs 'coeur altéré' | 'poète pieux'. And 'garde' itself
is undermined, in both its senses: if 'garde' is seen to refer back to a
particular bottle holding/keeping a literal wine for the poet's
delight, then it is not allowed its holding capacity: as 'garde' is
glanced over, so the bottle is forced to yield up what it holds to a
thirsty poet. If 'garde', on the other hand refers back to all bottles
which hold, not so much wine, as solace and life-giving properties,

then the disaccentuation of 'garde' casts doubts on the truth of that supposition. It is thus the treatment of 'garde' which initiates the progressively ironic cast of the final line, an irony which achieves an unrelieved ascendancy in the second tercet.

It is difficult, if not impossible, to assign any positional significance to the articulated e. Clearly it will not in normal circumstances occupy either positions 1 or 12, and only exceptionally will it be found at positions 6 and 7; but it is equally at home in all other positions. Of course there will be connections between the e's position and different syntactic constructions, as we have begun to see in our treatments of adjectival pairs and 'monosyllabic' present-tense verbs; but there is no way in which the position of an e can be a reliable predictor of anything more than a whole range of possible syntaxes. But again, it could be argued that the general position of articulated e's in relation to the circumflexity of the alexandrine does have some modal significance.

Of the 17 occurrences of the articuled e in 'Spleen': 'J'ai plus de souvenirs que si j'avais mille ans', for example, 6 belong to the first hemistich and almost double the number, 11, to the second. Four of the first-hemistich instances occur in the first ten lines of the poem and in three cases are balanced by a second-hemistich articulated e:

line 5   Cach*e* moins de secrets que mon trist*e* cerveau
line 6   C'est un*e* pyramide, un immens*e* caveau
line 9   Où comm*e* des remords se traîn*ent* de longs vers
line 10 Qui s'acharn*ent* toujours sur mes morts les plus chers

These lines provide us with a clue to what creates the peculiar heaviness and dragging density of Baudelaire's second hemistichs, qualities to which the articulated e contributes, providing at the same time its own falling, reflective (introspective) and often dispirited/dispiriting cadence: the presence of a noun qualified by a frequently preposed and frequently polysyllabic adjective. This consolidated nominality of the second hemistich is rarely to be found in the first: either the first hemistich is without a noun, or contains an unqualified noun; and even when that noun is qualified, it is frequently by a monosyllabic and relatively neutral adjective. These observations are intended only to indicate a tendency, not a compositional principle, but the tendency is obtrusive and does not relate solely to poems with a splenetic origin; a glance through 'Elévation', for example, or 'Parfum exotique' will confirm it. Anyway, as the *ennui* of 'J'ai plus de souvenirs' gets an even firmer grip on the poet's spirit, so second-hemistich occurrences of the articulated e take over, often underlining other forms of repetition (phonetic, syntactical) with its own repeatedness:

> Je suis un vieux boudoir plein de roses fanées,
> Où gît tout un fouillis de modes surannées,
> Où les pastels plaintifs et les pâles Boucher ...

or

> Rien n'égale en longueur les boiteuses journées,
> Quand sous les lourds flocons des neigeuses années

Here the articulated e's are agents of time's erasing power, enact the very evanescence of the nouns; or alternatively their protractive function predominates, giving an indefinitely receding outline to the adjectives.

The two other instances of the first-hemistich e in this poem are as structurally significant as they are expressively so. They occur in the last lines of the poem's two major sections (i.e. at lines 14 and 24). The first follows a line already quoted:

> Où les pastels plaintifs et les pâles Boucher,
> Seuls, respirent l'odeur d'un flacon débouché   (13–14)

and the second at the end of the poet's presentation of himself as the forgotten sphinx:

> Un vieux sphinx ignoré du monde insoucieux,
> Oublié sur la carte, et dont l'humeur farouche
> Ne chante qu'aux rayons du soleil qui se couche.

These are last-ditch attempts to reverse the overall trend of the poem towards second-hemistich articulated e's, to reintroduce a note of springiness into heavy-footed despair. The articulated e in the first hemistich often has an upward, lilting movement attached to it, a forward-looking readiness for experience:

> Je respire l'odeur de ton sein chaleureux
> ('Parfum exotique')

(how deep the articulated e makes the expectant inhalation), or a buoyant, resonating rapturousness:

> Qui chantent les transports de l'esprit et des sens.
> ('Correspondances')

Something of these modalities is to be found in the lines from 'J'ai plus de souvenirs', but not only is there an accompanying restriction in both cases – 'Seuls' and 'Ne ... que' – but the second hemistich also works to invalidate the embryonic zestfulness: the 'débouché' may signal a perfume's release, but it signals also its ultimate irretrievable loss, and the 'qui se couche' obliterates the very rays which are the source of song – the sphinx perversely chooses to sing only at the very moment when its song is vowed to extinction.

Finally, a brief mention should be made of one of the other positional functions of the articulated e, namely closure. The articulated e has a braking effect as well as a distributive one; because it ritualises poetic utterance, it is an ideal closing agent, either in the last lines of stanzas or, more especially, of whole poems. Here is a selection of Baudelairian final lines:

Le langag*e* des fleurs et des chos*e*s muettes   ('Elévation')

Ses parfums, ses chansons et ses douc*e*s chaleurs
('J'aime le souvenir . . .')

Tes appas façonnés aux bouch*e*s des Titans   ('L'Idéal')

Obscurcir la splendeur de tes froid*e*s prunelles
('Une nuit que j'étais . . .')

O ma si blanche, ô ma si froid*e* Marguerite
('Sonnet d'automne')

Etoil*en*t vaguement leurs prunell*e*s mystiques ('Les Chats')

These e's enable the poem to reverberate beyond its boundaries, into the silence of the reader's absorption; the articulated e is the point at which signification reaches into imagination, because it is itself in so many senses semantically dead. And at the same time it is a reminder of the rite which poetry is; being a purely enunciatory event of a purely poetic kind, it serves to recall, as do other conventions, that every syntactical sequence is informed or shadowed by an arbiter whose comprehension of language's communicative range seems inexhaustible.

My ambitions in this chapter have been necessarily modest. It is impossible to encompass, yet alone categorise, the varieties of structural and expressive function of the articulated (and elided) e, since each particular instance energises specific colourings and associations. I have tried to abstract some of the broad patterns of activity of the e, and to relate these to the central concerns of a particular poet, looking further afield only when need be. I have also tried to show one or two of the ways in which syntactic configurations affect, and are affected by, the nature of the e, and how far its position may be accounted significant. All these enquiries have been brief and provisional; but the e is bound into the very ontology of French regular verse and for that reason it should be considered as unflaggingly crucial to the verse's self-realisation in the imagination of the reader.

5

RHYTHMICITY AND METRICITY

HOPKINS'S 'THE WINDHOVER' AND MALLARMÉ'S 'LE TOMBEAU DE CHARLES BAUDELAIRE'

The more a text has design, the more it has designs – on the reader. But if design is multiplied beyond encompassment or is ambiguated, then the text's rhetorical effectiveness is sprung. But the 'springing' of rhetoric depends, of course, as much on the reader as on the text; the reader is always at liberty to persuade himself towards the perception of unity or consistency, or towards giving priority to one design over another. Rhetorical effectiveness can only ever be a result of a complicity, the complicity between a reader and a perceptible design. But such a complicity can only take place if the reader feels authorised to participate in it. That authority can come from many sources: an author hypothesised through the medium of a poet or narrator, generic conventions, recognisable and recognised formal principles, and so on.

Rhythm – and, for the moment, this term includes both rhythm and metre – is certainly one source of authority, since if it can be recognised, it allows the identification of the poem's semantic focuses and their articulations, and thus of the distribution of the poem's expressive and rhetorical resources. Rhythm is the informing design of the poem's power to communicate and makes its communication persuasive; rhythm, in short, guarantees that the poem means and means to mean; conversely, utterances without meaning can have no rhythm since they carry within them no principle of utterability; and as a corollary, utterances which have a patently emphatic or transparent rhythmic structure, even though they may semantically elude us temporarily or indeed permanently, equally have an inbuilt guarantee of their intelligibility and significance. The child's relationship with nursery rhymes, or hymns, may be peculiarly suspended between confidence in the text's intelligibility and actual non-comprehension; the nursery rhyme may be chanted, the hymn sung, with unabashable gusto, because the child, while not understanding, is a performer of the text's rhythmically self-evident coherence.

Adult readers of 'difficult' poetic texts are, in a sense, sophisticated versions of the child, sophisticated in that while they can also perform the text's intelligibility their own non-comprehension is now housed not in misconstruction or bafflement, but in an excess of comprehension which permits no resolution of itself. Rhythmic patentness in a difficult poem may represent for the reader not so much the sustaining drive of a self-resolving meaning and rhetorical purposefulness, as the simple armature onto which the proliferations and ramifications of ambiguated meaning are moulded; in this perspective, the rhythm does not positively activate or interpret complexity: it enables it, rather, as an uninterfering, but sustaining ground; in this perspective, rhythm stays on this side of meaning. But equally rhythm might situate itself on the other side of meaning, be the resolution towards which ambiguated meaning strives, a resolution either by virtue of its ability to organise and integrate, to synthesise, the texts' semantic productivity, or by virtue of its tendency to give priority to certain configurations of meaning over others, to read the poem into a primary meaning or meanings, which secondary meanings merely supplement, qualify or decorate. Equally, of course, rhythm may have no patentness, but instead a patent urge to exist; in other words, we may confront a text in which rhythmicity is visible, but its realisation invisible, in which the evident will to rhythm excites, and is excited by, the will to mean; the equivocations of a rhythmic presence are but signs of the unease of a meaning which cannot release itself from virtuality, but incites the reader to a revelation beyond the text, a revelation which includes the discovery of a deeper identity within rhythm's ambivalence. In Saussure's terms, rhythm may be no more than an accompanying guarantee of signification. But further than that, it may be an active negotiator between *signifiant* and *signifié*, or may itself constitute either a *signifiant*, inasmuch as it fantomatically means alongside verbal *signifiants*, or a *signifié* inasmuch as it proposes a meaning which is at one and the same time constituted of, and more than, the *signifiés* which individual textual items produce; indeed it may be the only *signifié* that a poem produces, if the poem's *signifiants* refuse their *signifiés* by signifying only other *signifiants*; the rhythm in this last instance is then the rhythm of the Idea of the whole text.

It is the difficult or obscure poem which peculiarly problematises rhythm and/or rhythmic function in the ways described above. And it is this problematisation that I wish to examine in analyses of Hopkins's sprung rhythm and the way it manifests itself in 'The Windhover', and of Mallarmé's rhythmically less controversial, but equally difficult, 'Le Tombeau de Charles Baudelaire'.

A brief description of 'sprung rhythm' is a necessary preamble to our scansion, or rather scansions, of Hopkins's 'The Windhover'; I postpone until a later paragraph an examination of sprung rhythm's implications. In a letter to R. W. Dixon of October 6, 1878, Hopkins wrote: 'In the winter of '75 . . . I had long had haunting my ear the echo of a new rhythm which now I realised on paper. To speak shortly, it consists in scanning by accents or stresses alone.' Sprung rhythm belongs to pure-stress (simple-stress) metres, in which the number of stresses per line alone defines the metre regardless of the number of accompanying unstressed syllables, and affiliates itself, according to Hopkins, with Greek and Latin lyric verse, Old English verse, and verse of the Elizabethan age, though it cannot be said to be derived from them.[1] It shares with Old English verse a cultivation of alliteration, though not raised to the same metrical principle, and other echoic patterns (assonance, internal rhyme, etc.); these help to point up and intensify the stresses and tend to override (acoustically) other syntactic particles so that the verse is more compressed. It should be said that the stress of pure-stress metre and sprung rhythm differs from the stress of standard or syllable-stress metre in that it is a sense-stress rather than a metrical one; it is not a stress in a repeated pattern (foot) to which the sense accommodates itself or by which sense is drawn out; it is a stress which expresses the sense, is demanded by the sense, that is to say, it is a stress not of a rhythmic, but of an expressive, nature and it is for that reason that it is more dramatic, more committed, more emotionally charged than a metrical stress; Hopkins describes the sprung stress as 'more *of* a stress' than that of standard rhythm 'in which less stress is laid' (letter to R. W. Dixon, 22 Dec. 1880). Hopkins's main justification for sprung rhythm is its naturalness; in his 'Author's Preface' (1883), he declares that it is the rhythm of common speech and written prose, of all but the most monotonously regular music (sprung rhythm is thus to be found in choruses, refrains, songs), that it is to be found in the folk-verse of nursery-rhymes, weather saws and so on, where phonetic erosion, particularly at the ends of lines, has had the effect of driving stresses together, and that it arises in standard rhythm when feet are reversed or the rhythm counterpointed.

It might be expected, given the quotation with which this

description began, and the differentiation of sense-stress from metrical stress, that sprung rhythm would have no room for the foot or for a scansion which notated any more than the sense-units in the line. But the metrical foot is central to Hopkins's prosodic thinking, even though he passes foot-scansion off as a mere convenience, an organising fiction. The reason for Hopkins's salvaging of the foot lies partly, perhaps largely, in his desire to explain sprung rhythm as a development out of standard rhythm, despite the availability of a pure-stress tradition, of which sprung rhythm could simply be seen as a revival. There can be no doubt that there are polemical motives in this move; Hopkins did not wish sprung rhythm to appear to be an *alternative*, even archaising prosody, which the syllable-stress poets of the nineteenth century could afford to disregard. After all, more was at stake than a mere metre; Hopkins treated poetic diction and prosodic concerns as inseparable and certainly Victorian poetic diction was in urgent need of reform. No, sprung rhythm needed to be seen as something inhering in standard rhythm, pressing to be released from it as an inevitable consequence of the practice of substantial poets. The stages of sprung rhythm's derivation from standard rhythm are: standard rhythm → reversal of individual feet → more thorough-going counterpointing of the given metre → sprung rhythm. The reversing of feet, particularly of the first, and of the foot after a caesural break in the line, is common practice; but when this reversal concerns two consecutive feet, and particularly if one of those feet is the second or the last, that is feet which, according to Hopkins, are 'characteristic and sensitive and cannot well be touched' ('Author's Preface'), then an alternative rhythm is superimposed on the 'ground' rhythm, so that we hear two rhythms at once: the spectral 'ground' rhythm and the actualised rhythm mounted upon it. This is counterpoint rhythm and it follows that the stresses of that counterpointing rhythm are in fact sense-stresses. If counterpointing is introduced to such an extent that the 'ground' rhythm disappears from perception, then the rhythm of the line is 'sprung'; only the counterpointing is perceptible and this rhythm is 'probably Sprung Rhythm'.

Although Hopkins acknowledges that rising rhythms (iambic, anapaestic), falling rhythms (trochaic, dactylic) and rocking rhythms (amphibrachic) are 'real and true to nature' ('Author's Preface'), he chooses to scan by feet in which the stress always comes first (i.e. only in falling rhythms) again for the sake of convenience (but whose, and what is to be gained by it?) and by analogy with the musical bar. Although 'for particular effects' ('Author's Preface'), Hopkins allows that any number of syllables may follow the stressed one in sprung rhythm, he in fact, and purely to install some (arbitrary?) notion of regularity, limits sprung rhythm to feet of between one and four syllables (monosyllable, trochee, dactyl and first paeon). 'And hence', Hopkins declares:

Sprung Rhythm differs from Running Rhythm in having or being only one nominal rhythm, a mixed or 'logaoedic' one, instead of three, but on the other hand in having twice the flexibility of foot, so that any two stresses may either follow one another running or be divided by one, two, or three slack syllables.   ('Author's Preface')

There is some spurious argument here. When Hopkins says that sprung rhythm has one rhythm (and cannot be counterpointed) and that standard rhythm has three, the three presumably refers to rising, falling and rocking; the one of sprung rhythm is falling. But when he attributes to sprung rhythm twice the flexibility of foot, he is treating standard rhythm as though it were scanned as his verse is (i.e. on a falling base only, and thus having only trochees and dactyls at its disposal). Moreover it should be noted that Hopkins here defends sprung rhythm in terms of its advantages as a *metrical-foot prosody*. In other words, however much Hopkins may appear to brush off foot-scansion as at best a convenient fiction, as a concession to standard-rhythm ways of thinking, he takes it seriously enough to justify sprung rhythm in terms of it, rather than treating it as an irrelevant and disfiguring constraint. Finally it should be said that Hopkins looks upon the feet of sprung rhythm as being isochronous and equal in stress-value; that is to say, where one foot is syllabically shorter than another, the 'missing' syllables are compensated for by pause and by a proportionate intensification of the stress. Sprung rhythm thus takes a variability of stress-strength for granted. I should add that it is too frequently argued that the traditional scansion of standard (syllable-stress) rhythms assumes that all stresses are equal; this is to do traditional scansion an injustice; it does not mark stress-variation because it is not its business to do so: that is the concern of the reader or reciter; the business of traditional scansion is to mark the *positions* of stresses, not to judge their relative strengths.

To this basic account of sprung rhythm, we must add some explanation of Hopkins's terminology and method of notation. 'It is natural in Sprung Rhythm', Hopkins tells us ('Author's Preface'), 'for the lines to be *rove over* that is for the scanning of each line immediately to take up that of the one before'. This is a kind of scansional enjambement and a way of dealing with unstressed syllables at the beginnings of lines so as to maintain the principle of the foot-initial stress and consistently falling rhythms. Hopkins allows two licences in sprung rhythm: rests, as in music, and *hangers* or *outrides*:

> that is one, two, or three slack syllables added to a foot and not counting in the nominal scanning. They are so called because they seem to hang below the line or ride forward or backward from it in another dimension than the line itself, according to a principle needless to explain here [!]
>
> ('Author's Preface')

The *hangers* or *outrides* are marked by a loop below the syllables concerned ⌣. Loops over syllables, ⌢, are *slurs*, tying the syllables together 'into the time of one' ('Author's Preface'). Little loops at the ends of lines indicate that the rhyme-sound runs on to the first letter of the following line. The mark ⌐ over two or three syllables indicates a reversed or counterpointed foot and should not be confused with the *quiver* or *circumflexion*, marked ⁀, which gives one syllable the value of nearly two. 𝄐 signals the equivalent of a musical pause; the syllable so marked should be dwelt on. In addition, Hopkins uses various marks to indicate differences of degree and quality in stress-value: ′, ″, ˇ, ˃, ˆ (this sequence is not a progression).

Armed with this information, let us proceed, without further ado, to a tentative scansion of 'The Windhover':

1. I caught this morning morning's minion, king-
2. dom of daylight's dauphin, dapple-dawn-drawn Falcon, in his riding
3. Of the rolling level underneath him steady air, and striding
4. High there, how he rung upon the rein of a wimpling wing
5. In his ecstasy! then off, off forth on swing,
6. As a skate's heel sweeps smooth on a bow-bend: the hurl and gliding
7. Rebuffed the big wind. My heart in hiding
8. Stirred for a bird, – the achieve of, the mastery of the thing!
9. Brute beauty and valour and act, oh, air, pride, plume here
10. Buckle! AND the fire that breaks from thee then, a billion
11. Times told lovelier, more dangerous, O my chevalier!
12. No wonder of it: sheer plod makes plough down sillion

13. Shine, and blue-bleak embers, ah my dear,
14. Fall, gall themselves, and gash gold-vermilion.

Notes on the scansion

Author's note: 'THE WINDHOVER. (Falling paeonic rhythm, sprung and outriding.) St. Beuno's, May 30, 1877'. Gardner's note: Each line has five main metrical stresses (Gardner, 1953, p. 221).

1. This line looks like an iambic preamble, an even-rhythmed, accentually 'neutral' pentameter, as the poet explains the circumstances of his encounter with the falcon, prior to the emotional and visionary engagement with it. The 'Author's Preface' (1883) does not, of course, allow an iambic scansion; strictly speaking, if we employ the scansion there suggested, this is a trochaic pentameter with anacrusis, and certainly the central dissyllables of the line – 'morning', 'morning's', 'minion' – consolidate any trochaic tendency. On the other hand, if we read this line with a rising rhythm we not only prepare the suspension and disjunction of 'king – | dom' ('this morn | ing morn | ing's min | ion king –') but we also as it were catch, or indeed launch, the upward and upward-soaring movement of the bird. But the standard rhythm of this line is already under assault, not for metrical reasons (e.g. counterpointing), but for acoustic ones: the insistence of the alliterative (m's) and assonant (or, i(n)) patterns tends to collapse stresses into each other, and to foreground them, while the repetition of 'morning' with its two different fields of reference – a particular morning, as time notation, and then morning in general, viewed more as atmosphere than temporal unit, more figurative than literal – will naturally lead to an augmentation of stress on the second, as the stress is passed on to a word with wider application: perhaps more properly 'morning morning's'.

2. Lines 1–2 are 'rove over', i.e. scanning runs on from one line to the next. The increased stress of feet with 'outriding' syllables ('dauphin', 'Falcon') and the difference between these feet and paeons are explained by Hopkins in a note to 'Hurrahing in Harvest': 'Take notice that the outriding feet are not to be confused with dactyls or paeons, though sometimes the line might be scanned either way. The strong syllable in an outriding foot has always a great stress and after the outrider follows a short pause. The paeon is easier and more flowing' (Gardner, 1967, p. 269). This line, like several others in the poem, is scansionally embarrassing because of the density of stressable items, and it might be surprising to find no stress marking on either 'dapple' or 'drawn'. A more satisfactory

reading of 'dawn-drawn' within Hopkinsian conventions might well be 'd<u>awn-drawn</u>'; the mark ⌐‾‾‾¬ is explained by Hopkins in a letter to Canon Dixon apropos of 'To what serves Mortal Beauty': 'the mark ⌐‾‾‾¬ over two neighbouring syllables means that, though one has and the other has not the metrical stress, in the recitation-stress they are to be about equal' (Gardner, 1967, p. 285). This device has much in common with what in other prosodic contexts is called 'hovering accent' (or 'distributed stress' or 'hovering stress'), a kind of compromise scansion in which stress is available to two adjacent syllables without being allotted to either, that is to say, a scansion which seeks to maintain the proper number of stresses in the line, but does not wish to commit itself to identifying their exact distribution. Though the concept of 'hovering accent' ostensibly leaves the choice of which syllable to stress to the reader, I suspect very much that 'hovering accent' resolves itself in the stressing of both syllables; in other words 'hovering accent' is a device for apparently maintaining a metrical norm while covertly empowering the reader to transgress that norm. The unstressedness of 'dapple' might be accounted for thus: after the pause which follows 'dáu<u>phin</u>', the voice rests from stressing as it looks for the next stress-peak, that is to say, that 'dapple' acts as a motivator of the next stress, is stress-compelling rather than itself being stress-receiving; such an explanation seems to me plausible, but it does have the disturbing implication that much unstressed material in Hopkins's verse is not 'intrinsically' unstressed, but merely a relief from the unremittingness of stress. Alternatively, we might account for the whole sequence, as given in our preliminary scansion – 'dápple – dáwn – dráwn' – as a rhythmic group, the massing of syllables around a central peak, a 'centroid' which is relatively more stressed than the syllables in its immediate vicinity; 'dawn' is the natural peak of this group since it continues the sequence 'morning – daylight – . . .'. But this is to let the notion of 'rhythmic group' momentarily supersede that of the metrical foot (for Hopkins's own distinction between these two notions, see Holloway, 1947, pp. 43–7), and to introduce the principle of the relativity of stress – both 'dapple' and 'drawn' are stressed, but less so relative to 'dawn' – to allow stressed elements to be marked as unstressed, paradoxically, for metrical and scansional reasons.

3.   Lines 2 and 3 are 'rove over'. There is some inconsistency in Gardner's marking of this line; 1953, p. 221 gives 'rolling' and 'underneath' single-stress markings ('ró<u>lling</u>', 'undernéath') with the note 'stresses so marked' (presumably in manuscript), while

1948, p. 228 and 1967, p. 266 give the double-stress markings that appear in our scansion, presumably on the basis of what Hopkins has to say about the effect of 'outrides'. Disquieting in this line is the non-stressing of 'level' and 'steady' and the accentual attention received by 'underneath'. Of syntactical and grammatical ambiguities in the poem we shall have more to say later, but if 'level' is an adverb attached to 'rolling', then its non-stressing can be better understood; but this makes the 'outride' of 'rolling', with the pause that follows, less comprehensible. If, however, we justify the 'outride' and subsequent pause by viewing 'level' as an adjective and the first element in the premodifying group 'level underneath him', then surely 'level' deserves a stress. The same conditions apply to 'steady': the syntactic segmentation:

Of the rolling level | underneath him steady | air

might make the non-stressing of 'steady' just about envisageable. On the other hand, the alternative segmentation:

Of the rolling | level underneath him | steady air

makes a stress on 'steady' unavoidable to my ear. The most 'natural' scansion of this line, a scansion unprejudiced, that is, by concerns for Hopkinsian prosody, would be:

$$\overset{x}{\text{Of}}\ \overset{x}{\text{the}}\ \overset{'}{\text{rol}}\overset{x}{\text{ling}}\ \overset{'}{\text{le}}\overset{x}{\text{vel}}\ \overset{x}{\text{un}}\overset{'}{\text{der}}\overset{x}{\text{neath}}\ \overset{x}{\text{him}}\ \overset{'}{\text{stea}}\overset{x}{\text{dy}}\ \overset{x}{\text{air,}}\ \overset{'}{\text{and}}\ \overset{x}{\text{striding}}$$

This sounds more like iambic hexameter with substitution of anapaest and fourth paeon (x x x '), at the first and third feet respectively. The scansion that we have opted for in our original version is necessitated by the maintenance of the five-stress norm and of the (according to Hopkins) underlying paeonic pattern, by the 'outrides' and their 'equivalence' to the paeon. In saying this, I do not wish to suggest that the reading of the line by Hopkinsian principles is impossible, but that, far from being a rhythm that moulds itself naturally to 'common speech', it often involves accentual distortion of the kind to be found in 'running rhythm' followed to the letter. And in this line we cannot refer ourselves to any notion of group rhythm and stress-centre simply because the groups themselves do not unambiguously emerge from the line.

4. Again there are inconsistencies in Gardner's various notes for this line: 1948, p. 228 indicates the 'outride' on 'there', but single-stresses 'High'; 1953, p. 221 provides no note on this line; 1967, p. 226 marks the 'outride' on 'there' and double-stresses 'High'. Again, following Hopkins's proposition that 'outriding'

augments stress, I have followed the last of these readings. Otherwise, this line is metrically uncontroversial. I would only add that the progressive abbreviation of the feet in terms of unstressed syllables (however isochronous the feet, or equalised by progressive augmentation of stress) – 'outride' + 2 unstressed syllables > paeon → dactyl → trochee → stress of 'wing' – enacts either a stalling movement in the bird's flight or a spiralling movement of ever-decreasing circles, depending on how 'rung upon the rein' is interpreted, at all events a movement of increasing stasis, an achievement of ecstasy in selfhood or self-concentration, which is then released into a sweeping and gliding flight in the following line.

5. Lines 4 and 5 are 'rove over'. This line is again metrically uncontroversial, but peculiar because of the juxtaposition of stresses in the two monosyllabic feet ' | off | , off | ' and following trochee 'forth on'. Thanks to their stresses, these adverbs have the force of imperatives; the bird is as if commanded into flight by a higher principle, that of its own inscape, or by the poet himself as he creates himself and his vocation through the bird; in other words, the poet commands himself to move into the making of his own poem by which he is 'selved' (see Sprinker (1980), pp. 3–15). And the modulation from 'off' to 'forth' is important; for whereas 'off' expresses a directionless, almost arbitrary, and uncaring movement away, 'forth' is filled with a sense of purpose, of enterprise, of calling.

6. Lines 5 and 6 are 'rove over', and in this instance the 'roving over' is not supported by any corresponding enjambement of the syntax; Hopkins writes, in his 'Author's Preface': 'and in fact the scanning runs on without break from the beginning, say, of a stanza to the end and all the stanza is one long strain, though written in lines asunder' (Gardner, 1967, p. 48). Hopkins might have added that scanning runs through stanzaic boundaries as well. This line is eccentric in that the 'outride' 'heel' would normally be a stressable element in the line, whereas other 'outrides' in the poem cover normally unstressable elements. If one took the unkind view that Hopkins uses notations not so much to identify metrical realities, but as a way of installing a metre, of circumventing elements which threaten the metre's existence, then the 'outride' would seem a convenient way of making extrametrical those unstressed syllables which exceed the paeon's limit of three; in this line the 'outride' would also seem to be a convenient way of slipping unwanted stresses under the carpet. But even allowing for the

extrametricality of 'heel', we are again, as with the third line, faced with a sequence of words containing more stressable elements than there are available stresses: 'smooth' and 'bend' are candidates for stress, though the case for 'bend' is not strong unless it is endowed with a verbal, actional impulse. As far as 'smooth' is concerned, and maintaining Hopkinsian conventions, perhaps 'sweeps smooth' would be a preferable scansion.

7. Lines 6 and 7 are 'rove over'. This line is metrically unproblematic and, taken on its own, leans heavily towards iambic.

8. Lines 7 and 8 – syntactic enjambement without 'roving over' – are the reverse of lines 5 and 6. The 'outride' 'of' deserves some comment; in normal circumstances the syntactic suspension of 'of' would attract some accentuation to it, accentuation which would be passed on to its repetition in 'the mastery of' and the syntactic segmentation would look like this: 'the achieve of, | the mastery of | the thing'. By extrametricalising the first 'of', that is by taking it out of stress circulation, Hopkins at one and the same time removes the threat of stress from it and allows us to treat the 'of' in 'the mastery of' as though it were a one and only appearance, and therefore, naturally, unstressed, producing the segmentation: 'the achieve (of) | the mastery | of the thing'.

9. This line is something of a scanner's nightmare. Lines 8 and 9 are 'rove over' without syntactic enjambement, unless one insists on a real break between octave and sestet, in which case the slack that we have attributed to 'Brute' must count as an anacrusis. Obviously every one of the nouns in this line is potentially stressable, as indeed is 'Brute'. In limiting myself to five accents for the line, I have considered that the coordinating 'and' projects 'valour' and 'act' into stress in a way that the commas after 'air' and 'pride' do not. The slur marked over 'oh, air' in Gardner, 1967, p. 267, tying the two syllables into the time of one, leads me to mark this compaction with a stress on 'air', which further deserves its accent as the generator of 'pride' and 'plume', and because it recalls the air and wind of the octave; 'pride' and 'plume' are, as it were, subordinated to 'air', or created out of it. And if I have stressed 'here', it is for three reasons: to suspend it as a *contre-rejet*, the better to project and halt the voice on 'Buckle', to give it prominence as a rhyme, calling forth its partners, and particularly 'chevalier' (though it would not be surprising to find Hopkins rhyming an unstressed syllable with a stressed one), and to give due weight to one of those deictic words, so crucial to the realisation and actualisation of moments of 'inscape' in Hopkins's work, where

'here' means 'in me' or 'in this bird'. But all these solutions are very much subject to the contingencies of my own reading and have no other authority.

10.   My particular scansion of line 9 means that lines 9 and 10 are not 'rove over' although they are syntactically enjambed. 'AND the fire that breaks from thee then': Gardner, 1948, p. 228, tells us that the B manuscript (copies made by Bridges, added to and emended by Hopkins) gives 'And', 'so that two scansions are possible: "Búckle! AND the fire that bréaks from thee thén, a bíllion" or "Búckle! AND the fire . . .", where "AND" takes a non-metrical stress. The latter reading seems preferable.' Gardner, 1967, p. 267, tells us that manuscript A (a book made up of autograph copies of poems sent to Bridges and pasted by him into a book) gives 'AND' and concludes: 'the intended expressional rhythm seems to be:

Búckle! AND the fire that bréaks from thée then, a bíllion

where 'AND' takes an extra-metrical emphasis'. Gardner's conclusions seem just; the capitalisation of 'AND' indicates what Holloway, 1947, p. 43, calls 'an emotional intonation', which, as Hopkins's lecture-notes explain, 'when not bound to the particular words will sometimes light up notes on unemphatic syllables and not follow the verbal stresses and pitches'. It is perhaps worth asking here whether this emotional illumination can be indicated other than typographically. Hopkins may make reading aloud an almost virtual condition of his verse's existence, but the capitalisation of 'and' can realise itself more efficiently in the mind of the silent reader than in any recitation.

Some change of mind is apparent in the quotations from Gardner about the scansion of 'from thee then'; 1947 favours 'from thee thén' while 1967 opts for 'from thée then' with the note (p. 268): 'the stress on "thee" seems essential if the pron. means "Christ our Lord" (to whom the poem is dedicated) or "my heart in hiding" (l. 7); but if "thee" is the bird the stress might fall on "then"'. 1953, p. 222 is more categorical: 'a stress on *thee* seems essential'. A stress on 'thee' seems to me to necessitate an identification of 'thee', to push the reader towards identification which, given the synthesising movement of the poem as a whole, strikes me as undesirable. To leave 'thee' unstressed is to maintain the multiplicity of potential reference. To stress 'then' is to reinforce the centrality of deixis as a way of focussing, and indeed producing, the moment of epiphany, of revelation and transformation.

11.   The only problem presented by this line lies in the interpretation of 'told'. 'Told' is the past participle of 'tell', but does 'tell' here mean 'tally' or 'express', 'describe'; if the former, then the absence of stress suits it well enough; if the latter, if the number of times of telling conveys the awesome and yet urgent ineffability of the fire's power, then that paradox and that wonder might well be thought to deserve a stress. And if 'told' were to be stressed and a five-stress-per-line norm to be maintained, then 'my' would be a candidate for yielding up its stress; but this would create, by the principle of Hopkins's metric, an unacceptably long sequence of unstressed syllables in the penultimate foot. Do the needs of scansion, in fact, *compel* us to leave 'told' unstressed and thus to interpret it in a particular way?

12.   Lines 11 and 12 are 'rove over', though there is no syntactical enjambement.

13.   Lines 12 and 13 enjamb syntactically, but are not 'rove over'. The scansion of 'blue-bleak' depends very much on the nature of the compound. If it is a compounding, in a single experience, of two separate adjectives, then both might deserve a stress or a 'blue-bleak' reading. The scansion that is offered adverbialises 'blue': the embers are bleak because of their blueness, of the iciness of their colour. The reverse reading – 'blue-bleak' – would not have the effect of adverbialising 'bleak', of course, since 'norms' of word-order would prevent it: when adjectives are qualified by adverbs, the adverb is usually preposed. Instead 'blue-bleak' would graph the sudden intensification of perception, as the poet moves from literal to figurative notation. If the need arose, 'ah' might yield its accent.

14.   Lines 13 and 14 are 'rove over' although, because of the parenthetic insertion 'ah my dear', there is little sense of syntactic enjambement. The scansion of the line given here is that provided by Hopkins himself in manuscript B. Hopkins presumably felt obliged to ensure the rather unusual reading 'themselves', to guarantee that galling is seen as an act of 'selving', of self-individuation. A more natural reading would surely be 'Fall, gall themselves, and gash gold-vermilion' (in which case, no 'roving over'). Hopkins is once again using metre to 'distort' enunciation the better to promote the interpretation that chimes with his purposes. Scansion is again an expedient for 'loading' the line; the flexible, or rather, amenable rhythms of sprung rhythm are called upon to impose a metrical imperative on the reader that sprung rhythm, by its nature, cannot do.

These notes on scansion are not designed to cast doubt on either the rhythmicity or greatness of this poem; they are designed to uncover the compromises and inconsistencies in an essentially dualistic prosody which makes scansion a series of rhythmic transactions, where rhythm itself is negotiable. Hopkins, however much he may seem to disparage foot-scansion by arbitrarily selecting a falling rhythm for sprung rhythm, obviously puts much store by metre, and by a metre governed by the foot rather than by stress alone; and he makes it quite clear that it is by metrical presence alone that verse distinguishes itself from prose:

The repetition of feet, the same or mixed, without regard to how long, is *rhythm. Metre* is the grouping of *a certain number* of feet. There is no metre in prose though there may be rhythm.

(Notes on 'Rhythm and other structural parts')

The foot, then, is the unit of rhythm and rhythm itself is merely a sequence of feet. What 'raises' rhythm to metre is the fact that the number of consecutive feet in a line is fixed and repeated from line to line; in other words, not only is the integrity of the line metrically crucial, but the metre of sprung rhythm is reckoned not by the number of stresses but by the number of feet, and these feet, if we are to take account of the 'Author's Preface' are not free variations, but a limited number of variations on a single, falling, principle. Holloway, 1947, p. 57, footnote 17, is right to emphasise that sprung rhythm is actually sprung *metre* and simply not a refusal of metre; but she is wrong when she asserts that 'Hopkins's method of scansion was never intended for a true representation of the rhythmic nature of verse' (p. 50); Hopkins's method of scansion may not have been intended as a true representation of the nature of rhythm, but it is, I am sure, intended as one way of representing rhythm wrought up to metre. And let us not be led into believing that metre is simply a handy grid which can be laid over the line without disturbing its accentual structure: we have seen in our notes on the scansion of 'The Windhover', and particularly in the treatment of 'dapple-dawn-drawn' (2), 'the rolling level underneath him steady air' (3), 'told' (11) 'gall themselves' (14), how metre can work, at the very least, as a disambiguating influence and, at most, as an imperative which drives enunciation into configurations which are unnatural to it. How can Milroy (1977) state: 'Rather than requiring him to resort to grammatical liberties in order to observe its rules, sprung rhythm allows Hopkins to escape from the restraints of traditional syllable-counting rhythms and metres' (p. 116) and, a few pages later, unselfconsciously concede, in relation to 'The Wreck of the Deutschland':

It has often been noticed that sprung rhythm enables Hopkins to use juxtaposed full stresses. This is not the case in *flint-flake* and *black-backed* in the above quotation (which are required by the five-foot line to carry only one primary stress each), but it is commonly used and is one of the most striking features of Hopkins's poetry.   (p. 120)

And the view, expressed by Ong (1949, p. 125) among others, that Hopkins's idiosyncratic prosodic concepts ('outrides', 'roving over', etc.) and marks are designed to serve the workings of the pure-stress economy and the recitational immediacy of the verse, needs to be qualified by the remark that they equally serve the installation and maintenance of a metrical discipline. For, as we have seen, 'roving over' is a way of consolidating metrical consistency by ensuring that all feet can be falling – its artificiality as a device is pointed to by the fact that all poem-initial, and possibly stanza-initial, slacks have to be treated as instances of anacrusis – while 'hovering' accents allow two potential stresses to be collapsed into one, again for metrical purposes, and 'outrides' make syllables, which might otherwise cause scansional embarrassment, extrametrical (I think particularly of 'skate's heel', line 6, and 'the achieve of', line 8).

But the fundamental ground on which the case for Hopkins's espousal of pure-stress principles is most often made is the distinction between speech-stress or sense-stress on the one hand, and metrical stress on the other. Let us listen to the account given by Ong (1949) of this distinction:

But in sense-stress patterning the difference between prose and verse is less marked because sense-stress rhythm differs from running rhythm in this important psychological feature: whereas emotion does not naturally reassort words so that the alternating stress is placed evenly to produce running rhythm, emotion does naturally heighten the irregular sense stresses and in doing so can assert its tendency to rhythm by balancing the weight of the segments of speech of which these sense stresses form nuclei.
                    (p. 114)

To maintain this distinction, which makes plenty of theoretical sense, one would have to insist that those lines of Hopkins's which fall out as, say, iambic pentameters (e.g. the opening line in 'The Windhover') are not to be thought of as 'iambic pentameters', because what motivates their stresses is not the demands of a metre, but the pressure to utter. This distinction can only emerge in, but cannot be guaranteed by, recitation. But at any rate, in our own discussion of the scansion of the first line of 'The Windhover', we could see how Hopkins's acoustic effects (internal rhyming, alliteration etc.) positively urge stress out of words (but does metre do anything different?) and encourage stress variation. But even in accepting the distinction, we should remember this about traditional metrical scansion: it makes metrical stress available to sense-stress; in other words, in recognising a syllable as metrically stressed, we are equally recognising that it is potentially sense-stressed; we are equally recognising that its stress value may be lesser or greater than other stresses in the line – as I have already said, traditional scansion does not assume that all stresses are equal; its business is to mark the *position* of stress, not its strength. But just as metrical stress can be sense-stressed, by the same token sense-stresses can be metricalised. It is round this proposition that I wish to argue.

What would an 'untutored', 'natural' sense-stress reading of 'The Windhover' look like, what stresses would what syntactic segments gather round? Perhaps something like this emerges:

No. of
stresses

4   I cáught | this mórning | morning's mínion|, kíng-

3   dom | of daylight's dáuphin,| dapple-dawn-drawn Fálcon|, in his ríding

4   Of the rólling | lével underneath him | steady aír, | and stríding |

4   Hígh there|, how he rúng | upon the réin | of a wimpling wíng |

4   In his écstasy! | then óff, | óff | forth on swíng, |

5   As a skáte's heel | sweeps smóoth | on a bów-bend|: the húrl | and glíding |

4   Rebúffed | the big wínd|. My heárt | in híding |

5   Stírred | for a bírd, | – the achíeve of|, the mástery of | the thíng! |

6   Brute beáuty | and válour | and áct, | oh, aír, | príde, | plúme | here

5   Búckle! | AND the fíre | that breáks | from thee thén, | a bíllion

3   Times told | lóvelier, | more dángerous, | O my chevalíer! |

4   No wónder of it |: sheer plód | makes ploúgh | down síllion |

3   Shíne, | and blue-bleak émbers|, ah my deár, |

4   Fáll, | gáll themselves, | and gásh | gold-vermílion. |

Where a metrical-foot reading encourages questions about the stressability or non-stressability of individual lexical items, a sense-group reading has no such concerns: it seeks out the sense-groups as they would obtrude in speech and asks which syllable in each group carries the *principal* sense-stress; this principal sense-stress acts, as it were, as the gravitational centre, the point of focus, of other stressed material in the group. The reading above suggests a 4-stress-per-line norm, established in the first five lines, deviated from persistently in the emotionally charged, exclamatory first tercet, but reinstated as a predominating principle in the second tercet; the rhythmic groups vary between a lower limit of one syllable and an upper limit of six. This seems to me to endow the verse with sufficient rhythmic discipline for one to have no doubts about its status as verse (leaving aside the acoustic effects and regularity of rhyme scheme), and the deviations from four-stresses-per-line would either merely define the parameters of the norm or be explicable in terms of special expressive effects. But this account bears little relation to the scansion on which we have based our discussion. Even though this sense-group scansion only identifies the primary stress in any group and thus allows for any number of secondary stresses to be realised in recitation, it would not satisfy Hopkins because the rhythm is not sufficiently marked (that is, it does not endow the rhythm with a true selfhood, does not endow it with an authority which is beyond authoriality), does not impose that oratorical delivery that Hopkins envisaged; if stress is indeed a manifestation of instress –

> Since, tho' he is under the world's splendour and wonder,
> His mystery must be instressed, stressed
>
> ('The Wreck of the Deutschland', st. 5)

– and if instress is the energy which actualises an object's inscape and embodies the force which inscape exerts on the mind and emotions of the perceiver, and if inscape is the apprehension of an object's irreducible individuality and essence, and of Divine pattern working through the variety of individuations, then the rhythm of the verse must express, on the one hand, the subjective idiosyncrasy of the perceiver of inscape and the time-bound relativity of the perception, and, on the other, the inescapable and timeless imprint, or authority, of God's hand, in inscape. The fact that Hopkins bases his choice of consistently falling feet on musical practice is of significance here: isochronous or stress-compensating rhythms involve the discovery of temporal and accentual consistency, order, pattern, underneath what at first seems a highly variable and contingent rhythmic surface. At all events, in the light of our sense-group scansion we should, I think, disagree with

Hopkins's assertion that sprung rhythm is not counterpointed, a view which has persisted:

A poem of sprung rhythm, then, is one in which any 'patterning' of stresses exists only in the immediate, actual rhythm, without reference to any restrictive, controlling meter. (Malof, 1970, p. 17)

Does sprung rhythm, after all, have a metrical nature? The answer to that question might seem to depend on whether one attributes an a-priority or an a-posteriority to Hopkins's scansional solution. That is, do we assume that Hopkins wrote according to his scansional solution or that he wrote according to one rhythmic principle (pure-stress) which he then accommodated to a metrical principle, creating idiosyncratic metrical concepts to get around certain problems? The evidence so far points to the latter. But in fact this question does not matter, for it is clear that Hopkins did wish to exert some control over the way his poems were read, and a kind of control which often involves a distortion of natural accentual and syntactic values; this I take to be an impulse to 'metrify' his verse, an impulse which the choice of a metrical scansion only served to consolidate. And the metrifying impulse of his verse is heard in counterpoint with the kind of sense-stress reading which we have suggested. That is to say that we hear leisurely, unforced or unheightened, non-emphatic, non-oratorical natural rhythms of speech in counterpoint with a 'metrified', wrought-up, altogether denser, occasionally non-natural rhythmic code.

But in saying that Hopkins was fatally and perhaps inevitably attracted towards a metrical justification of sprung rhythm, we should remind ourselves just how much his prosodic 'innovations' equally pushed against metrification. We have suggested that Hopkins's sprung rhythm is grounded in the foot and the repetition of a certain number of feet per line. This implies that the integrity and identity of the line are of some metrical significance. And yet 'roving over', which is metrical in the sense that it does not necessarily coincide with syntax (e.g. those examples in the 'Notes on scansion' where there is a non-coincidence of 'roving over' and syntactic enjambement) and that it preserves the integrity and consistency of the falling foot, is anti-metrical in that it undoes the integrity of the line and produces a stanza which is 'one long strain'. This equally has the effect of undermining the privilege of rhyme, both as special acoustic effect and as marker of the line-terminus, reducing it to the level of all other stanza-internal music, alliteration, assonance, and so on. And the 'outrides', for all their ability to dispose of unwanted syllables or to introduce metrical variation within the already broad flexibility of Hopkins's basically four-foot system, do demetricalise as much as they extrametricalise: we should take seriously Hopkins's comment that they 'are so called because they seem to hang below the line or ride forward or backward from it in another dimension than the line itself' ('Author's Preface'), even though he offers us no further explanation. It is as though Hopkins were trying, through 'outrides', to push the stressed syllables that precede them out of the line, into a third dimension, to make them resonate beyond the poem into the pure and absolutely non-metrical stress of inscape; the pauses that follow 'outrides' underline the culminativeness of their stress, the achievement of penetration and realisation that stress can be. Stress here is not so much a prosodic mark as a moment of epiphany. That stress is a thrust towards inscape is made clear by Hopkins in a letter to Patmore of November 7th, 1883, in which he defines stress as 'the making of a thing more, or making it markedly, what it already is; it is the bringing out its nature'. And it is equally clear that Hopkins aimed at as great a sense of stress density and intensity as possible, which took him beyond metre's accentual capacity; metre, for example, assumes that unstressed syllables are separate phonetic events and as such they may be inclined to draw the voice off the stress; Hopkins for his part maintains that the tendency to *slur* unaccentuated syllables contributes to the emphatic distinctness of stressed syllables (letter to Patmore, Nov. 7, 1883), with the implication that we should, as readers, indeed slur, the better to stress. Alliteration also helps to augment stress; unaccented syllables which alliterate with a following syllable will drive the voice more insistently into the stress, while an accented syllable will, by alliterative linkage, proportionately increase the stress of a following accented syllable. Finally, a large number of Hopkins's lines contain more stressable elements than can be accounted for by the metre; however much a scansion of the line may be able to subdue its superfluous stressability, no reading of the poem can avoid restoring some of that stress density, or simply increasing the intensity of the stresses, beyond metrical requirement, on those syllables which the metre allows as stressed.

Hopkins's rhythms therefore seem caught rather awkwardly between the metrical and the non-metrical, a conventionalised rhythm and a rhythm of immediate utterance, an accentual pattern unjustified by sense and an occurrence of accent dictated by sense.

Hopkins's verse, in short, is slung somewhere between a metre which does not do justice to 'natural' rhythms and 'natural' rhythms which cannot forego the form-giving and heightening authority of metre. Charles Hartman (1980) sees this simply as a confusion:

The fact remains that Hopkins badly muddles together accentual meter, isochronous prosody, and a foot system appropriate to neither. But the third was forced upon him by prosodic tradition, and the first two are easily confused. (p. 33)

I do not think that Hopkins's 'muddle' is a muddle of incomprehension, but a real ambivalence deriving from a wish to reconcile the accentual and the accentual-syllabic; nor do I think the foot system was 'forced upon him', but rather that he was impelled to choose it. I would reiterate that sprung rhythm, as Hopkins presents it to us, is an essentially ambiguous, dualistic prosody, where rhythm itself has an inbuilt margin of negotiability; and the Hopkinsian accent is neither a metrical stress nor indeed a sense-stress but a metricalisation of sense-stress, a metricalisation made necessary not only by a more general need for an 'authority' which might be stress-giving rather than merely stress-registering, but also by a specific need for a code which would be sense-directing and sense-guaranteeing, when sense itself was not immediately available. For how is sense-stress to go about its business if sense is constantly ambiguated by equivocations of syntax and grammatical status? And where is rhythmicity to locate its area of operation, if its interpretive function is radically curtailed? Indeed does not one of the attractions of metricity lie, for Hopkins, in its potential independence from sense? These questions can only be answered after we have established the nature of the syntactic and grammatical ambiguities in 'The Windhover'.

Notes on grammar and syntax

In the following notes on grammatical and syntactic ambiguities in 'The Windhover', I naturally leave out of account those semantic ambiguities inhering in words whose grammar and syntax are unambiguous – e.g. 'I caught' = 'I captured': 'I caught' = 'I caught sight of'. I do not pretend to exhaust the possibilities, merely to indicate some of them.

1. 'this morning morning's': 'this morning' is an adverbial phrase, but because of its repetition, it takes on the function also of

a premodifying adjectival phrase, that is to say 'morning's minion' is a peculiarly 'this morning' kind of 'morning's minion'.

1–2. 'king/dom of daylight's dauphin': 'dauphin of the kingdom of daylight'? 'Kingdom of the dauphin of daylight'? 'Kingdom of a daylight dauphin'?

2. 'dapple-dawn-drawn': 'drawn (pulled, attracted) into/ towards the dappled dawn'? 'Silhouetted, etched by the dappled dawn'? 'Dappled (Falcon) drawn by the dawn'? 'Drawn with a pattern or marking like the small dappled clouds at dawn'?

3. 'rolling level underneath him steady air': the problems of syntactical segmentation and grammatical status in relation to this sequence have already been explored (see 'Notes on scansion' above). 'striding': is this a participial noun = '(in his) striding' or simply a present participle?

4. 'how': = in what manner – 'I caught ... how he rung upon the rein'? Or a purely exclamatory 'how' accompanied by syntactic disjunction – 'I caught ... etc. / how he rung upon the rein ...!'?

5. We have already discussed the imperative, verbal dimension of the adverbs 'off' and 'forth'. 'on swing': it is not clear whether this is a curving, but back-and-forth, movement ('on a swing') or a single arc-like movement ('in a swinging curve').

6. 'heel': 'the rear-end or bottom part of the skate'? Or a verbal noun = 'As a skate's leaning ...'? 'on a bow-bend': 'on (in) a curve like a bent bow'? Or more verbally, 'in a curve like a bow being bent'? Or 'in a figure of eight, like a tied bow', where 'bend' is either the bends (loops) in the figure, or again the action of 'taking the bend', 'going round the loop'?

8. 'the achieve of': is this a telegraph version of 'the achievement of' i.e. something already achieved? Or does 'achieve' retain a verbal thrust, that is to say, function as an imperative or optative with a high aspirational and projective charge?

9. Is this line an enumeration from beginning to end, or do the final three nouns ('air', 'pride', 'plume') stand in a complex permutational set of appositions to the first three nouns? Are the nouns nominative or vocative?

10. 'Buckle' is the word which has perhaps received most critical attention from commentators. For our purpose, it is sufficient to ask whether it is a verb or noun, and if it is a verb, whether it is indicative, imperative or optative.

11. The problem presented by 'told' has been dealt with in the 'Notes on scansion' (see above).

12. 'No wonder of it': 'There is nothing wonderful about it'? 'It

is not to be wondered at' (i.e. it is no cause for surprise)? 'No wonder derives from it'?

12–13. 'sheer plod makes plough down sillion/Shine': 'sheer plod(ding) makes the plough in the furrow shine'? Or is 'plough down' a modifier of 'sillion', so that 'sheer plod(ding) makes the furrows, down which the plough has passed, shine'?

13. 'blue-bleak': ambiguities here are discussed in the 'Notes on scansion' (see above).

14. 'and gash gold-vermilion': is 'gash' here an intransitive verb with 'gold-vermilion' acting as an adverb? Or is 'gash' transitive and 'gold-vermilion' a compound object? One might further ask whether 'gold-vermilion' is indeed a simultaneous compound, or a process, a movement through a colour-range, beginning with 'gold' and ending with 'vermilion'.

Can a poem so beset with ambiguities about grammatical and syntactical functions be read with rhythmic conviction, if rhythm is in any way sense-giving? Of course decisions can be made to cope with any of the problems, but such decisions must be recognised as provisional. Of course metrical indications supplied by Hopkins can be applied to resolve some of the questions, but Hopkins is no less a reader of his own verse than we are. Of course the text is not unremittingly problematical, but the oases of ease are subject to the same rhythmic ambivalence as the rest of the text: what is the nature of their accentuation, what is the nature of their accents, how much like an iambic pentameter is a Hopkinsian iambic pentameter?

But there is, after all, a simple way to cut the Gordian knot, merely by shifting our ground from an either/or approach to ambiguity, to a both/and one. Jacob Korg (1977) discusses a more general source of the apparent dualism in Hopkins's verse:

On the one hand, he appreciated the imitative power of words, which makes them consistent with God's creation; but he also saw them, less consciously, as units of a symbolic system that gives them an inherent semantic power to diverge from reality. (p. 978)

In other words, not only does Hopkins seek to use language representationally or mimetically, to convey the wonders of God's creation, to instress through language the inscape of the world around him – and one thinks here of his exercises in onomatopœia, of his propensities for common speech and dialect – but he also seeks to dissociate language from reference, to make it self-referential, the better to make stand forth its own inscape – and one thinks here of those Hopkinsian dicta to be found in his notes on 'Poetry and Verse' e.g.:

Some matter and meaning is essential to it [verse] but only as an element necessary to support and employ the shape which is contemplated for its own sake.

or:

Poetry is in fact speech only employed to carry the inscape of speech for the inscape's sake – and therefore the inscape must be dwelt on.

The language of verse is not only a way of making manifest God's presence in the universe, but is itself a manifestation of God. And one might argue that the duality of these enterprises is expressed in the dualism of rhythmicity (pure-stress rhythm) with its essentially expressive and imitative concerns, and metricity (foot metre) with its peculiarity to verse and verse's corporealisation of language. And the reconciliation of this dualism, the synthesis of apparently contradictory directions, is to be achieved only if rhythmicity and metricity are seen as the two terms of a metaphor, whose conjunction produces a third term, beyond identification but not beyond apprehension. But how is this relationship in metaphor to be distinguished from any other effect of counterpoint, in which two principles are simultaneously active? Counterpoint is a relationship of tension, not of identification. In counterpoint one principle dominates the other, is laid over the other, and is experienced as deviation or variation, not as the instigator of a third dimension; and the effects of counterpoint are local rather than thoroughgoing. Finally, counterpoint exists precisely because we can identify an alternative rhythm with confidence; the ambiguities of Hopkins's syntax and grammar frequently leave us not knowing whether we are in the world of metricity or the world of rhythmicity.

What I wish to propose, then, is this: the 'rhythm' of Hopkins's 'The Windhover', as of many of his other poems, lies beyond either metricity or rhythmicity, as a knowledge to be reached for or intuited. We might say that 'rhythm' is in God's hands, or in the sui generis or quiddity of inscape which is neither the variability of the perceiver (rhythmicity) nor the patternedness of consecrated utterance (metricity), but a blend of both. 'Rhythm' in this sense is the poem's objective, the subject of both the poet's and the reader's interrogation of the world by language and interrogation of language. If stress, and patterns of stress, have the power to draw us to epiphany, they can have that power only on two conditions: first that they resist codification, since codification would vulgarise and deindividualise the epiphanic experience, and secondly and relatedly that they do not, even at the moment of revelation, reveal *themselves*; in other words, they must be absorbable into what they reveal; they do not create epiphany so much as coincide with our achievement of it. Metricity and rhythmicity are thus approaches to a 'rhythm' which can only emerge from their conjunction; it is a 'rhythm' which both by virtue of its sacral function and by virtue of the protean nature of the language which produces it, must remain tacit and virtual; rhythmicity and metricity actualise its absence and are the basis from which we go in search of it; and in the moment of our discovery of it we will equally recognise our inability to transcribe it. 'Rhythm' here is the pattern of the reader's insight, of a revelation which by definition cannot be communicated. The Hopkinsian poem is a facilitating structure, and in that sense it is priestly; the priest can neither afford to express himself, to interpose the obstacle of his own authority, nor yet rely on the self-evidence of a pre-ordained word; he must inspirit, by the mediation of his own infinitely adaptable example. 'Rhythm' is the common goal which *can* only be reached by a multiplication of routes corresponding to the multiplication of readers.

These proposals about the tacitness of Hopkinsian 'rhythm' may seem to contradict Hopkins's own insistence that his poems be read aloud, just as our emphasis on syntactical and grammatical ambiguity and the consequent ambiguity of the 'visible' rhythms seems to deny Hopkins's wish for a rhetorical or oratorical delivery, since periodicity depends on rhythmic definition. To answer the second of these contradictions first, we might suggest that Hopkins himself retreated from his demand for a rhetorical recitation; the two passages in which he affirms the rhetorical nature of sprung rhythm occur in a letter to Robert Bridges, written during sprung rhythm's infancy, the letter of August 21st, 1877. Just over ten years later, in the notes which accompanied 'Spelt from Sibyl's Leaves' and were sent to Bridges on December 11th 1886, we find a significant change of position:

Of this long sonnet above all remember what applies to all my verse, that it is, as living art should be, made for performance and that its performance is not reading with the eye but loud, leisurely, poetical (not rhetorical) recitation, with long rests, long dwells on the rhyme and other marked syllables and so on.

These words imply a much more contemplative procedure, where recitation is not so much a dramatic interpretation as a ruminative inhabitation of the text, a heavily paused, interrogative process. And this allows us to resolve the first contradiction: recitation is necessary to Hopkins's 'programme' for his poetry, not as a realisation or actualisation of the poem, condemned to failure by the poem's essential unreadability, nor as a dramatisation of the poem for the benefit of others, but as a careful palpation of the text, an elicitation of its 'rhythm' which will be at the same time its meaning, an elicitation which involves the reader in an act of self-creation as a reader, aided by metricity and rhythmicity perhaps, but left to travel the last part of the way on his own.

We have already used a vocabulary of Hopkins's poetry which assorts well with the poetry of Mallarmé: tacit, virtual, absent, quiddity. Many similarities between the poets suggest themselves: their mutual interest in philology and particularly in the onomato-pœia of etymology and in unsuspected etymological kinships, their cultivation of idiosyncratic syntaxes, the acoustic excess of their verse, their favouring of the sonnet, the unmistakable connections between Hopkins's inscape and Mallarmé's symbol, their oscillations between a referential and self-referential language. But it is not my business to examine the ramifications of this comparability; others have done that (e.g. Jane Kressler (1976)). I wish to suggest that, like Hopkins, Mallarmé pitches rhythm as it were beyond the text, but that he does it not by setting up interferences between metricity and rhythmicity so that a third 'rhythm' is produced, but by creating a gap between syntax and the syntax-orientated rhythms which flesh out the metrical mould (for remarks on the implicitness of rhythms within metre in French verse, see Prefatory remarks, pp. viii–ix). In other words, in Mallarmé's poetry the rhythmic pattern remains patent throughout; what is brought into question is its function in relation to syntax. For the purposes of this discussion, I will limit myself, as in my treatment of Hopkins, to an analysis of a single poem, 'Le Tombeau de Charles Baudelaire', offering, as prelude, a scansion of it:

Le temple enseveli divulgue par la bouche	2+4+2+4
Sépulcrale d'égout bavant boue et rubis	3+3+3+3
Abominablement quelque idole Anubis	6+3+3
Tout le museau flambé comme un aboi farouche	4+2+4+2
Ou que le gaz récent torde la mèche louche	4+2+1+5/ 4+2+4+2
Essuyeuse on le sait des opprobres subis	3+3+3+3
Il allume hagard un immortel pubis	3+3+4+2

Dont le vol selon le réverbère découche	3+6+3
Quel feuillage séché dans les cités sans soir	3+3+4+2
Votif pourra bénir comme elle se rasseoir	2+4+2+4
Contre le marbre vainement de Baudelaire	4+4+4
Au voile qui la ceint absente avec frissons	2+4+2+4
Celle son Ombre même un poison tutélaire	1+5+3+3
Toujours à respirer si nous en périssons	2+4+6

This poem presents very few scansional problems and those that there are relate so closely to syntactic ambiguities that they will be dealt with under that head. Mallarmé's verse has a patent and conventional rhythmicity which acts as a guarantee of its intelligibility and its in-orderness. The rhythm is where we are immediately at home without knowing why, because the syntax, evidently articulated as it is, and clearly the producer of the rhythmic measures, does not confirm the rhythm's continuity and constantly disarticulates itself against the rhythm; its elisions, suspensions, dislocations, regressions, asyndeta, syllepses, synecdochic figures seem to catch out rhythmic assumptions, require rhythm to justify its ability to absorb them and pattern them in the sequence of the line. And I would emphasise *sequence*. In its urge to demonstrate that the Mallarméan poem is the autotelic and self-reflexive object, criticism highlights processes of superimposition, echo, progression equalised by regression, everything designed to make the poem a *space* of meaning, simultaneous with itself at all points; and there are plenty of justifications for doing this. But it begets the habit of leaving rhythm to one side; for although individual rhythmic measures (hemistichs) are equally susceptible of redisposition in structures of parallelism, complementarity, substitution and so on, rhythm is primarily a temporal experience, and its temporality, functioning in tension with the spatiality of the constantly self-recuperating linguistic structure, is part of what Mallarmé would call 'la seule dialectique du vers' ('Solennité'). Against a process of signification which works through an almost infinitely permutable set of *equations*,[2] rhythm sets the promise of consecutively unfolded meaning.

Before pushing this enquiry further, we should familiarise ourselves more with the particular syntactical difficulties to be found in 'Le Tombeau de Charles Baudelaire'. It is only gradually that the rhythm's function as confirmation and periodisation of the poem's syntax is thrown into question. There are certain disturbing factors in the first stanza, it is true: the sequence 'bouche/Sépulcrale

d'égout', rather than 'bouche d'égout sépulcrale', is odd and its
oddness is heightened by the dislocating force of the line-terminal
juncture; 'sépulcrale' is lifted into a space of its own and its field of
influence and figurative colouring thus extended; our sense of disjunction, of the 'égrènement' of lexical units may suggest 'dégoût'
in 'd'égout', as the initial noun in an appositional phrase 'dégoût
bavant boue et rubis'. 'Abominablement', by virtue of its position
at the head of a line and its occupation of a whole hemistich, is,
equally, more distributed and its point of application left in some
doubt – does it modify 'bavant' or 'divulgue' or is it some kind of
pre-modifier of 'quelque idole Anubis'? 'Quelque idole Anubis' is
unusually distanced, as grammatical object, from its verb
'divulgue'. And the absolute construction of the last line has an
element of ellipsis in it – 'Tout le museau flambé comme [par] un
aboi farouche' – which allows the simile to attach itself to other
syntactical elements e.g. 'divulgue ... quelque idole Anubis ...
comme un aboi farouche'. But these features do not prevent a
consecutive reading of the stanza, where word-order defines
grammatical status and the order of syntactic units corresponds to
the on-flowing temporality of rhythmic measures.

It is the first line of the second stanza which threatens the
stability of the whole syntactic structure. Is this first sentence a
main clause, coordinated with the main clause of the first stanza?
Or is it a clause subordinate to the main clause 'il allume hagard
un immortel pubis', in which case the 'que' operates as a conditional conjunction (= si). Gill (1967) favours the former
reading, which leads him to treat 'il allume hagard...' as a
parenthetical qualification:

Tout n'est pas clair encore dans ce deuxième quatrain, mais on peut au
moins indiquer, à l'aide de quelques explications de détail et d'une ponc-
tuation un peu appuyée, la forme syntactique et le sens littéral: ou que le
gaz récent [moderne] torde la mèche louche, essuyeuse – on le sait – des
opprobres subis (il allume un immortel pubis, hagard [farouche?], dont le
vol découche selon le [à chaque] réverbère).   (p. 56)

This, of course, has retrospective consequences for the first
stanza:

La proposition dont le mot 'divulgue' est le verbe principal est parallèle,
grammaticalement, à la proposition avec laquelle elle est coordonée, celle
(concessive? hypothétique?) qui ouvre le deuxième quatrain ... Le verbe
'divulgue' doit être, par conséquent, comme 'torde', un subjonctif (con-
cessif? hypothétique?).   (pp. 50–1)

Gill notes that the use of a subjunctival main clause without 'que' is archaic but not exceptional in Mallarmé's work, and he suggests that this first sentence is doubly archaic in that the subject and object are inverted i.e. it should be read 'quelque idole Anubis ... divulgue ... le temple enseveli' rather than vice versa (this proposal is backed up with other examples of Mallarméan inversion). Most other commentators opt for the latter syntactical pattern.

But if 'il allume' is coordinated with 'divulgue', does that coordination help us to identify the referent of the pronoun 'il'? It is generally assumed to refer back to the first available masculine noun (i.e. 'le gaz'). Schulze (1976), however, equating 'allume' with the action of Baudelaire's artistic 'phares': –

> C'est un phare allumé sur mille citadelles
>
> ('Les Phares', line 39)

– identifies 'il' as Baudelaire, the interred poet, which again has consequences for the reading of the first stanza:

Il wäre soviel wie der Dichter also Baudelaire, und *allume ... un immortel pubis* müsste soviel wie 'Schaffen eines bedeutenden oder gar unsterblichen Werkes' besagen. Das Wort *immortel* wirkt in dieser Hinsicht schon sehr plausibel. Wegen der syntaktischen Äquivalenz müsste aber auch *Le temple enseveli divulgue ... quelque idole Anubis* eine nach verwandte Bedeutung haben, d.h. *Le temple enseveli* müsste soviel wie 'der (tote) Dichter Baudelaire', *divulgue* soviel wie 'schafft, veröffentlicht, stellt dem Publikum vor' und *quelque idole Anubis* soviel wie 'sein Werk' bedeuten.

(p. 173)

Schulze justifies his interpretation of 'le temple' as poet by reference to Biblical views of the human body as the temple of the Holy Spirit.[3] He further suggests that 'quelque idole Anubis' should be related to Baudelairian images of vampiric women:

> A la très-chère, à la très-belle
> Qui remplit mon cœur de clarté,
> A l'ange, à l'idole immortelle,
> Salut en l'immortalité!   ('Hymne')

where the vampire is the 'chien volant', the 'renard volant', the bat (corresponding with the dog-headed, or jackal-headed Anubis).

Schulze's suggestion has many virtues, but does not seem to me to require the insertion of a new, implied, subject at 'Il', if the gas-lamp itself is to be understood as the poet; and the reasons for doing this latter are threefold: the 'phare'-like quality of the street lamp and its power of illumination, its creative and controlling capacity ('selon le réverbère') and the fact that 'réverbère' rhymes with 'Baudelaire' and 'tutélaire' and is similarly tri-syllabic. And the power of the gaslight seems to me to give more authority to an interpretation of 'essuyer' as 'wipe away, efface', rather than as 'undergo, endure', supposing that 'la mèche' of line 5 is a figurative presentation of the gas-flame (e.g. Austin, 1973, p. 196); the gaslight, by its 'illumination', cancels out the shame or insults which bourgeois morality might heap upon the prostitute. Besides, it seems to me unlikely that Mallarmé would indulge in the near-pleonasm of 'essuyeuse ... subis'; true, there is a distinction between what the lamp undergoes and what the prostitute undergoes, but 'subis' alone is sufficient to suggest both aspects. If 'la mèche' is a synecdochic substitute for the prostitute herself (the play of light 'twisting' the prostitute's hair into different shapes), as 'pubis' is to be in line 7, then the pleonasm 'essuyeuse (sufferer) . . . subis' would be real; 'essuyeuse' as 'wipe away, erase' again indicates the efficacity of poetry, as it transforms and transcends the underhand and degrading, through the hair itself, as it becomes the trigger of an expansion of consciousness far beyond the confines of Paris ('La Chevelure'); as we have already seen in our chapter on the articulated e, 'prostitution' is itself a poetic principle for Baudelaire. Gardner Davies (1950, pp. 171–3) also interprets 'essuyer' as an erasing process, but it is erasure by darkness, by hiding; for Davies 'la mèche' refers to the wick of the old-fashioned oil-lamps which the gaslamps have supplanted and which gave out such a feeble light that any sordid goings-on were enveloped in gloom. This interpretation has had relatively little support.

The only other potential source of syntactic disquiet in this second quatrain is 'hagard'. Either 'hagard' belongs to 'il' (the fierce and uncompromising light paralleling Anubis's fierce and uncompromising bark) but has undergone adverbialisation by its displacement to a post-verbal position; or it belongs as an anticipatory adjective to the 'pubis', in which case it syntactically enjambs the caesura, or isolates itself by virtue of the caesura the better to underline its transformation into 'immortel'.

The first tercet too has its displacements. 'Votif', it is generally assumed, is an epithet of 'feuillage', the funerary wreath. But there is no syntactical reason why it should not be an epithet of 'soir', in which case 'soir' would be that time of day proper to thoughts of death and of the spiritual life, proper, too, to a contemplative *recueillement*; the eternal day of Paris has no room for such frames of mind. At all events, 'votif', placed at the head of the line like 'sépulcrale' before it, provides a tonality for the whole of the sestet;

the adjective's attributional capacity is disseminated over a larger linguistic area. 'Vainement', it is equally assumed, is the postponed adverb of 'se rasseoir'; the 'elle' figure will sit in vain because the tomb does not return what it has taken (Davies, 1950, p. 179), because the rites paid to the dead, who neither see nor hear, are unavailing (Austin, 1973, p. 198). But it seems to me that 'vainement' might function as a kind of adverbial epithet of 'marbre' (which is itself an elided form of 'le marbre du tombeau de'); in other words the marble monument is pointlessly trying to hold or imprison Baudelaire, who is always elsewhere, in his work, in the mind of the 'mourner' and so on; the tomb is empty. It may also be that 'vain' has something of 'vaniteux' in it too; monuments answer the needs and self-satisfactions of the living, are no more than a convenient form for memory; the dead for their part would have other monuments, their works, which are not monuments but part of the currency of existence. The function of 'vainement' is dependent, of course, on the interpretation of 'elle'. Is 'elle' the prostitute, referring back, by syllepsis, to 'un immortel pubis' (Davies, 1950, p. 176)? Is 'elle' an anticipatory pronoun, leaving identification in suspense until the arrival of the noun 'son Ombre même' (Austin, 1973, p. 198)? Or does 'elle' refer to poetry itself (Gill, 1967, p. 56)? Gill's account of the whole tercet is as follows:

Où la Poésie pourra-t-elle demeurer dans un temps qui n'en a cure? Bannie de la cité, où trouvera-t-elle un refuge? Quel feuillage séché dans les cités sans soir [nos cités éclairées au gaz] pourra bénir, votif (comme elle [la Poésie veuve de son poète] pourra se rasseoir – vainement – contre le marbre [du monument] de Baudelaire).   (p. 56)

This quotation brings our attention to the syntactical ellipsis in the tercet's second line. Has a 'pourra' simply been omitted – 'comme elle pourra se rasseoir' – or is the elision more extensive, as Davies (1950, p. 178) suggests: 'Quel feuillage pourra bénir le marbre comme elle pourra le bénir en s'y rasseyant'?

The syntax of the first line of the second tercet is usually assumed to run: 'absente avec frissons au voile qui la ceint', although it is possible that 'avec frissons' qualifies the verb; certainly this latter pattern makes 'avec frissons' easier to interpret, as the quivering of the veil, the vestigial sign of a presence or the adumbration of the veil's being rent – 'Est-ce le voile dans le temple qui tremble et va se déchirer, montrant une absence de Déesse? Car dans le temple de l'avenir il n'y aura plus de divinité que nous-mêmes' (Gill, 1967, p. 60). 'Absente avec frissons', on the other hand, suggests other

Mallarméan phrases like 'sa presque disparition vibratoire' ('Crise de vers') or 'centre de suspens vibratoire' ('Le Mystère dans les lettres'), that is to say, a shimmering vibration between presence and absence, object and Idea, figure and phantom, 'celle' and 'son Ombre même', a mode of meaning by infinite dialectical play. The second line, it is usually assumed, is made up of a demonstrative pronoun ('celle'), referring back to 'elle', and two appositional phrases 'son Ombre même' and 'un poison tutélaire': the prostitute is Baudelaire's very shade and a tutelary poison, inasmuch as she is guardian of the tomb and morally poisonous, and/or inasmuch as she is to be identified with Baudelaire's 'other' shade – *Les Fleurs du Mal* – which is poisonous because it is morally undermining, but tutelary because it is morally undermining only for those whose morals deserve to be undermined. But the permutations of the line's three units are in fact multiple: 'son Ombre même' need not be appositional so much as definitional i.e. it need not be 'The prostitute, Baudelaire's very shade', but rather 'This thing which is Baudelaire's shade'; or indeed it need not be Baudelaire's shade at all, but her own i.e. the prostitute (or rather) her very shade, is a tutelary poison, because her shade is *Les Fleurs du Mal*. It could equally be argued that it is not necessarily 'celle' which is the 'ground' (pro)noun to which the other nouns are in apposition; either 'son Ombre même' or 'un poison tutélaire' could be the 'ground' noun, particularly if we assume that the first line of the second tercet belongs with the syntax of the first tercet. Furthermore, the grammatical status of 'même' is by no means clear. Might not the line be read trimetrically, thus:

Celle son Om/bre même un poison/tutélaire   4+5+3

i.e. *Les Fleurs du Mal* or indeed the prostitute can *even* be described as a guardian poison. Might not this 'même' also be the 'même' missing from 'si' in the line following: 'Toujours à respirer (même) si nous en périssons'? This would involve another scansion:

Celle son Ombre même//un poison tutélaire   4+2+3+3/5+1+3+3
Toujours à respirer si nous en périssons   2+4+6

and would cast 'un poison tutélaire/Toujours à respirer' as a parenthesised, anticipatory explanation of 'périssons'.[4] But even if this seems a little far-fetched, there is no doubt that 'même' can afford to be absent from the final line because it is present in the penultimate.

It is clear from this brief analysis that the room for prosodic ambiguity in the poem is very small, largely because the semantic and syntactic ambiguities usually do not have any prosodic repercussions: rhythmic measures merely mark syntactic segments without making assumptions about the way the segments are articulated. On the contrary, the rhythm enacts a continuity, a transparency, which runs like a gloss and sense of purpose through the complex and meandering syntax. This might be to imply that the rhythmic configurations read the poem and release a meaning, even while the words in the syntactic chain refuse to do so. But if this is true, what kind of meaning is rhythm?

It is easy enough to argue that the Mallarméan poem is a passage of signifiers, that words operate a continual process of handing themselves on and handing themselves back, so that each lexical item is the intersection of projection and recall. If we separate out from the first stanza, for example, the principal phonetic protagonists, we discover an intricate network of cross-reference, with some items (particularly 'abominablement' of course) privileged by their more extended participation in that phonetic network:

|ā| temple, enseveli, bavant, abominablement, flambé
|a| par, la, sépulcrale, bavant, abominablement, Anubis, aboi, farouche
|e| sépulcrale, égout, flambé
|i| enseveli, divulgue, rubis, abominablement, idole, Anubis
|ɔ| abominablement, idole
|u| bouche, égout, boue, tout, farouche
|y| divulgue, sépulcrale, rubis, Anubis, museau
|b| bouche, bavant, boue, rubis, abominablement, Anubis, flambé, aboi
|f| flambé, farouche
|l| temple, enseveli, divulgue, la, le, sépulcrale, abominablement, quelque, idole, flambé
|v| enseveli, divulgue, bavant

This is one of the reasons why words never properly accede to the business of signification; the insistence of phonemic recurrence means that signifiers can never reach their signifieds before being qualified and compounded by those other signifiers which their phonetic structure gives them access to. And complicating this phonetic interpenetration are the relationships of items in particular lexical sets; thus, for example, in this first stanza, the lexical set of 'utterance' produces: divulgue, bouche, égout, bavant, museau, aboi. A second reason why the signifier cannot reach its signified is, of course, the disjunctiveness of Mallarmé's syntax; if words are to signify punctually, then they must be supported by a word-order which justifies the immediate ascription of significance by ordering meaning as it occurs. Syntax, in Mallarmé, is not a way of *un*folding meaning in the 'correct' order, according to the grammar that meaning has already chosen, but of *in*folding meaning in a structurally complex entity, in which grammar is not yet fully resolved.

It might, at first sight, seem that the strategies of postponement in the Mallarméan text are a very denial of a temporal reading process; the Mallarméan text seems to demand, not to be read, but rather to be 'read through', so that it may be 'read' after it has completed itself, that is, so that its items can then be variously arranged and variously interpreted; in a sense, such an approach assumes that the Mallarméan poem does not mean, but rather must be made to mean. The reading of the Mallarméan poem would be a traversal and encompassment of a space which would then constitute the parameters of the poem's semantic productivity. This would also entail the treatment of rhythm as a sequence of separable units themselves susceptible of any number of structural re-arrangements. The episodic nature of Mallarmé's syntax may indeed encourage such a view, but rhythm also, as we shall see, plays out a drama of loss and recovery, follows an itinerary of changing projections of thought.

The French alexandrine is at one and the same time an agent of conjunction and disjunction, inasmuch as it is both rhythmical (hemistich-internal *coupes*) and metrical (hemistich junctures). Whereas within the hemistich, the *coupe* is a moment of articulation, of drawing together and sequencing, the caesura and the line-ending are potentially moments of disarticulation and division, moments when metrical imperatives can peremptorily cut into the syntactic chain and redistribute its elements. The hemistich-internal *coupe* is a sense-making of syntax, while the metrical juncture can be desyntactifying in the sense of making grammatical units absolute or dispersing syntactical context. It is noticeable in 'Le Tombeau de Charles Baudelaire' that many hemistichs are made up of a noun or verb + qualifier, e.g. 'Le temple enseveli', 'divulgue par la bouche', 'Tout le museau flambé', 'Ou que le gaz récent', 'dans les cités sans soir', 'Au voile qui la ceint', etc.; it is equally noticeable that many of the syntactical disorientations and losses of sequence are created by the caesura or line-terminus, e.g. 'par la bouche / Sépulcrale d'egout', 'Abominablement | quelque idole Anubis', 'dans les cités sans soir / Votif', 'Votif pourra bénir |

comme elle se rasseoir', etc. As we read Mallarmé, we never lose a
sense of a syntactic direction, but at the same time we are aware
that rhythm lies in the hands of a power beyond syntax, in the
metrical structure of the poem itself and in a principle of rhythmic
combination, which are models of mind.

If the hemistich represents a limit of syntactic coherence, then it
is the rhythm of hemistichs which precisely encodes the rhythm of
the whole poem's elusive coherences and the modal values attached
to them. The hemistich central to this poem, though not quantita-
tively the most frequent, is the 2+4 combination. It is central
because, on three occasions, it governs the whole line (1, 10, 12),
the first of which initiates the poem and the last two of which are a
consolidated return after the interruption of other hemistich combinations – 4+2 at line 4, and, possibly, line 5, and 3+3 at lines 2
and 6. It is central, too, because it is the hemistich which predominates in the sestet and because its tetrasyllabic element is the
poem's subject 'de Baudelaire' (line 11) – it could be argued that
this last tetrasyllabic measure derives from 4+2, but the tetrasylla-
bles of line 11 grow out of the preceding 2+4's of line 10.

The first line provides the backdrop for the whole poem: buriedness and utterance and the proportionality of utterance's power to
the buriedness of the utterer. The 2+4 pattern is a pattern of
mathematical doubling, of expansion, liberation, dissemination.
After this first line, it is driven underground, until its reappearance
at line 10, when again it occupies both hemistichs of the line. Line 2
installs another kind of hemistich, another kind of discourse – 3+3.
In its repeated form here, as in line 6, it has something of a
parenthesising force, a matter-of-fact explanatoriness (endorsed in
line 6 by the confident 'on le sait'), evenly paced and equilibriated.
It is the only hemistich common to all stanzas, acting as a stabiliser
after moments of rhythmic destabilisation (lines 9, 13), allowing
utterance to re-initiate itself from a source of reflective quietude;
the non-repeated 3+3 hemistichs are essentially moments when the
image is stilled and focussed, moments of unruffled consciousness.

The 6 hemistich, though it occurs only three times (if we include
its appearance in the trimetric line 8), is crucial to the dynamics of
the other two-accent hemistichs, and is as much a space of potential
catastrophe as of potential triumph. It has these features because of
its essential undecipherability and promiscuity. It is difficult to tell
whether it is white or black, whether it is the aggregate of all
divisions of six, or whether, on the contrary, it is a number void of
smaller units, a rhythmic emptiness. And if it is the former, it is

impossible to tell which combination it is the aggregate of $-3+3$ or $4+2$ or $2+4$ or $1+5$ – that is, with which combination it is in complicity. 'Abominablement' would seem to be the sum of $3+3$, but the probability of this affiliation does not, ironically, help to stabilise it; for, if the hemistich is the limit of syntactic coherence and metrical juncture is the source of syntactic disorientation, the single-word hemistich cannot, by its very nature, be syntactically coherent and indeed is totally dependent for its syntactic connections on cross-junctural relationships. 'Abominablement', therefore, is, on the one hand, the gravitational centre for the first stanza's phonetic structure and the aggregate of the hemistich which dominates the stanza's two inner lines; on the other hand, it is a principal agent of the stanza's syntactic dissolution. This particular 6, then, sets the rhythmic structure of the poem two tasks: a) to affiliate the 6 with the key $2+4$ hemistich and b) to restore to the 6 its syntactic coherence.

The second time the 6 occurs, in line 8, it still has connections with the $3+3$ hemistich, but it is now a $3+3$ cracked apart by the 6. This splitting of the $3+3$ by the 6 is an indication not only of the much smaller part that $3+3$ will play in the poem thereafter, but also of 6's dissociation of itself from the role of passive aggregation. Equally it has recovered its inner syntactic coherence and its coherence within the syntactic chain.

When 6 finally appears, as the last hemistich of the poem, it is not only a syntactically integrated clause, but also both an aggregate of $2+4$ *and* a final step in an expanding mathematical progression. That the clause it contains is a restrictive conditional of an ostensibly negative kind only adds to its savour; for it can hardly act as a restriction to that which it is the sum of, and its conditionality is gainsaid by its presenting itself as an increase; 'si nous en périssons' is the final exhalation of a poem and of a reading of Baudelaire which promises a 'toujours' of self-surrender.

Having taken these steps forward through the poem, we must now go back to line 4 and the introduction of the $4+2$ hemistich. This hemistich is usually a combination of a noun + adjective or adjectival phrase – '...museau flambé', '...aboi farouche', '...gaz récent', '...mèche louche'(?), '...cités sans soir'. The only exception is 'un immortel pubis' to which we shall return. $4+2$ is, not surprisingly, something like the reverse of $2+4$, in that it is a contracting hemistich where the contraction is connected with an aggressive movement, often of eruption, or of brashness, or of unassimilatedness. $4+2$ and $3+3$ are the crossover points between stanzas one and two, but although 4+2 hangs on into the first tercet, it is ousted by the re-emerging 2+4 from the second. This overall career of 4+2 suggests a gradual process of muting and taming; the potentially obstructive, and vulgar, nature of the hemistich, drawing attention to itself by its self-assertiveness, is absorbed into an increasingly phantasmal text. In 'un immortel pubis', the dissyllabic element again has an eruptive energy, an energy of shock and disembodiment, which diverts the claims of 'immortel' into a wry notion of the age-oldness of the prostitute's profession. And it is precisely a vindication or redemption of this 'immortel' that the prostitute sets out in search of, and achieves, as her immortality loses its professional colouring by embedding itself, as a quiddity, in a poetic *œuvre*; and this transformation is paralleled by the transformation of a highlighted synecdoche, mobile and capricious under the street lamps, into a full, but unidentified, figure, seated in respectful repose by Baudelaire's tomb ('comme elle se rasseoir' – 2+4).

The function of the two 1+5 hemistichs derives less from their innately dramatic polarisation of syllabic proportions than from their immediately preceding measures. The 1+5 of line 5 is preceded by a 4+2, so that the monosyllabic measure of 'torde' represents a pinnacle, thrown into relief by the caesural break, of the contracting movement of 4+2. But at the same time, of course, it initiates a rhythmic movement which runs counter to 4+2, a movement which is part of the process whereby the brashness of the contemporary city is assimilated into the poetic enterprise of spiritual expansion. The 1+5 of line 13, on the other hand, succeeds the 2+4 of the previous line, reinforcing it by taking it a step further, highlighting the prostitute's presence and generative force – 'Celle' corresponds to 'absente'; the prostitute is proportionately more present as Baudelaire's spirit, as she is more absent as a purely emblematic funeral monument – and increasing her disseminating power as she becomes identified with the poet and his work – the oscillatory half-existence expressed by 'avec frissons', the very interface of life and death, leads to the emergence of that shade in which is realised a truly integrated life-in-death, and for us, as readers, a death-in-life. It should also be recalled that both instances of the 1+5 hemistich are followed by a 3+3, which brings them back into the purview of quiet reflection.

Finally we must turn to the two trimetric lines, 8 and 11, lines which relocate rhythmic consciousness, which stand outside the dramatic interplay of hemistichs we have just discussed. The *trimètre* is significant in the rhythmic economy of Mallarmé's poems in that it submerges hemistichiality and minimises metricity; there is no question of there being an accentuable sixth syllable in either of these lines. In doing this, the *trimètre* momentarily opens up the possibility of pure rhythmic construction. In line 8, for example, we should remind ourselves that the hexasyllabic measure is not a hemistich, but a nonce creation, precisely 'selon le réverbère', which has the power to manipulate other measures. The measures in such lines may, of course, *allude to* measures in regular lines, but they should not be confused with them: while a tetrasyllabic element, for example, in a regular alexandrine has the hemistich as its immediate metrical referent and can only be combined with a dissyllabic element, a tetrasyllabic element in a *trimètre* has the whole line as its metrical referent and may be combined with elements of 5 and 3, or 4 and 4, or 2 and 6, etc. In approaching lines 10–11 therefore, we must recognise that though the tetrasyllabic measures of the *trimètre* (line 11) take up the tetrasyllabic measures of the previous line, they do so in a different rhythmic dimension: in escaping from over-restrictive principles of combination, in having a much larger unit, the line, as their metrical perspective, they can be moments of divagation, of intellectual arabesque, of rhythmic free-thinking. Despite the apparent setback of 'vainement', and the prostitute's apparent exclusion from the tomb expressed in 'contre', line 11 conveys, rhythmically, a unison, an acquiescence in the presiding pervasiveness of 'de Baudelaire'; for, after all, if we feel some adversativeness in the preposition 'contre', that, too, is declared to be 'vain'. Though the line may ostensibly express the non-emergence of Baudelaire and the futility of the prostitute's vigil, from another point of view, it does the opposite: the sense of resistance and exclusion in 'contre' is shown to be equally futile; Baudelaire assimilates the prostitute, just as she absorbs him; the barrier of the marble tomb-stone is broken down by the pivotal 'vainement' which as much speaks of Baudelaire's infiltration of all space as of any inaccessibility. The rhythmic concord of this line gives some hint perhaps of one of the *trimètre*'s essential characteristics: its ability to make rhythm available to fantasy. Released temporarily from the constraints of metricity with its peculiarly binary methods of ordering imaginative experience, whether they involve equation, contradiction, polarisation, or declaration and qualification, the *trimètre* can occupy an in-between, a space where categories are dissolved or do not yet obtain, where all is yet to be imagined in a rhythmically undefined respite from metre. The *trimètre* offers the opportunity of creative contingency, the untendentious sequence of thought in pure propulsion.

The *trimètre* is only a respite from metre, since all must converge in the total metrical structure which the sonnet is. But that intellectual fantasy, which the *trimètre* is and which is pure rhythmicity, is itself installed in the metrical frame of the poem, as a consistent subcurrent: besides the two 'true' *trimètres* (lines 8 and 11), there are three-accent *tétramètres* (lines 3 and 14) and a line whose syntactic structure is clearly ternary (line 13). This ternary subcurrent guarantees that the metrical orderliness of the poem is accessible to rhythmic meandering, to the impulses of free association.

Rhythm in the Mallarméan poem, then, enacts processes of mind and imagination which are at once responses to textual material and motivators of textual material. In other words, rhythms which by their general lack of equivocation guarantee an intelligibility of text are also instruments whereby the mind makes itself intelligible, makes manifest its operations. Roughly speaking, 'Le Tombeau de Charles Baudelaire' emerges from a 2+4 pattern, which is, as it were, the rhythmic occasion of the poem which the poem then seeks to repossess and extend after exploring all its modulations. And here we should remind ourselves of the whole drama of meaning which the Mallarméan poem acts out: the text of the poem trespasses on the immortal tacit poem – 'penser étant écrire sans accessoires ni chuchotement mais tacite encore l'immortelle parole' ('Crise de vers') – in order to reconstruct or re-activate that tacitness in the silence of the blank space which opens, interrupts and closes the poem – 'significatif silence qu'il n'est pas moins beau de composer que les vers' ('Sur Poe'). Put another way, the pure and virtual operations of mind and imagination use the mediation of the poem to recover themselves. Rhythm, therefore, which is the operation of mind made audible, the rhythm of ideation, is not so much a resource of text, as a source and destination of text, a tacit signifier which, through the play of its activities in text, seeks to become its own, equally tacit, signified. Within this itinerary from an anterior signifier to a posterior signified, the text institutes a play of signifiers whose sole function is to complicate infinitely their own potential signification in order to postpone a signified which, by definition, lies beyond them.

Mallarmé's poem does not present us with a search for a meaning in a search for a rhythm, as Hopkins's does. Rather, it presents us with a rhythm, a structure of ideation, seeking to enact the potentialities of its operations by allowing itself to be textually interfered with. We are in the habit of describing the rhythms of French verse as registering syntactical movements, as being that which actualises the periodisation and articulations of syntax. Rhythm, in short, is meaningful because it confirms the sense of, and is made sense of by, the syntactic chain. In 'Le Tombeau de Charles Baudelaire', the relationship between rhythm and syntax is much more tenuous; true, the two measures of the Mallarméan hemistich may indeed perform a syntactic continuity, but this continuity is constantly vulnerable to dislocation by metrical juncture or by the rhythmic syncopation of the *trimètre*; and, besides, Mallarmé's syntax itself, by disjunction and other moves to ambiguate its relationships, expresses a desire to go its own way. Rhythm thus joins syntax, not as a confirming agent, not in the confidence that segmentation is also an act of articulation, but rather in the knowledge that segmentation is as disjunctive as it is conjunctive, and that accentuation, the point at which rhythm becomes present, is also the point at which syntax momentarily ends without projecting anything. In this way, rhythm and syntax intersect one another, rather than moving along hand in hand.

Inasmuch as rhythm has a temporal dimension and inasmuch as the Mallarméan poem is the project of mind to repossess itself in its tacitness, so 'Le Tombeau de Charles Baudelaire' can be said to have a direction and to propel us towards a sense of something achieved. But the fact is that the achievement lies in the silence on the other side of the poem, that the last line is not a destination, but a verbal perimeter, so the relationship between syntax and rhythm is not so much a relationship of causality as of inference. Rhythm completes syntax, not by confirming it and sustaining its sense, but by informing it and complementing it. The ostensible enterprise of the poem – to find a suitable monument for Baudelaire's tomb – is the occasion for a set of reflections about Baudelaire which, in turn, are the occasion for the mind to suggest the shapes of its capacity to think about Baudelaire. Such shapes of mental capacity cannot, by their nature, be described at all intimately, and our analysis of the 'drama' of hemistichs can be no more than an attempt to trace the interplay of structures of aspiration and expansion, of jarring contraction, of steadied vision, the dialectic of plenitude and vacuity, the creative mobility of rhythm unconstrained by metrical juncture. Such expressive resources are obviously part of the rhythmic and metrical structure of any poem in regular verse, but their function in Mallarmé is crucially different, in that they do not simply endorse meaning but rather produce it, are the medium through which the text is passed, in order to rediscover itself in thought. And rhythm, in the inclusive sense, is that alone which can gather the poem into the web of its articulations; bound into the poem's very structure by metricity, but installed in the poet's/reader's fantasising imagination by its rhythmicity, part of the poem's temporal texture, but also both anterior and posterior to it, rhythm becomes what the poem means, namely the tacitness of Baudelaire in the thought performed by the poem.

We have considered two difficult poems in which the complex relationships of rhythmicity and metricity add up to an overall rhythm, which as much transcends the poem as informs it. In the case of Hopkins, the poem's rhythm was caught in the unresolved conflict between rhythmicity and metricity, and the poem's meaning was to be sought in the resolution of that conflict pitched beyond the poem. In Mallarmé's poem, there is no such conflict, though rhythmicity and metricity function with different effects; instead, the poem's rhythm is generally unequivocal, but is mystified and projected beyond the poem by its ideating thrust, evident in its oblique relation with syntax. In the following chapter, we shall examine how free verse, and in particular the free verse of Jules Laforgue's 'Solo de lune', delivers rhythmicity and metricity into a no man's land of polymorphousness, by educating the reader out of metricity without indicating any reliable rhythmic alternative.

6

RHYTHMICITY AND METRICITY IN FREE VERSE

LAFORGUE'S 'SOLO DE LUNE'

'Une heureuse trouvaille avec quoi paraît à peu près close la recherche d'hier, aura été *le vers libre*, modulation (dis-je souvent) individuelle, parce que toute âme est un nœud rythmique'. In expressing the view, in 'La Musique et les lettres' (1894), that free verse was, as it were, specially designed to release each poet's unique 'chant profond', Mallarmé was thoroughly in line with the thinking of his contemporaries. Far from the poem's releasing a rhythmic structure set somewhere beyond language, and beyond the poet, as a constellation of meaning to be achieved through strenuous reflection, through supplementation of the text by blank space, as in the Mallarméan enterprise, rhythm was, in free verse, to be a direct outcrop of the poet and indistinguishable from any other aspect of his utterance; Gustave Kahn tells us, in his 'Préface sur le vers libre' (1897): 'Depuis longtemps je cherchais à trouver en moi un rythme personnel suffisant pour interpréter mes lyrismes avec l'allure et l'accent que je leur jugeais indispensables'. The *verslibristes* of the late nineteenth century envisaged a verse in which every modulation in the poet's psychic and organic condition, every creative impulse, conscious and unconscious, by definition unique and unrepeatable, would find its corresponding realisation in a perfectly adapted line of verse, itself necessarily unique and unrepeatable. Unfortunately there are insurmountable obstacles to such an enterprise: no individual, poet or otherwise, can possess language – or rather, the more language is possessed, the more others are dispossessed of it; this kind of free verse imagines a rhythmicity so variably intrinsic to its every utterance that it could not be unearthed, with the consequence that the reader must either take rhythmicity on trust, or discover a rhythmic principle or model, which necessarily alienates the utterance from itself. Any poetry which proposes an understanding of the poet (rather than of poetry) as its objective, is doomed to failure, particularly when the reader is invited to create his own poem by the very indeterminacy and ambiguity of the text he has in front of him. Filliolet (1974) exposes the paradoxicality and self-contradictoriness of free verse, when he writes of it:

Sa nouveauté tient dans un pari: celui de ne pas être reconnu comme fait poétique. D'où son errance entre deux écueils: la création de structures trop diffuses pour être perçues, le figement de modèles qui se veulent éphémères pour être toujours renouvelés.   (p. 71)

The solution to this particular dilemma seems to me to lie in the kind of free verse to be found in Laforgue's *Derniers Vers*, namely: to set one's verse close enough to familiar prosodic models – that is to write a *vers libre* which often has the look of *vers libres classiques* – for those models to supply a contractual framework, a degree of rhythmic visibility and a basis for prosodic transaction, and at the same time to deprosodify them, to reveal their non-metrical potentialities; and to prevent the 'congealment' of the models by requiring the reader to redefine them at each appearance, even though they may seem to be repeated within the course of the poem, simply because the lines in question do not quite perfectly confirm them. Laforgue's lines encourage the reader to reach through to a prosodic model and then to withdraw from that model immediately it is identified. In other words, Laforgue's verse enacts a process of prosodic re-education; it is much less an 'errance', than an itinerary from the metrical to the non-metrical in which the metrical retains an orientating capacity. Free verse is not so much 'metre undone' as 'learning to undo metre', not so much 'rhythm made wayward' as 'rhythm redistributed'.

It was not in Laforgue's nature to subscribe to the version of free verse which we have outlined above. He could hardly seek to make himself possessable through his verse, since he was not in possession of himself. He is Pierrot, masked beyond knowledge, caught in the limbo between a contempt for the provincial or suburban everydayness of the bourgeoisie, and an idealism reached for, but not really believed in; he is the acrobat in attitudes, the juggler with concepts; moon-lover, his expressionless floured face is a measure both of his ironic detachment and total vulnerability. The kind of poetry which could cope with the succession of masks assumed by the hypertrophic dandy and dilettante, will-less, afloat in the fluid and ungraspable present, had to be peculiarly available, available to changes of tone and register, to sudden deviations, tangents, afterthoughts, and above all uncommitting, predicting nothing. And yet it also had to be sufficiently poised, in a formal sense, to maintain its self-reflexive quality and to give leverage and discipline to its irresistible ironies. Having no tongue of his own, Laforgue cultivates all other tongues, is ventriloquial, intertextual, quotational: his is a poetry of borrowing, but the borrowings are so improvised, so associatively produced, that we never lose our sense of the poem's first-hand quality; as Pound puts it, in 'Irony, Laforgue, and Some Satire' (1917):

He is, nine-tenths of him, critic – dealing for the most part with literary poses and *clichés*, taking them as his subject matter; and – and this is the important thing when we think of him as a poet – he makes them a vehicle for the expression of his own very personal emotions, of his own unperturbed sincerity. (p. 282).

It is hardly surprising, then, that Laforgue's free verse should localise its pains and pleasures in a structure whose impulses and characteristics are equally localised. His poetry is not a poetry of expatiation or development, of sustained periods, but of the staccato, the spasmodic, the highly episodic; in his verse, momentum is generated by repetition, by a mechanism which facilitates a series of new beginnings from the same point, rather than by the articulations of an unfolding syntax. His free verse operates predominantly at the level of the line, re-sensitising the line by sapping its metricity; it is never far from regular structures and the attitudes embedded in them; but it leans on the ready-made the better to make it only approximate, vulnerable to corrosive prosodic innuendoes. And rhyme, now irregular and improvised, functions both as the motor of association of ideas, and as a constant cue to the text for merciless self-scrutiny.

As a preamble to further reflections about free verse and Laforgue's 'solutions' to its problems, and as a way of focussing these reflections on textual instances, I offer below a traditional scansion of the seventh of the *Derniers Vers*, 'Solo de lune', or as near to a traditional scansion of it as the poem allows.

No. of syllables			Rhyme/rhyme gender (the mark ' indicates a repeated rhyme-word)	
8	Je fume, étalé face au ciel,	2+6/2+3+3	a	m
11	Sur l'impériale de la diligence,	5+6	b	f
11	Ma carcasse est cahotée, mon âme danse	3+4+2+2	b	f
4	Comme un Ariel;	4	a	m
5	9	Sans miel, sans fiel, ma belle âme danse,	2+2+3+2	b'	f
11	O routes, coteaux, ô fumées, ô vallons,	2+3+3+3	c	m
9	Ma belle âme, ah! récapitulons.	3+1+5	c	m

	8	Nous nous aimions comme deux fous,	4+4	d	m
	8	On s'est quitté sans en parler,	4+4	e	m
10	8	Un spleen me tenait exilé,	5+3/2+3+3	e	m
	9	Et ce spleen me venait de tout. Bon.	3+5+1/3+3+2+1	(d)c	m
	8	Ses yeux disaient: "Comprenez-vous?	4+4	d	m
	8	Pourquoi ne comprenez-vous pas?"	2+6	f	m
	11	Mais nul n'a voulu faire le premier pas,	2+4+5	f	m
15	10	Voulant trop tomber *ensemble* à genoux.	3+4+3	d	m
	4	(Comprenez-vous?)	4	d'	m
	6	Où est-elle à cette heure?	3+3	g	f
	6	Peut-être qu'elle pleure …	2+4	g	f
	6	Où est-elle à cette heure?	3+3	g'	f
20	10	Ch! du moins, soigne-toi, je t'en conjure!	1+2+3+4/3+3+4	h	f
	10	O fraîcheur des bois le long de la route,	5+5/3+2+2+3	i	f
	16	O châle de mélancolie, toute âme est un peu aux écoutes,	2+6+2+3+3	i	f
	3	Que ma vie	3	j	f
	3	Fait envie!	3	j	f
25	16	Cette impériale de diligence tient de la magie.	5+5+2+4	j	f
	8	Accumulons l'irréparable!	4+4	k	f
	8	Renchérissons sur notre sort!	4+4	l	f
	12	Les étoiles sont plus nombreuses que le sable	3+5+4	k	f
	12	Des mers où d'autres ont vu se baigner son corps;	2+5+3+2	l	f
30	8	Tout n'en va pas moins à la Mort.	5+3	l	f
	4	Y a pas de port.	4	l	f
	8	Des ans vont passer là-dessus,	5+3/2+3+3	m	m
	9	On s'endurcira chacun pour soi,	5+4	n	m
	10	Et bien souvent et déjà je m'y vois,	4+3+3	n	m
35	8	On se dira: "Si j'avais su …"	4+4	m	m
	12	Mais mariés de même, ne se fût-on pas dit	3+2+7/5+7	o	m
	8	"Si j'avais su, si j'avais su! …"?	4+4	m'	m
	6	Ah! rendez-vous maudit!	1+3+2/1+5/4+2	o	m
	6	Ah! mon coeur sans issue! …	1+2+3/3+3	m	f
40	6	Je me suis mal conduit.	6	o	m
	7	Maniaques de bonheur,	3+4	p	m
	9	Donc, que ferons-nous? Moi de mon âme,	1+4+1+3	q	f
	9	Elle de sa faillible jeunesse?	1+5+3	r	f
	8	O vieillissante pécheresse	4+4	r	f
45	10	Oh! que de soirs je vais me rendre infâme	1+3+4+2/4+4+2	q	f
	4	En ton honneur!	4	p	m
	8	Ses yeux clignaient: "Comprenez-vous?	4+4	d'	m
	8	Pourquoi ne comprenez-vous pas?"	2+6	f'	m
	8	Mais nul n'a fait le premier pas	2+2+4/4+4	f'	m
50	9	Pour tomber ensemble à genoux. Ah! …	5+3+1	(d')f	m
	5	La Lune se lève,	2+3/5	s	f
	5	O route en grand rêve! …	2+3	s	f
	14	On a dépassé les filatures, les scieries,	5+4+5	j	f
	9	Plus que les bornes kilométriques,	4+5	t	f

55	14	De petits nuages d'un rose de confiserie,	5+3+6	j f
	12	Cependant qu'un fin croissant de lune se lève,	3+4+2/3/3+6+3	s' f
	10	O route de rêve, o nulle musique …	5+5/2+3+2+3	t f
	8	Dans ces bois de pins où depuis	5+3/3+2+3	o m
	7	Le commencement du monde	5+2	u f
60	5	Il fait toujours nuit,	5	o m
	9	Que de chambres propres et profondes!	3+2+4	u f
	8	Oh! pour un soir d'enlèvement!	1+3+4/4+4	v m
	8	Et je les peuple et je m'y vois,	4+4	n' m
	8	Et c'est un beau couple d'amants,	5+3	v m
65	8	Qui gesticulent hors la loi.	4+4	n m
	8	Et je passe et les abandonne,	3+5	w f
	8	Et me recouche face au ciel.	4+4	a m
	9	La route tourne, je suis Ariel,	4+5	a m
	10	Nul ne m'attend, je ne vais chez personne.	4+3+3	w f
70	11	Je n'ai que l'amitié des chambres d'hôtel.	6+2+3	a m
	5	La lune se lève	5/2+3	s f
	5	O route en grand rêve!	2+3	s f
	5	O route sans terme,	2+3	x f
	5	Voici le relais,	5/2+3	y m
75	8	Où l'on allume les lanternes,	4+4	x f
	8	Où l'on boit un verre de lait,	3+5	y m
	6	Et fouette postillon,	2+4	c m
	6	Dans le chant des grillons,	3+3	c m
	8	Sous les étoiles de juillet.	4+4	y m
80	4	O clair de Lune,	4	z f
	14	Noce de feux de Bengale noyant mon infortune,	1+6+3+4	z f
	9	Les ombres des peupliers sur la route …	2+4+3	i f
	6	Le gave qui s'écoute, …	2+4	i f
	6	Qui s'écoute chanter, …	3+3	e m
85	13	Dans ces inondations du fleuve du Léthé …	7+2+4	e m
	5	O Solo de lune,	3+2	z f
	5	Vous défiez ma plume,	3+2	z f
	7	Oh! cette nuit sur la route;	1+3+3/4+3	i f
	11	O Etoiles, vous êtes à faire peur,	3+3+5	g/p m
90	7	Vous y êtes toutes! toutes!	5+2	i f
	8	O fugacité de cette heure …	5+3	g' f
	6	Oh! qu'il y eût moyen	1+5	A m
	12	De m'en garder l'âme pour l'automne qui vient! …	5+4+3	A m
	7	Voici qu'il fait très très-frais,	4+3	y m
95	6	Oh! si à la même heure,	1+5	g f
	11	Elle va de même le long des forêts,	5+3+3	y m
	6	Noyer son infortune	2+4	z' f
	8	Dans les noces du clair de lune! …	3+5	z' f
	7	(Elle aime tant errer tard!)	4+3	B m
100	8	Elle aura oublié son foulard,	5+3	B m
	12	Elle va prendre mal, vu la beauté de l'heure!	6+4+2	g' f
	8	Oh! soigne-toi, je t'en conjure!	1+3+4	h' f

11	Oh! je ne veux plus entendre cette toux!	1+6+4	d m
11	Ah! que ne suis-je tombé à tes genoux!	1+6+4	d' m
105	11 Ah! que n'as-tu défailli à mes genoux!	1+6+4	d' m
	10 J'eusse été le modèle des époux!	3+3+4	d m
	16 Comme le frou-frou de ta robe est le modèle des frou-frou.	5+3+4+4	d m

This scansion is only approximate and cannot, by the nature of the verse, but be approximate. Since the verse gives no indications about the status of the *e atone*, I have used the principles that apply to it in regular verse; but there is no reason to suppose that I am right to do this; and merely by practising *syncopes* and *apocopes* in a systematic fashion, the whole balance of the poem would change: many of the lines which in my reading seem parisyllabic would become imparisyllabic and vice versa. If we imagine a *césure épique* in the second line for example, with the final e of 'diligence' becoming extra-numerical, then we create a 5+5 decasyllable; if we pursue the same policy with line 55:

De petits nuag(es) ‖ d'un rose de confiserie

then we produce a thirteen-syllable line 5+2+6. But why stop there? Why not generalise *syncope* and *apocope*:

D' p'tits nuag' d'un ros' d' confis'rie

thus allowing the magnificent emergence of a totally unsuspected, but non-disruptive octosyllable?

But even the octosyllable is potentially subject to further abbreviation. In the treatment of double vowels, I have again followed the principles which obtain in regular verse, except where colloquial elision points to the habits of synaeresisation of current speech, as in line 31:

ja pɑ də pɔʀ

where I assume that 'y' is a semi-consonant. But if we have colloquialised line 55 by practising syncopes and apocopes, it would be only consistent to reduce the diaeresis of 'nuage' to synaeresis, to treat the 'u' as a semi-consonant, thus nɥaʒ and thus a seven-syllable line. Equally one might ask whether line 41 is a seven-syllable line (ia of 'Maniaques' a diaeresis) or a hexasyllable (ia a synaeresis: manjak). Beneath every meticulously articulated, ritualised, poetic enunciation lurks a careless and colloquialised enunciation which would make a nonsense of the line's numericity. In effect, doubts about the status of the *e atone*, and hesitations about synaeresis and diaeresis, destroy numericity and thus rob it of a prosodic function. But, of course, such doubts and hesitations do not bedevil absolutely every line, and every reader is free to discover a numericity appropriate to his own reading. I have, at any rate, assumed that my scansion has some validity, and made structural observations on the basis of it. Nonetheless we should recognise that this kind of free verse, though it is line-related, is, in its capacity as a scenario for multiple possible readings, non-numeric.

But even if we could establish a reliable number of syllables for each line, we would still have to confront the problem of rhythmic segmentation. Filliolet (1974) provides a timely reminder of the source of the problem: 'Pourtant, on n'insiste pas assez sur le fait que ces unités accentuelles restent, avant toute réalisation par la parole, virtuelles' (p. 67). This remark is, of course, only relatively true of regular verse, since major verse junctures (line-ending, caesura) do act as imperatives for accent. But it is true of line-internal and hemistich-internal (i.e. secondary, optional) accents where the reader has some choice about whether and what to accentuate. Free verse, it seems to me, exacerbates the virtuality of accent, by allowing, or indeed encouraging, the coexistence of 'intensive' (poetic) and 'extensive' (prosaic) readings; I can hardly agree with Filliolet (1974) when he writes:

Par l'hétérométrie et la valeur donnée au blanc final, . . . le vers libre offre donc à celui qui écrit la possibilité d'*actualiser* pour le lecteur les structures rythmiques de son énoncé, structures qui, en quelque sort, *participent alors à l'énonciation.*   (p. 67)

This observation may be true in that variation of line-length in free verse is certainly a way of manipulating accent, its frequency and nature, and in that short lines in particular can be used to segment larger utterances and increase the density of accent. But in longer lines the problem of accentuation is doubled by the difficulty of not knowing whether to try and encompass the line as a complete unit by reducing the incidence of accentuation and thus lengthening its measures (extensive reading), or whether to accentuate with a frequency comparable to that obtaining in shorter regular lines and thus to encourage the view that long lines are compounds of shorter ones (intensive reading). Thus, for example, faced with line 22:

O châle de mélancolie, toute âme est un peu aux écoutes

do we read, minimally, $8+8$, or at most $8+2+6$ (extensive reading), or do we segment maximally, producing a $2+6+2+3+3$ scansion (intensive reading), and thus imply that the line is not so much a sixteen-syllable line with eight-syllable hemistichs as a combination of two octosyllables, each with its own rhythmic identity?

But even when lines are short the problem is not swept away; a simple hexasyllable like:

Où est-elle à cette heure?　　　　　(line 17)

may still leave us wondering whether to read it as 6 or 3+3, the former implying that free-verse lineation is indeed expressively segmented prose, the latter that this is a true verse hexasyllable (or separately lineated hemistich). Of all this, we shall have more to say later. It is sufficient for the moment to demonstrate how problematical the scansion of 'Solo de lune' is and how provisional and partial my account of it must be. And these brief remarks reveal, too, perhaps, how far, at least in the passage cited above, Filliolet is a prey to the free-verse fallacy explored in the first paragraph of this chapter; much nearer the truth, and a fitting conclusion to these paragraphs, is the observation Filliolet makes, a few pages later in his article, about Rimbaud's celebrated 'J'ai tendu des cordes de clocher à clocher; etc' ('Phrases', *Illuminations*):

Dans cette phrase isolée sur la page, qui pour nous mérite le nom de vers du fait de son fonctionnement globalisant, plusieurs structurations rythmiques se superposent, s'associent, plaçant le lecteur devant une sorte de 'mobile' dont les figures se décomposent à l'instant même où son attention a réussi à les figer dans une organisation donnée.　　　　　(p. 69)

I would like to approach the demetrification of the metrical model in Laforgue's verse by first considering some of the ways in which free verse can redistribute or relocate its prosody, remembering that the strength of these alternative prosodies is proportional to metricity's loss of a controlling interest. In *French Verse-Art*, I drew attention to the centrality of tone in free verse's construction of semantic play:

... the pursuit of *expression*, as against a submission to the interpretative powers exercised by conventional prosody itself, has given special prominence to tone, as against prosodic structure, as the multiplier and compounder of meaning. It is perhaps significant that one of the more potent strains of early free verse was one which explored modes of irony (Laforgue, Pound, Eliot) ... and that French free verse grew out of Symbolism, out of a movement which might be said to have overtaxed the purely lexical and syntactic sources of semantic multiplicity.　　　　　(p. 183)

The orchestration of tone can itself be a source of prosodic structure. Laforgue's heavily paratactic and endstopped verse, while it may sometimes produce excessively jagged, stop–start effects, does allow him to use end-of-line punctuation as a consistently applied value system, a real part of the line's prosody. Most characteristically Laforgue's utterances oscillate between the energising exclamation mark and dissipating *points de suspension*. The exclamation mark, most frequently syntactically motivated by imperative, optative or exclamatory (Que ..., que de ...) constructions, promises urgency, emotional commitment, but allows us to suspect an inflatedness, an exasperated wish to make significant that which too stubbornly is unnoteworthy; the exclamation mark is both an acknowledgement of the real pressure of personal feeling and the observance of an etiquette, the visible sign of feelings *expected of* the poet. Can we distinguish between the two in practice? That depends a little on our response to *points de suspension*. These, too, seem to me to have an essential duality; they betoken a shrug of the shoulders, a loss of interest, the inability to sustain the communicative impulse. But they can also have a more positive colouring: in the stanza (lines 80–5), in which *points de suspension* have something like a monopoly of the punctuation, they seem to signal rapt concentration, giving aura to sensations, isolating them in their distinctness, and protracting their effect in the poet's spellbound oblivion of all else. And whatever their expressive colouring, *points de suspension* have another important prosodic function: they provide a closure which is no closure, which lets the line gently into the blank space following it and prolongs line-terminal pause, thus countering the staccato quality characteristic of lines governed by other punctuation. Aside from the stanza already quoted (lines 80–5) and the final stanza, which is markedly inclined to the exclamation mark, neither form of punctuation has a noticeable ascendancy; we might suggest that the exclamation mark predominates between lines 21 and 45 and again between lines 94 and 107; on the basis of this observation and the oddity of the stanza between lines 80 and 85, we might further suggest that the exclamation mark belongs particularly to the theme of the failed love-affair, while *points de suspension* are characteristic of the coach-ride motif, but this cannot be a hard-and-fast distinction. What I would also propose is this: when the two punctuations are joined, in the composite mark '!...' not only are the two thematic concerns unconsciously, subliminally, joined, but also the negative aspects of both forms of punctuation become paramount; that is the mark '!...' betokens a fundamentally factitious emotionalism which is shrugged off in spiritual inertia. This cannot, of course, be demonstrated.

But this particular punctuational play is not only structurally effective by its conspicuous activity alone; it is equally effective by its conspicuous absence. And it is conspicuously absent from the first sixteen lines of the poem, where the poet installs his two themes in a spirit of insouciant reportage, and from lines 66 to 79, where the poet recovers some of his equanimity in a resigned indifference (lines 66–70) and in a neutral, uninvolved registration of phenomena around him (lines 71–9). One might also note the absence of this loaded punctuation in the final line of the poem; here the laconic and pointedly ill-adapted image establishes a purgative distance between the poet and his preceding concerns. Finally, it is perhaps significant that the apostrophes, with which the text is interspersed, regularly refuse exclamatory or suspensive punctuation, the exceptions being the composite mark at line 52 and the *points de suspension* at lines 57 and 91; it would seem that apostrophe is a gesture of withdrawal, of withdrawal into the hermetically sealed world of self-regarding invocation. And it is to apostrophe that I now wish to turn, and in particular to the structural and prosodic patterns it creates with the supportive exclamations 'Oh!' and 'Ah!'.

One of the personae adopted by the poet in 'Solo de lune' is Ariel (lines 4, 68), whose significance is explained by Laforgue in a passage in the *Mélanges posthumes* (1903):

Je ne trouverai beau et pur que ce que j'imagine et ce dont je me souviens – ce qui peut arriver et ce qui a été. Je me sens comme un Ariel au-dessus du Présent – l'odieux et quotidien et importun Présent – ainsi pour la femme et tout. Oh! qui jettera un pont entre mon cœur et le Présent. C'est que le souvenir et le rêve sont l'art d'enchâsser les moments, de les prendre en eux ébarbés du moment d'avant et du moment d'après, des regrets et des appréhensions qu'eût ainsi ce moment. Aux paysages il enlève le trop froid et le trop chaud et tous les ennuis du corps – l'âme seule est prise. Et ne vivre qu'avec son âme . . . Ah! ne vivre qu'avec son âme!   (pp. 70–1)

Herein perhaps lies a further explanation of a free verse prosody which never strays too far from the habits of regular verse. Regular verse, it might be argued, exists continuously in the interstitial gap between echo and anticipation, memory and projection; the very recognisability of its structure means that it is permeated by anteriority, and those mnemonic artifices which make it memorable at the same time enact the processes of memory; and equally the artifices of regular verse are the agents and instruments of fantasy, imperiously drawing the imagination forward into a world of its own construction, authorising all manner of association, fulfilling wishes in textual actualisations. But by its very refusal of, or failure to find a home in, regularity, Laforguian free verse cannot produce moments 'ébarbés ... des regrets et des appré-hensions', those negative forms of memory and anticipation which fix the present as an existential condition, as a space difficult to inhabit, precisely because past and future are experienced not as freedoms, as avenues of escape, but as corroding forces, eating away at the soul's integrity in the moment. The present, inescap-able, is 'importun' because it is not a point of radiation backwards and forwards, but a last retreat ('aux abois') in which the soul is besieged by missed opportunity and unrealisable desire.

The signals of the 'regrets' and the 'appréhensions' are the two exclamations 'Ah!' and 'Oh!' which appear in the passage above and which poignantly punctuate 'Solo de lune', as they do the *Derniers Vers* as a whole. The definitions of these two exclamations provided by *Le Petit Robert* make little distinction between them: 'Ah!' is described as '1. Interjection expressive, marquant un sentiment vif (plaisir, douleur, admiration, impatience, etc.). 2. Interjection d'insistance, de renforcement', while 'Oh!' is defined as '1. Interjection marquant la surprise ou l'admiration. 2. Interjec-tion renforçant l'expression d'un sentiment quelconque.' But in usage, and in Laforgue's usage in particular, 'Ah!' is clearly past-related, with an 'if only' modality, expressing a sense of failure:

> Ah! rendez-vous maudit!
> Ah! mon coeur sans issue! ...
> Je me suis mal conduit   (lines 38–40)

> Ah! que ne suis-je tombé à tes genoux!
> Ah! que n'as-tu défailli à mes genoux!   (lines 104–5)

while 'Oh!' is future-related, jussive or optative in modality, expressing a wish whose fulfilment is by no means guaranteed:

> Oh! qu'il y eût moyen
> De m'en garder l'âme pour l'automne qui vient! ...
>   (lines 92–3)

> Oh! soigne-toi, je t'en conjure!
> Oh! je ne veux plus entendre cette toux! (lines 102–3)

These observations make doubly significant Laforgue's use of 'Ah!' in the passage from *Mélanges posthumes*, because the phrase 'ne vivre qu'avec son âme' seems projective and optative, the goal of an enterprise. But the 'Ah!', on our evidence, would indicate that this wish is already cursed with pastness, that it is a wish remembered and a futility acknowledged, rather than a still possible project.

'Solo de lune' does not take place entirely in a past and a future, or in a present peculiarly vulnerable to regret and apprehension. It takes place also in the present of a coach ride, a present precisely 'Sans miel, sans fiel', that is to say without feelings of sentimental nostalgia or aspiration, or of bitterness, a present which because of the dynamism of the coach and the poet's elevated position ('sur l'impériale de la diligence') is almost omnitemporal or atemporal, expanding into cosmic space and releasing the poet into contemplative quietude. Ariel then becomes the mediator between the poet and the moon, a corridor-persona through whom the poet might achieve the non-relative, non-contingent, total suspendedness of the sterile moon, the 'nombril du Néant'. It is only fitting that the sign of this kind of present should be the apostrophic zero, the O, the very figuration of the moon, the vocative which entails no dialogue, which absorbs otherness into *solo*.

> O fraîcheur des bois le long de la route,
> O châle de mélancholie, ...   (lines 21–2)

> O route en grand rêve!
> O route sans terme   (lines 72–3)

But the apostrophic 'O' installs another persona, that of 'poet'; as Culler (1981) points out, 'O' is a call which dramatises a calling: 'The poet makes himself a poetic presence through an image of voice, and nothing figures voice better than the pure *O* of undifferentiated voicing' (p. 142), for every apostrophe is in some sense an invocation of the muse. 'O' may be the way in which a poem installs itself in its own temporality, in the *durée* of writing or uttering, a linearity which outwits linearity by regression, recapitulation, redundancy, expectation and all kinds of laterality; but prosodic regularity, even of the reduced kind we find in the *Derniers Vers*, is the creator of a gap of self-consciousness, the gap of making (as opposed to simply saying), and in a context of abrupt tonal change, self-interruption and paraded intertextuality, that gap is sufficient to turn any utterance into a parody of itself. The persona which offered the promise of self-consolidation is undercut by others which make it just another agent of self-dispersal. The coach-ride may outstrip time's motion or anticipate time with its own momentum, but this momentum is as subject to interruption as any

other of the poet's moves; the road may be endless but the stamina
of the horses is not: after the wishful apostrophe:

> O route sans terme

we fall back, arrested in reality by:

> Voici le relais

It is not, I am sure, fanciful to suggest that 'Oh!', 'Ah!' and 'O'
are an essential part of the prosody of 'Solo de lune'; the pattern of
their occurrence is itself a rhythm of modality and temporal
perspective. That pattern is as follows: line 6: O...ô...ô, 7: ah!,
20: Oh!, 21: O, 22: O, 38: Ah!, 39: Ah!, 44: O, 45: Oh!, 50: Ah!, 52:
O, 57: O...ô, 62: Oh!, 72: O, 73: O, 80: O, 86: O, 88: Oh!, 89: O,
91: O, 92: Oh!, 95: Oh!, 102: Oh!, 103: Oh!, 104: Ah!, 105: Ah!
The prosodic status of these words is underlined by the fact that the
vast majority of them – 24 instances out of 29 – are line-initial and
take their place alongside other anaphoric patterns. The broad
disposition of these words would seem to be this: in the first fifty
lines, the changes are rung, as the three 'mentalities' jockey for
position; between lines 51 and 103, 'Ah!' drops from sight and 'O'
and 'Oh!' compete for supremacy; at first 'O' has the upper hand –
up to line 85 it makes six appearances and 'Oh' makes one – as the
poet is able to inhabit with some consistency the outlawed world of
the coach ride and to forget all obligations to the loved one; he is for
the moment the master of his own loneliness and free to embroider
on sensations of landscape. But the magic does not last: the poet
loses faith in the capacity of his own writing to engineer an
alternative temporality; the very solo which was to be the guarantee
of this withdrawal into the refuge of his own text cannot be
sustained:

> O Solo de lune,
> Vous défiez ma plume

The poet relapses into an awareness of contingency, in which text
can only express a separation and not an absorption. And in these
circumstances, the image of the loved one infiltrates his meditation
and 'O' has to yield to 'Oh!' – between lines 92 and 103 there are
four consecutive occurrences of the exclamation. And once 'Oh!'
has reinstalled itself, 'Ah!' becomes an inevitable complement; the
ability to project wish and desire depends on a foundation in the
past, a foundation which does not exist; as the poem closes, 'Ah!'

reasserts itself and delivers 'O' and 'Oh!' into the limbo of pure utterance.

The slippage of 'O' to 'Oh!' in the stanza which occupies lines 86–93 bears further examination, because it reveals some confusions of function. At line 88: –

> Oh! cette nuit sur la route

– one might have expected 'O', since the line refers to the poetic present of the coach ride and since the line is embedded between 'O Solo de lune' and 'O Etoiles'. The use of 'Oh!' already marks the coach-ride as fantasy, as something wished for but unachieved; and it introduces a subjective emotional response, a human personality, into a passage which otherwise leans towards the disembodied voice of purely poetic rapture. And if one admits 'Oh!', why not rather 'Ah!', a night which has already all but passed and whose memory the poet would wish to salvage or safeguard? By the same tokens, and conversely, one might have expected 'Oh!' at line 91: –

> O fugacité de cette heure . . .

– which would have led into the optative formulation of line 92:

> Oh! qu'il eût moyen

Or alternatively one might have expected 'Ah!', a lament for the passage of the exquisite moment, which the poet then attempts to reverse, to counter, by the forward projection of 'Oh!'. Instead we find an apparently ill-adapted apostrophic 'O', which makes 'fugacité' an object of contemplation, which seems to wish to suspend that fugitivity in the amber of poeticised utterance, or to make it the very source of a different kind of flux, the constantly self-replenishing flux of poetic verbalism. At all events, it appears that in this stanza, the crux of conflict, there is some crossing of wires, whereby 'O' and 'Oh!' lose their power to differentiate and are destabilised. But this destabilisation has already been adumbrated in an earlier stanza (lines 41–46), the only other stanza in which the two terms appear together:

> O vieillissante pécheresse,
> Oh! que de soirs je vais me rendre infâme
> En ton honneur!

It is difficult to account for the 'O' here; we could suggest, perhaps, that the 'O' in this instance should not be confused with others, that it is a *real* vocative, a real impulse of address, rather than an apostrophic vocative, which as much addresses the muse, or itself, as the object named, or addresses a space adjacent to the object. But 'vieillissante' projects the loved one into the future, a future of ageing which the poet as good as wishes on her. Does not this make 'Oh!' more appropriate? Or does the poet indeed cast the loved one momentarily as his muse, in which case the following two lines take on a very different colouring: the disreputability of poetry is proportional to the disreputability of its source of inspiration. The ambivalence of 'O' and 'Oh!' in these two verse contexts highlights the ambivalance between an authority without author and an author without authority, an ambivalence which informs not only the poetic attitudes throughout the poem, but the poem's prosody, a regularity as much relied upon as tampered with.

If confusions between 'O' and 'Oh!' are in part explained by their being phonetically identical, this phonetic identity should not blind us to fundamental differences of syntactical and prosodic opera-tion. 'O' is not a separate exclamation and has no existence apart from the noun which it endows with apostrophic force. In other words, it is always integrated into a syntactical unit, and conse-quently into a prosodic measure, larger than itself; it cannot therefore take an accent, wherever it occurs in the line:

> O routes, coteaux, ô fumées, ô vallons   2+3+3+3
> (line 6)

If we were to read this line as a regular alexandrine, with a caesura after the sixth syllable and counting the unelided *e atone* of 'fumées', thus:

> O rou|tes, coteaux, ô || fumé|es, ô vallons   2+4+2+4

or perhaps:

> O routes, coteaux, | ô || fumé|es, ô vallons   5+1+2+4

the enjambement at the caesura, by momentarily suspending ô and enforcing an accent on it, would in fact change its function: it would drift from apostrophic marker towards exclamation ('Oh!'). In normal circumstances, the O of apostrophe confirms the poeticity of the text, not only by virtue of its being a figure peculiar to poetic utterance, but also because it contributes to the 'measuredness' of the rhythm: it is an isolated syllable which refuses to isolate itself metrically and thus to create the metrically eccentric, or at least infrequent, monosyllabic measure. In the Laforguian example, of course, the non-accentuation of the medial 'ô' produces either an eleven-syllable line scanned 2+3+3+3 or an alexandrine (counting the *e atone* of 'fumées') with a displaced caesura: 5∥7; if the regularity of the alexandrine option is insisted upon, then it entails a transformation of the status of 'ô': instead of being the marker of a supra-personal poetic authority and a poeticising figure, it functions as an exclamatory and depoeticising intervention of authoriality. It is typical of Laforgue's prosody as a whole that it renders unto metricity with one hand what it removes from metricity with the other; the processes of compliance and deviation cannot be put apart.

'Oh!' and 'Ah!' operate very differently. They are self-sufficient utterances which look to wrench themselves out of the syntactic chain and can only achieve their full rhetorical force by occupying a rhythmic unit to the exclusion of all else. Laforgue fully exploits their disruptive potential by emphasising their supernumerariness at the same time as their expressive ineluctability; in fact their supernumerariness acts as a pledge of their urgency; they must be added because they can neither be omitted nor postponed. Perhaps the most striking example of this phenomenon is to be found at line 50, where 'Ah!' is line-terminal:

> Pour tomber ensemble à genoux. Ah! ...   5+3+1

The 'Ah!' here is triply disruptive: it creates adjacent accents which are awkward in any event, but particularly awkward at a point of stanzaic closure; it introduces a nine-syllable line after a sequence of three octosyllables; and it diverts the potential *rimes embrassées* into the structurally slapdash dfff by submerging the pair 'vous/genoux'. Laforgue is indeed a poet of the afterthought and he makes no attempt to lessen the conspicuous 'addedness' of the interjection; prosodically 'Ah!' has a casualness, a prosaicising effect which we may suspect is a disclaimer of a very real emotional pressure; as 'Ah!' is prosodically inadmissible so is its charge of feeling. On the other hand, 'Ah!' marks the unpredictable intervention of a voice beyond the reach of prosodic exigency, of an author behind a poet, or another consciousness responding to the writing consciousness, a voice of randomness and relativity undercutting the complacent ordainedness of poetic formulation. The casualness of addition is more apparent in a line which corresponds very closely in effect to line 50, namely line 11:

> Et ce spleen me venait de tout. Bon.   3+5+1/3+3+2+1

'Bon' is disruptive in the same three ways that 'Ah!' is in the previous example. A voice concludes after the verse has come to its conclusion, and again it is difficult to tell whether the 'Bon' is an endorsement of the verse which paradoxically unbalances the verse, or whether 'Bon' is part of a competing prosody which is attempting to divert the regular verse structures into its own makeshift and wayward patterns: if the latter is the case then the octosyllable preceding 'Bon' is made to endorse the prosodic dislocations which 'Bon' engineers; in other words 'Et ce spleen me venait de tout' is a willing platform for 'Bon', enters into complicity with it and thus identifies itself as part of a different prosodic code. As readers, we suddenly find ourselves in a situation in which we can no longer trust the ostensible regularity and conformity of regular verse.

Equally a whole line may be presented as an afterthought, disturbing the balance of the stanza and once again diversifying voice. Line 16:

(Comprenez-vous?)

is a phatic addition, a check on communicative efficiency, confirming the interlocutor's continuing attention. But who is the interlocutor? Is it the loved one, or the reader, or a question addressed by the poet to himself and parodying the loved one's question at line 12? And do the brackets indicate a *sotto voce* of earnest solicitousness or of winking slyness? Or not *sotto voce* at all? 'Solo de lune', like the majority of Laforgue's work, is a poem of monologue and dialogue, involving the reader as a potential interlocutor; the reader can thus never locate himself in the text, since at any moment he may be thrust from the text by being addressed by it; thus he finds himself totally without privilege and *point de repère*, as subject to manipulation and textual double-cross as any persona within the text. Furthermore, because the Laforguian text is ventriloquial, quotational, intertextual, it is already a meta-language; we must therefore beware of believing that with any exclamation or offhand remark like 'Bon' we are breaking through to a real voice, or to an irreducible presence behind the process of fabrication; on the contrary, there may be no situations to penetrate through to, no person behind textual 'personality'; one can only get as far as the changing disguises, the shifts between different *kinds* of situation denoted by different *kinds* of text, in an infinitely recessive allusiveness.

But if Laforgue is a poet of afterthought, he is equally a poet of forethought. The line-initial exclamation is likely to be as prosodically disturbing as the line-terminal one. In lines 104-5, for example:

> Ah! que ne suis-je tombé à tes genoux!   1+6+4
> Ah! que n'as-tu défailli à mes genoux!   1+6+4

The 'Ah!'s' are like anticipatory enunciations added to decasyllables, as the 'Oh!' of line 103 is; they anticipate or introduce decasyllables, which by their very presence they undo. The reader has two ways of coping with the superfluity of these exclamations. The line-initial exclamation differs from the line-terminal one, in that it can be assimilated into the following measure and its accent removed; surrendering its exclamatoriness, it becomes something more like an anacrusis, a reflective liminary sigh:

> Ah – que ne suis-je tombé | à tes genoux!   7+4

But this assimilative manœuvre is self-defeating in the sense that it connives in the creation of an unequivocally eleven-syllable line. Alternatively, the reader can maintain the decasyllable at all costs, but this entails confirming 'Ah!' in its isolation and in its rhythmic abruptness; of course there are cosmetic ways of minimising its prominence or justifying its isolation e.g.:

> (Ah!) que ne suis-je tombé à tes genoux!

which would reduce its articulatedness, or make it more of an aside, an accompaniment to the line, rather than a part of it. Laforgue leaves it to the reader to cook the books if he so wishes, but will not let him conceal from himself that he is indeed cooking the books.

If I dwell a little on this prosodic chicanery, it is to emphasise two things: first that Laforgue's prosody, no less than Hopkins's, is a matter of transaction and negotiation. But whereas with Hopkins one has the feeling that the transaction is part of a common assault on the recalcitrant text by both poet and reader, that they share an objective, namely a sense-making construction of the text, with Laforgue the objective is concealed behind a protean front which changes with each attempt to fix it, and because the poet refuses to participate in the transaction, though he provides the transactability, so the reader derives no satisfactions from his suggestions. And the commerical image of transaction is perhaps peculiarly apt, because no poetry casts prosody in such a mercantilist light as Laforgue's; even though his poetry depends on the postures and cultural assumptions locked into the various forms of regular verse, it equally and continuously withdraws from circulation the currency of its numbers. Understanding cannot be bought with scansion; scansion is in some sense an acquisitive instinct which possesses its object by enforcing the assumption that poetry is a record, a fair copy, of what has already found a form; Laforgue would have us read his poetry as if it were the first draft of something which could only be revealed in the writing, and for that reason refused any further drafts; which is not to say that the poet begins writing without a *motif*:

Une poésie n'est pas un sentiment que l'on communique tel que conçu avant la plume. Avouons le petit bonheur de la rime, et les déviations occasionnées par les trouvailles, la symphonie imprévue vient escorter le *motif*.   (*Mélanges posthumes*, pp. 129–30)

In the second place, and relatedly, all free verse is more or less the desire to make experience simultaneous with the act of writing; the reading eye moves at the pace of the pen, does not merely read through what the pen has already completed. This impulse to remove anteriority from the text is of course not to remove memory from the text; but when traces of regular prosody are found in free verse we should imagine them not as structures chosen to inform utterance, but as structures remembered in the act of uttering; in other words moments of regularity in free verse are not moments of compliance, but moments of coincidence, of *déjà vu*, carrying with them no structural responsibilities, but inevitably injecting into the poem reminiscences of tone, context, cultural association, and habits of echo and anticipation. Of course, all this is a question of dosage and degree, but I would suggest that even in Laforgue's free verse, where regular patterns seem to dominate whole sequences of lines, the regularity is something encountered, played with, and its authority conspicuously borrowed. It is generally assumed that each free-verse poem creates its own prosody and that that prosody may be an amalgam of several different prosodic principles operating within the poem. Already we have noticed that the play between 'Oh!', 'Ah!' and 'O' constitutes a rhythm, and that these words have specific prosodic implications and consequences, just as different kinds of punctuation have. We might also point to the elements of regular prosody – derived in large part from 'Arabesques de Malheur' (No. 52 of *Des Fleurs de bonne volonté*), an embryonic form of 'Solo de lune', about which we shall have more to say later – as factors contributing to the poem's overall prosody. But to suggest that a free-verse poem has a prosody, however eccentric or however multiple its derivation, seems to me wrongheaded, in so far as it implies that the free-verse poem does *possess* its prosody. Given the instability of the *e atone*, doubts about synaeresis and diaeresis, and whether a verse or a prose segmentation should be practised, the most that a French free-verse poem can possess, it seems to me, is the ambiguity of its prosody. But does the free-verse poem seek to possess anything? Would it not be truer to say that what characterises free verse is not what it has, but what it allows, not what it resolves, but what it marshals, not the emergence of a prosody, but the interferences of prosodies, not a structuring principle, but a principle of structures. If Laforgue's verse vibrates between authority without authoriality and authoriality without authority, it is because these are the parameters of a prosodic field of activity ranging from all kinds of given prosody to all kinds of nonce prosody, which are mutually validating and invalidating; but the field of activity is what is important, not a product. Perhaps these propositions can best be demonstrated by reference to Laforgue's stanzas.

In regular verse, poems are usually homostrophic. Each stanza is a link in a homogeneous chain, guaranteeing structural continuity, tonal consistency and, once again, underlining the anteriority of the text. Each stanza has its end built into its beginning, is a mechanism of self-completion. A sequence of stanzas is a repeated rehearsal of particular procedures of disposition, organisation and interpretation, a repeated reminder of a pedigree. And the motor of the stanza is a prosody, finding a shape; once the shape is found, the stanza ends; the stanza has no option on its end, cannot really make anything expressive out of it, cannot enforce it; the stanza does not end, so much as undergo its end. The free-verse stanza is quite different. Usually without pedigree, theoretically infinitely elastic, guaranteeing no structural continuity but, on the contrary, constantly throwing the reader into the unpredictable, it ends because there comes a point at which it can properly circumscribe the field of its own structural/prosodic activity and because that field of activity must be activated by an act of closure. That end cannot be anticipated, other than visually, because the structural/prosodic activity is only defined in the act of ending, it cannot itself beget an ending. One might argue that in rhymed free verse, rhyme can still act as an imperative for ending; but rhymed free verse is free-rhymed verse, so that although rhyme carries within itself a principle of completion, it cannot set a time or place.

Let us consider the structural activity in the stanza which runs from lines 66–70. Lines 66–7 are bound together by their octo-syllabicity, by the repetition of 'Et', by the exclusivity of the first-person perspective, and by their forming a complete sentence.

Line 68 is related to these by continuity of theme – the coach-ride – and to line 67 in particular by rhyme. But it installs a pattern of syllabic increase which pushes it into structural collusion with lines 69–70; it is syntactically related to line 69: both have the pattern 3rd person + verb, 1st person +verb, and together they constitute a sentence; it rhymes with line 70. Lines 69 and 70 are related by their common trimetricity and by commonness of theme. Overlying these relationships are acoustic connections created particularly by |a|, |ã|, |u|, |ɛ|, |ʃ|, |s|.

The following stanza (lines 71–9) has an equally complex structural organisation, and I content myself this time with a graphic representation of it:

Sentence	Main clauses with subordinates	Repetition, verbal + syntactic		Rhyme	Syllabicity	Theme
1	1		La lune se lève,			
			O route en grand rêve.		5	
			O route sans terme,			
2	2		Voici le relais,			
			Où l'on allume les lanternes,		8	
			Où l'on boit un verre de lait,			
	3		Et fouette postillon,		6	
			Dans le chant des grillons,			
			Sous les étoiles de juillet.		8	

This representation leaves out of account acoustic patterning, but it is sufficient to show that the free-verse stanza is given its density, or integrity, by what it enables, not by what it confirms; even after its close, it is still a stanza in the process of formation; and the rhyme-scheme which might in other contexts be called upon to define the stanza, is itself as much in search of definition as other structural elements; the inexactitude of some of the rhymes (terme/ lanternes), the rhyming of singulars with plurals, masculines with feminines, make the rhyme itself makeshift, ad-libbed, arrived at rather than imposed or conformed to; it is just another structure which has found itself, and must compete for existence with other structures. In other words the free-verse stanza, as we see it here, is a stanza in search of stanzaicness; it is an organisation, or rather an organisational principle, which alerts to organisation without prescribing it.

We have spoken of the Laforguian poem as a first draft, and of its denial of anteriority. But of course, in a strict sense, 'Solo de lune' like the other *Derniers Vers*, does have a previous existence, in the abandoned project for a collection entitled *Des Fleurs de bonne*

volonté, which was superseded in 1886 by Laforgue's 'discovery' of
free verse; Michael Collie (1977) comments: 'What we now have as
Des Fleurs de bonne volonté is no more than a writer's notebook,
"un répertoire pour de nouveaux poèmes"' (p. 59). As we have
already mentioned, it was 'Arabesques de malheur' from this
collection which acted as a source for some sections of 'Solo de
lune'. 'Arabesques de malheur' is a six-stanza poem in octosyllables, whose stanzas, in *rimes embrassées*, are alternately masculine and feminine; Pia's (1970) notes reveal how uncertain
Laforgue was as to the 'proper' order for these stanzas (p. 558),
which is hardly surprising: a poet of the changeable could not but be
a poet of the interchangeable; Laforgue does not lean on argument
or narrative, to arrive at conclusions; he deals in the disordered
aperçus of memory and projection, in the waywardness of association, to arrive at a kind of finality which is no more than a tenuous
moment of self-mastery on the brink of further dissolution. But
Pia's further observation: –

Les vers de ce poème, sauf ceux du quatrième et du dernier quatrains, ont
été repris par Laforgue dans les vers 8–15, 32–35, 42–45 et 47–50 de la pièce
des *Derniers Vers* intitulée *Solo de lune*.　　　　　　　　　　　(p. 559)

– is a little misleading; the first lines of the fourth stanza:

> Oh! comme on fait claquer les portes
> Dans ce Grand Hôtel d'anonymes!

are taken up at lines 69–70 in 'Solo de lune', although here they
serve as an image of alienated loneliness rather than as the image of
the proudly exhibited legitimacy of the touristic couple, which they
are in 'Arabesques de malheur'. Similarly the final stanza contains
lines crucial for 'Solo de lune':

> Si on ne tombe pas d'un même
> Ensemble à genoux, c'est factice,
> C'est du toc. . .

But once again, 'Solo de lune' supersedes the thought expressed
here, presenting a critique of this kind of idealisation of equality,
making its peace with compromise. These adjustments of view
demonstrate, I think, that 'Arabesques de malheur' is not so much
a source or a first version of 'Solo de lune', but a quotation within it,
an intertext, and this distinction is important for the formal status
of those stanzas which are borrowed.

　　In alluding to material in 'Arabesques de malheur', 'Solo de lune' again changes the order of its stanzas: the first stanza of 'Arabesques' occupies lines 8–11 of 'Solo de lune', the second lines 42–5, the third lines 32–5, the fifth lines 12–15 and lines 47–50; 'Arabesques de malheur' is, as it were, imperfectly recalled in the writing of 'Solo de lune', recalled as a set of moves, without sequence, but full of consequence. And the stanzaic integrity of the 'Arabesques' stanzas is unpicked and rewoven, often into larger units, so that though the rhyme-scheme may remain the same, it acquires a structuring function in place of its structural one, and can only be artificially separated from the ongoing improvisation of and with rhymes, of which it is now a part. The third stanza of 'Arabesques de malheur', for example, runs:

Des ans vont passer là-dessus;	5+3
On durcira chacun pour soi;	4+4
Et plus d'une fois, je m'y vois,	5+3
On ragera: "Si j'avais su!" ...	4+4

Its equivalent in 'Solo de lune', at lines 32–5, shows that drift towards temporisation which we have already noted: the more abrupt, final and unequivocal 'durcir' gives way to the more gradual, imperceptible and relativised 's'endurcir', just as the more violent 'rager' yields to the muted, reflective 'se dire'. And the syllabic increase created by 's'endurcir' and by the insertion of 'déjà' destroys the isosyllabicity and with it the alternation of 5+3 and 4+4 segmentations which counterpoint the enclosed rhyme-scheme. In 'Solo de lune', the two middle lines introduce, through their heterosyllabicity, a groping prosody in which vestiges of the octosyllable may be reached for through individual measures, but which install the prosaic gait of a mind that has lost or abandoned the initial metrical impulse, the better to create room in, or dupe, a destiny. So often in Laforgue one finds these transitional prosodic stutterings, as one kind of enunciatory authority is shaken off and an alternative, more promising or more appropriate, authority is looked for. These are the moments when the disguise is changed, when we would feel that we were seeing the poet disarmed, more nakedly himself, were these moments not equally motivated by manipulative strategies; thus the pentasyllabic first measure of line 33 imitates that of line 32, only to deny us the expected following trisyllable; while line 34 opens with a tetrasyllabic measure which promises a return to octosyllable, only to veer off into a hexasyllabic continuation, adumbrating perhaps the three hexasyllables at the close of the stanza. And additionally, of course, these four lines surrender what stanzaic identity they may have had to a much larger unit.

Much the same could be said of the transformation of the second stanza of 'Arabesques de malheur':

> Que ferons-nous, moi, de mon âme,
> Elle de sa tendre jeunesse!
> O vieillissante pécheresse,
> Oh! que tu vas me rendre infâme!

As it appears at lines 42–5 of 'Solo de lune', this stanza is compelled to surrender its 2 lines + 2 lines syntactic structure, and become part of a 3 lines + 3 lines structure. And the new binarity is a binarity of increased scission: by the addition of the conversational 'Donc', like 'Bon' an erratic discourse particle whose prosodically disintegrative function far outweighs its semantic value, and the substitution of 'faillible' for 'tendre', the first two lines of the 'Arabesques' stanza become part of an imparisyllabic triplet (7, 9, 9) which thus differentiates itself radically from the following triplet of syllabically diverse, but parisyllabic lines (we may note in passing how Laforgue's reformulation of 'tu vas me rendre' to 'je vais me rendre ... en ton honneur' spreads the culpability). In fact, then, this stanza operates more naturally as a pair of tercets (pqr/rqp) than it does as a quatrain enclosed by a further rhyme pair (p/qrrq/p), that is to say, as a group of three temporarily unrhymed lines which find their way to stanzaic justification by encountering partners in the second syntactic movement. All traces of the stanzaic integrity of the original quatrain have been effaced.

We have already paid some attention to the other 'transcriptions' of stanzas from 'Arabesques de malheur', particularly those at lines 8–11 and 47–50 where stanzaic disturbance is engineered by the addition of the afterthoughts 'Bon' and 'Ah! ...' But we should stop to ask whether a regular or near-regular stanza can, by definition, exist in free verse, even though its lines may seem to be isosyllabic and its rhyme-scheme conventional. And this entails first asking whether a line which, for example, has eight syllables can be called an octosyllable, that is to say, a metrically motivated line. We have already referred to the ambiguating effect of the *e instable* and of doubts about synaeresis and diaeresis, about prosaic and poetic segmentations. But our point of departure must be still more fundamental.

Marjorie Perloff (1980), in her article on the line, suggests that Beckett sometimes wrote 'unlined' verse: '[Beckett] is rarely thought of as a poet ... Yet ... the rhythms of recurrence in his work are marked' (p. 867). Conversely some modern lineated poetry is, she implies, merely decorated prose: 'the line qua line, used without any particular concern for the forms of recurrence intrinsic to verse, and the relation of these forms to the structure of meaning, has become no more than a surface device meant to arrest our attention as readers' (p. 861). Many modern commentators, myself among them, would argue that verse is verse precisely because of the special kind of attention that the reader brings to it, and that this special kind of attention is generated by lay-out, by lineation. In other words nothing is intrinsic to verse apart from its relation to the page on which it is, or can be, written; its peculiar margin, its refusal of 'prose' margins, marks its organisation as structurally significant and activates the white paper around it. And the language of verse does not derive its characteristics, its obtrusiveness as music and its polyvalent forcefulness as meaning, from qualities which the language of itself makes conspicuous; verse is not a special kind of language within language, but primarily a structure which incites us to make its language special, to foreground its physical and acoustic features and, in doing this, to enlarge its semantic productivity. A passage of prose may potentially be more insistently and regularly rhythmic than a passage of verse, but since this fact is not highlighted, nay produced, by lineation, so it will not 'count', may be treated as accidental, may indeed be overlooked. Conversely a passage of verse may be rhythmically indeterminate or non-rhythmical, but because of lineation its non-rhythmicity will be part of its *raison d'être*. But one must insist that a characteristic more essential to the line than any consideration of metricity or rhythmicity, is that it *combines and divides*; it introduces junctures into the syntactic chain which may coincide with syntactic junctures but need not, segmenting syntax in order to release certain expressive capacities which would otherwise be ignored; in other words, crudely put, the effect of lineation is to transform language's functionality into an expressivity.

Definitions of verse which emphasise notions of combination and division, it might be objected, betray assumptions about the visibility of verse, its writtenness. But any oral production of a poem will make little verse-sense if it does not, as it were, propose a writeability, and besides, it simply must be accepted that our habits of perception are intimately geared to the writtenness of our culture; as Filliolet (1974) puts it:

Le support de l'écriture existe désormais, et existe au point de ne jamais se laisser oublier. Ce qui signifie, rythmiquement parlant, que les mots sont visuellement isolés ou groupés afin de constituer des complexes perceptifs. Or, comme nous l'avons déjà dit avec D. Delas (1973, p. 164), 'l'émergence du poétique visuel impliquait en premier lieu la dislocation de la métrique normative dont la rigidité bloquait l'évolution'. De nos jours le poème est donc vu dans un rythme avant que d'être lu dans un rythme ... (pp. 65–6)

These remarks seem to me just and illuminating. But regardless of the ascendancy of the written page, no rhythm or metre can achieve existence without perceptions of combination and division having first taken place; and such perceptions are perhaps more essential in French verse than in English, because, in French verse, the line is itself the unit of recurrence, rather than being the product of recurrent units. Prosody in French regular verse, as Cornulier points out (1982, p. 39), emerges only by virtue of contextual evidence and confirmation:

La définition que les métriciens dits générativistes donnent du vers en tant que 'réalisant' un certain *schéma abstrait* est donc insuffisante, puisque, pour qu'une expression soit un vers, il ne suffit pas qu'elle 'réalise', par exemple, le schéma abstrait *x x x x* (en ayant 4 syllabes); il faudrait compléter cette définition en ajoutant – et c'est l'essentiel – qu'elle doit réaliser le même schéma métrique que des vers voisins.

But Cornulier's notion of contextuality seems a rather restricted one. Might not intertextuality, too, provide the context? Are we not predisposed by the history of our own reading to recognise 8-syllable lines as metrical octosyllables, or twelve-syllable sequences as alexandrines? And is it not lineation itself which activates, or indeed imposes, this predisposition? Our answer must be a qualified 'yes', qualified because Cornulier is nonetheless right to emphasise that French metrical norms are extrinsic to the line, or rather that they must be extrinsically recognised before they can become intrinsically motivating, and that such recognitions are immanent to any given text. It is much easier for English rhythms to suggest themselves as intrinsic, simply because the recurrent units which create the rhythms are smaller than the line itself; French lines, on the other hand, particularly those without any internal articulation (caesura), that is lines 'à rythme interne libre' like the hexasyllable, the heptasyllable and the octosyllable, must establish their metricality, and their metrical normativeness, by reference to external factors, context (including intertext), the circumstantial evidence of rhyme, stanzaic formation, linguistic and stylistic features.

Bearing this in mind, let us confront that central problem which confronted the French *verslibristes* in the later 1880s: how to write non-metrical verse, or rather how to establish in the reader's mind that their verse might be non-metrical. After all, there is no reason, in logic, why a line of (by chance) eight syllables should be a metrical octosyllable rather than an utterance or sequence of syntactical segments which happen to add up to eight syllables. Unfortunately that very principle so necessary to confirm free verse as verse, to solicit the right kind of readerly attention, to activate those mechanisms of combination and division which peculiarly reward readerly attention, namely lineation, is equally the very principle which tends to metrify any circumscribed sequence of syllables. No avenue of escape lay in the direction of imparisyllabic lines or radical enjambements, which might destroy linear outline by encouraging the disaccentuation of line-terminal syllables, since these things had already been endowed with metrical status in the isosyllabic sequences of the *vers libéré* practised by poets like Verlaine and Rimbaud. In the Anglo-Saxon world, non-metricity is easy enough to establish: it parades itself in the refusal of recurrence; lineation may induce a rhythmic sense in the reader but cannot induce metricity in the text; and as metricity is denied, so rhythmicity may be relocated, may be found in other patterns of recurrence (lexical, syntactic, phonetic). In French verse, because rhythms are syntax-related and because metricity operates only at the level of the line, as a principle of numericity rather than rhythmicity – a metrical definition of the octosyllable stipulates eight syllables with an accent on the final (rhymed) syllable, it does not stipulate the rhythmic measures of which those eight syllables are composed – so *any* sequence of syllables is rhythmable and if that sequence is lineated, it is also metrifiable. French free verse was free to multiply its locations of rhythmic principles, as Laforgue does in patterns of punctuation, in his arrangements of exclamations and apostrophe, or in his treatment of the stanza, but while the line continued as metrically identifiable, it would enjoy an inescapable rhythmic priority. It was clear to Gustave Kahn, Laforgue's close friend and perhaps the theoretical stimulus behind Laforgue's adventure into free verse, that the tyranny of the syllable, and of a line identified solely by numericity, must be brought to an end. Broadly speaking there were two ways of achieving this. The first need not detain us, since we have already referred to it on several occasions: the destabilisation of the syllable by equivocations about the *e atone*, and about synaeresis and diaeresis. We should add that though the poet may wish us to see these equivocations as irrelevant, since the counting of syllables is irrelevant, as products of his own carelessness, we must, as readers conditioned to recognise number as a potential source of rhythmicity, interpret these same equivocations as strategies of avoidance. Edouard Dujardin (1922) may have declared 'Le vers libre ne modifie pas, il *ignore* le nombre des syllabes' (p. 14), just as Laforgue wrote to Kahn in July 1886 'J'oublie de rimer, j'oublie le nombre des syllabes ...', but this does nothing to change the countability of syllables, or the impulse to count; free verse cannot oblige us to ignore syllables, it can only encourage us to modify the significance we attach to numericity. The second way is that pursued by Kahn in his 'Préface sur le vers libre', which serves as a prologue to his *Premiers Poèmes* (1897); here he attempts to provide an alternative to a line-prosody by privileging units both smaller and larger than the line, namely the individual measure and the stanza. I borrow my description of this attempt from *French Verse-Art*:

Kahn sought to achieve his end by increasing the directness of the relationship between measure and stanza, so that the structure of the stanza was actually referable to a significant pattern of measures, and not to the grouping of lines or a rhyme-scheme. In other words, the line had to be minimised, if not eradicated, as a mediator between measure and stanza, as that which determined both the possible combination of measures *and* the nature of the stanza; to do this, Kahn needed to suggest, in a rather English way, that the line was not so much the key to, as the accidental result of, the arrangement of measures within it, that it had no stipulative function. This is how he expresses these ideas: 'Comment l'[le vers] apparenter à d'autres vers? par la construction logique de la strophe se constituant d'après les mesures intérieures du vers qui dans cette strophe contient la pensée principale ou le point essentiel de la pensée' (p. 27) ... And, more fundamentally, he attempted to undo the notion of number, of syllable count, as a principle of line organisation; what this involves is the establishment of a new principle for combining measures which is not numerical, but musical: 'Pour assembler ces unités et leur donner la cohésion de façon qu'elles forment un vers il les faut apparenter. Les parentés s'appellent allitérations, soit union de consonnes parentes ou assonances par des voyelles similaires' (p. 27). It equally involves not counting syllables beyond the boundaries of the measure. By this latter I

mean that while Kahn *must* count, must use number, to distinguish his
measures, and particularly his dominant measures [Kahn favours the
cohesive recurrent measure, the *leitmotif*-measure as a device of rhythmic
structure], he wishes the reader to forgo the process of aggregation; . . . put
another way, a measure of three syllables in a twelve syllable line is of
exactly the same nature as a measure of three syllables in a decasyllable, or
octosyllable, or pentasyllable; it does not owe its significance to the
measures it is combined with and what they add up to.   (pp. 197–8)

So Kahn makes, or seems to make, some allowance for numericity,
but it is a numericity of an extremely localised kind, a numericity
which promotes inter-linear reading rather than justifying
lineation.

Kahn's manœuvre for bypassing the line by giving prominence to
units smaller and larger than the line can work, paradoxically, at
the level of the line itself. Lines which are longer than a familiar
norm (i.e. over twelve syllables) or shorter (i.e. less than five
syllables and thus difficult to segment, to endow with a rhythmicity)
still function as lines understood as units of combination and
division, but not as lines understood as self-sufficient metrical units.
Laforgue uses tetrasyllabic or trisyllabic lines in 'Solo de lune' with
sufficient frequency for us to be aware of them as one pole of
non-metricity; lines like:

Comme un Ariel   (line 4)

or:

En ton honneur   (line 46)

are non-metrical (a) because there is no isosyllabic context to
establish their tetrasyllabicity as metrically determined and (b)
because they have no inner rhythmic structure, they enforce no
combination of measures (though they enforce a lexical combination), no fractioning of themselves into complex units. Thus in
order to make their tetrasyllabicity count, to endow it with metrical
value, we must view these lines as rhythmic segments of units larger
than themselves. In other words, in giving these lines metrical
status, we are denying their status as metrical lines, and in a sense
denying their status quite simply as lines.

Equally, and as we have already seen, we must demetrify (reduce
the accentuation of) longer lines, read them extensively, as prose, if
we are to maintain their integrity as lines, and not allow them to
become simply the accidental or convenient amalgams of shorter
lines. It may indeed be structurally illuminating to see line 25:

Cette impériale de diligence tient de la magie   5+5+2+4

the last line of a stanza, as the synthesis of rhythmic elements within that stanza, as the combination of a 5+5 decasyllable, corresponding to the 5+5 decasyllable that the first line of the stanza may be (line 21), and of a hexasyllable which draws together the trisyllabic lines 23–4. But this leaves line 25 peculiarly unrelated to the other sixteen-syllable line in the stanza, line 22, which we have already discovered is, if anything, a combination of octosyllables and which has no apparent metrical bearing on its immediate context. Similarly we may find it productive to see the final line of the poem:

Comme le frou-frou de ta robe est le modèle des frou-frou

5+3+4+4

as a combination, not of two kinds of octosyllables, but of measures which play some part in the preceding lines of the stanza: the tetrasyllabic measures with which lines 104–6 close and which echo the closing measures of lines 102–3, and the trisyllabic measures with which line 106 opens. But these justifications of an intensive reading cannot hide the fact that they attribute to these sixteen-syllable lines an essentially factitious identity, whereby the line is altogether too much the sum of its parts. I do not wish to disqualify an intensive reading; but we should recognise what repercussions such a reading has for the long line.

We are thus left with a contradictory pair of formulations. In order to underline the longer line's integrity as a line, we are compelled to demetrify it, in the sense of de-intensifying its accentuation and allowing an extensive (prosaic) reading of it, which leaves us more with an awareness of the number of its measures than an awareness of its overall number of syllables. Conversely, in order to underline the shorter line's integrity as a line, we are compelled either to overmetrify it (i.e. to endow it with a second accent), if such a thing is possible, e.g.:

Y a pas de port   2+2 (line 31)

or:

O clair de Lune   2+2 (line 80)

or, if such a thing is not possible, to fabricate a metrical context for it by adducing other examples of lines of identical length within the poem, with, ideally, some inbuilt metricity; such a manœuvre as this latter is bound to court suspicion, partly because any system of numericity is so difficult to establish in free verse, and partly because free verse's variability and unpredictability cast doubt on any attempt to create norms or models, or to suggest that any line has anything more than its own particular existence in its own particular verse-context; a perfectly tenable view of the line in free verse is that it can neither confirm anything nor project anything. Otherwise the short line is open to treatment as a non-metrical fragment of a larger utterance which may or may not be metrical, a fragment whose lineation marks a certain lexical combination and a certain urge to expressivity, but does not constitute it as a line in any metrical sense.

If we have used the short and the long line to polarise certain tensions in free verse, between extensive and intensive readings, between the non-metrical and the metrical, between the line as fragment and the line as compound, we should acknowledge that the same tensions operate, if less visibly, in lines of the middle range whose potential metricity is much more firmly established. Any octosyllable, for example one of those 'borrowed' from 'Arabesques de malheur':

> Un spleen me tenait exilé

not only offers itself as a typically ambivalent metrical octosyllable: 5+3/2+3+3, but equally as a compound of measures whose real *raison d'être* is not that they belong to this particular octosyllable, but that they echo measures of the same length in their immediate vicinity, or again as a 'prose' fragment which happens to be countable as an eight-syllable unit and whose only accentuation corresponds to the act of lineation itself, occurring on the last syllable of the line. How mistaken it would be, in the light of this range of possibilities, to assume that those stanzas in 'Solo de lune' which resemble most closely octosyllabic quatrains from 'Arabesques de malheur', namely lines 8–11 and 47–50, are octosyllabic quatrains, slightly disturbed by a final added syllable; true, the extra syllables do have a disturbing effect, but what they disturb is already only an octosyllabic stanza in one of its guises, a guise that has no priority over others. And how mistaken it would be to assume that line 36:

> Mais mariés de même, ne se fût-on pas dit   3+2+7/5+7

is an alexandrine, with a displaced *césure enjambante* at the fifth syllable. Might it not equally be the compound of a 'metrical' pentasyllable and a 'metrical' heptasyllable, or simply a sequence of twelve 'prose' syllables with one major syntactical juncture within it?

Similar questions might be asked about all lines. Laforgue's free verse eases us out of metrical ways of thinking, out of a certain panic to restore to prosodic respectability those lines which might strike us as aberrant, by polarising our reading between the short line which is a fragment and metrically no line, and the long line which can only be read as a line if it is demetrified or re-metrified in a prose direction, in the direction of casual utterance. If this kind of free verse tugs us both towards lineated prose and towards standard verse structures, it does so not by creating a restless oscillation, but by encouraging the reader to occupy a stable territory of looser prosodic thinking where the imperiousness of regular prosody has been left behind, but its applicability not forgotten. The free-verse poet, after all, is only trying to raise the reader's level of prosodic tolerance and to foster the ability to entertain more prosodies concomitantly.

This chapter has been unavoidably selective in its treatment of free verse and in its analysis of 'Solo de lune'. But it has achieved its purpose if it has done something to reveal the taxing, but rewarding, finesse of Laforgue's verse-art, the way in which free verse may relocate structural and prosodic principles in odd corners of the text and the fundamental rethinking of stanzaic function necessitated by free verse. Above all, though, it has sought to demonstrate that the notion of lineation and the notion of line, in a metrical sense, are not coextensive in free verse; lineation is an attention-inciting principle of combination and division, where the attention incited is an attention-to-verse; the line, in a metrical sense, is a spatially isolated or isolatable sequence of words which fulfil certain prosodic stipulations extrinsically established so that they may be intrinsically motivating. Such a distinction seems easy enough to make in theory, but in practice we are loath to admit that lineation is a more fundamental condition of verse than the metrical line, and for that reason are equally loath to surrender the metrical line to lineation, when there is the slightest chance of maintaining its metricity. This seems peculiarly perverse, since lineation is a ground-state which encompasses metricity in all its degrees, along with non-metricity in all *its* degrees. And it is only the faint-hearted reader who views with dread the contamination of the former by the latter.

CONCLUSION

CHOICE AND AUTHORITY IN VERSE

Verse is one of the most highly coded,[1] if not *the* most coded, kinds of discourse, and it is a kind of coded discourse in which, paradoxically, the codes operate to give the text pure performance value, that is, the poetic text does not reveal its origins in a competence; the poetic text is understandable as the manifestation or realisation of a set of codes and yet is ultimately irreducible, unparaphrasable, and is subject to processes of abstraction only if its parts are separated and considered in isolation. The reasons why the poetic text is, relatively speaking, a surface structure whose deep structure is invisible, a *parole* without a *langue*, are that its codes are so manifold that they are non-coincident, and that at any given point in the text one code may have predominance over the others; in other words the codes operate in a complex permutational structure of shifting priority. In regular verse, for example, the following, by no means exhaustive, set of codes is active: lineation (as a code of a certain kind of readerly attention); metricity, which entails numericity; rhythmicity; rhyme; codes of other acoustic patterns; a rhetorical code (code of figures); a grammatical and syntactic code (including peculiarly poetic forms of grammar and syntax e.g. inversion, ellipsis, iteration, special punctuational usage); a dictional code (code of register); a generical code (attitudes and treatment consonant with the poem's being elegy, ode, satire etc.); a formal code, which may relate to the generical but need not (the overall structures of fixed forms such as the sonnet, triolet, haiku, stanzaic structures of non-fixed forms). It might be proposed that the classical ideal in poetry is the satisfaction of all codes at all points in the poem. But, by the nature of things, such an ideal is unattainable, because at every point in the poem one or more of the codes will be more determining than the others, and the determining codes are never consistently the same. Thus, in the regular French line, at the rhyme position, the rhyme code, metrical code and stanzaic code will have a natural ascendancy: it will be more important that the word in the line-terminal position rhymes, that it can carry an accent, that it is masculine or feminine, singular or plural, that it confirms a certain rhyme-scheme, than that it is rhetorically, generically, syntactically or semantically consistent, or that it has acoustic connections with words *within* the line. In a celebrated passage, Valéry describes a similar set of codal stipulations:

> Je cherche un mot (dit le poète) un mot qui soit:
> féminin,
> de deux syllabes,
> contenant P ou F,
> terminé par une muette
> et synonyme de brisure, désagrégation;
> et pas savant, pas rare.
> Six conditions – au moins! ('Autres Rhumbs')

It is generally agreed that the word Valéry was looking for was indeed discovered: 'rupture' in the final stanza of 'Les Grenades':

> Cette lumineuse rupture
> Fait rêver une âme que j'eus
> De sa secrète architecture.

But we can see, supposing that the problem of rhyme-sound did not require solution (although 'architecture' may have already been in Valéry's mind), that not all these conditions are equally imperious; the sixth and third are mere desiderata, the fifth leaves some area of play, the first and second intimate that the poet is loath to change the rest of the line, to lose the feminine form of 'lumineuse' and the softening and protracting effects of the articulated e's. But the only condition which is obligatory is the one which relates to the alternation of rhyme-gender (given that this particular poem complies with that 'rule'), namely the fourth.

This hierarchy of codes will change as different locations within the poem are considered. At every point in the sequence of the text, the fulfilment of some of the codes will be obligatory, while the fulfilment of others will be merely desirable. In the line from Baudelaire's 'Harmonie du Soir', for instance:

> Valse mélancolique et   vertige!

the codes of rhetoric and numericity would seem to be the paramount considerations for satisfactorily filling the gap; the poet needs a three-syllable sequence, and, to fulfil the chiastic pattern noun + adjective + adjective + noun, he needs an adjective. Thus what is required is a trisyllabic adjective which will complete the tetrametric structure by bringing an accent with it. Other considerations would be semantic and acoustic ones: since 'vertige' is related in sense to 'valse', is an effect of 'valse', so the looked-for adjectives should have semantic affiliations with 'mélancolique', possibly as of effect to cause; and since, furthermore, 'vertige' has acoustic connections with both 'valse' (|v|) and 'mélancolique' (|i|), we might expect the looked-for adjective to do likewise; but these needs are not so pressing as the first-mentioned. The adjective which fills the gap is 'langoureux' which fulfils all conditions, relating acoustically to 'mélancolique' through |lã| and to 'valse' through |l| only.

Of course I do not wish to give the impression that the writing of poetry is an unrelenting and strenuous process of gap-filling, or that the text is put together word by word. But it remains true that the reader must regard each word as chosen, for some effect or other, and that the reader is free to test each word as choice, by the simple expedient of substituting and assessing alternatives. But critical analysis has tended to concern itself little with choice, other than in specific instances, usually highlighted by the existence of variants. Our sense of the poem as a sequence of interrelated choices is thus extremely undeveloped, as is our sense of the mutations of those conditions which govern choice and of the poem as a shifting web of changing priorities. And yet it is these things which, it might be argued, constitute the very essence of poeticity and the secret of poetry's irreducibility. And because we are not attuned to choice and its principles, so our sense of what is not chosen, of what is resisted or simply ignored is equally undeveloped. And yet what is omitted not only defines the 'choiceness' of what is chosen, but is, as it were, the shadowed side of the poem, is part of the poem's potentiality, or something the poem constantly alludes to.

One of A. E. Housman's *Last Poems*, for example, begins with the stanza:

> Tell me not here, it needs not saying,
> What tune the enchantress plays
> In aftermaths of soft September
>   Or under blanching mays,
> For she and I were long acquainted
>   And I knew all her ways.

(the 'enchantress' is Nature). In the fourth line here we might ask if 'blanching' is the best word, whether 'whitening' or 'blossoming' or 'paling' or 'fading' might not be preferable. The iambic tetrameter (with its alternating unrhymed feminine endings and rhymed masculine ones) stipulate a dissyllable with falling rhythm and all our alternatives fit the bill (supposing 'whit'ning' and 'bloss(o)ming'). 'Blanching' has the 'advantage' of an archaising poetic flavour, of including in its range of meaning the two directions 'whiten' and 'discolour' ('fade', 'pale') and of being acoustically affiliated to '*en*chan*tress*' and '*a*fterm*a*ths', so that the blossoming of the mays is not only like a spell cast over them, but already has something melancholy and twilit about it; 'blanching' also has overtones of deathliness and fear, so that the notion of the springlike is betrayed. None of the alternatives has this same versatility; 'blossoming' is too singleminded and is made redundant by the fact that we understand 'blossoming' in 'may' (may=blossoming hawthorn). 'Whiten' is too neutral and purely colouristic. 'Fade' and 'pale' are only one dimension of 'blanch', but would assonate with the masculine rhymes (and the first feminine ending) and thus have a poignant contrastive relationship with their youthfully capricious overtones (plays, mays, ways). Thinking about these alternatives helps us to define the appropriateness of 'blanching', but it makes the alternatives available too, as potentialities offered by the verse-structure. And this is a principle which it is important to underline: in prose, and in free verse as we shall see, choice cannot be rationalised or justified by the pressure of codes to the same degree that it can in regular verse, and for that reason our awareness of choice is less activated; in regular verse, on the other hand, choice *can* be rationalised and justified by the pressure of codes and, for that reason, so can alternative, non-utilised choices; in regular verse, the chosen always opens on to the left aside, includes it as one of its own potentialities (assuming, of course, that the left aside satisfies the dominant code's stipulations). Thus, in this particular instance, 'fading' and 'paling' and, to a lesser extent, 'whitening' and 'blossoming', are present in 'blanching' by virtue of the fact that the play of codes allows them, that there is no technical reason for refusing them. And equally, of course, in a poem like this, in which unrhymed lines occur, we shall often hear 'avoided' rhymes: hear, for example, a 'remember', trying to answer 'September', or a 'betraying' trying to establish itself as a partner for 'saying'.

But if critical analysis has not paid sufficient attention to the patterns and repercussions of choice, nor has it offered any suggestions about the changing significance of choice. We have proposed that choice is less visible in prose and free verse, because the structures which motivate them are less visible. But do we mean by that that choice is less significant in prose and free verse? Or, put more generally, is it true to say that the more limited the field of choice, the more significant the choice made? Is it a more deliberate, a more committing, a more meaningful act to choose one from two, rather than one from fifty-two? And if there is no principle of choice to refer to, and therefore no alternative, might this not mean that the item in question was somehow, inescapably, the only possibility, the absolutely necessary word, brooking no second thought? Presumably the answer to these questions depends on one's critical leanings; the more intentionalist one's persuasions, for example, the more likely one is to argue that all choices are equally significant. Faced with this line from Baudelaire's 'Parfum exotique':

Des hommes dont le corps est mince et vigoureux

we might justifiably suppose that 'vigoureux' belongs to a fairly limited family of possibilities: 'langoureux', 'amoureux', 'généreux', 'ténébreux' etc., some of which are not particularly plausible, while 'mince' might be replaced by a much larger set of items: monosyllabic adjectives applicable to the human body. Can we say that we respond more vividly to 'vigoureux' as choice because we are aware of what it is competing with and that a consequence of our response to it as choice is precisely the covert activity of those competitors? Can we say that we respond to 'mince' less as choice, because its paradigmatic field is so large, and that we are thus less likely to envisage alternatives? Or, on the contrary, can we propose that because the field is large, the choice is more crucial, more purposeful, even though the pressingness of alternatives escapes us? I leave these questions open. It is not my concern to provide answers, but to draw attention to the complexity of attitude and response within poetry's protean codedness.

Free verse only complicates these issues, able as it is to allude to the codes of regular verse to almost any degree, and to create its own. I have suggested that verse's irreducibility is connected not only with the very multiplicity of its codes, but also with the fact that they may stand in relations of conflict one to another. In regular verse, it is easy to imagine how such conflicts might occur, particularly in poetry which has a significant element of parody, satire, irony. But conflict of code is almost the *raison d'être* of free verse, inasmuch as its very foundation, lineation, will tend to run against other codes naturally associated with lineation, i.e. metricity, numericity. And individual codes find themselves caught in a process of de-codification and re-codification, in which they may retain some codal authority, but cannot impose the conditions that they can in regular verse; they are, as it were, in conflict with themselves. In these lines from 'Solo de lune', for instance:

> O Solo de lune,
> Vous défiez ma plume,
> Oh! cette nuit sur la route;
> O Etoiles, vous êtes à faire peur,
> Vous y êtes toutes! toutes!
> O fugacité de cette heure . . .

we can see that a rhyme code operates, but we find it hard to assess its conditions: it allows half-rhyme (lune/plume), rhymes between singulars and plurals (route/toutes) and between masculine endings and feminine endings (peur/heure). This already much enlarges choice. But it may be that other conditions and freedoms from conditions also apply. And because the stanzaic code does not operate systematically either, even though stanzas come into existence, the end of the line is free to associate itself with any foregoing rhyme-word or to become, in its turn, a rhyme-giver. This opens up virtually the whole lexicon. And since the code of numericity works at best haphazardly, if it works at all, so we cannot say at what point in the line the rhyme should emerge; in other words, any end of line allows us to choose another rhyme simply by adding another syllable or so, e.g.

> Vous y êtes toutes! Oh! Malheur . . .

We thus find ourselves confronted by a code, apparently exerting pressures of choice, but these pressures cannot be related to any conditions and can only retrospectively and by chance be said to potentiate alternatives. Free verse is code-governed and yet none of the codes is ever finally ratified, nor do they, for that reason, have any stipulative capacity. Rhyme in free verse has an authority which it is incapable of asserting; it may be *endowed*, retrospectively, with a determining force, by readerly consent, but it cannot of itself exert that determining force.

What effect does this have on choice and the idea of alternatives? Consider the following line from 'Solo de lune':

> Renchérissons sur notre sort!

Since 'sort' is the rhyme-giver, since nothing binds us to an octosyllabic line, despite the octosyllabicity of the preceding line, since Laforgue's dictional code is so varied, we might envisage, say, 'destin' or 'destinée', or 'fortune', or 'condition' as alternatives to 'sort'. But we should recognise that we are simply thinking of synonyms, that is to say we are accepting the meaning of Laforgue's own word as the stipulator. But there is no reason of a prosodic kind why we should not expand the paradigmatic field to include any noun appropriate to 'renchérir sur'. If however we do imagine that the line does have some prosodic principle working in it, that it is eight syllables long for a reason (apart from the repetition of the first-person plural imperative form) which we cannot understand (but which the poet can), then the monosyllabicity of 'sort' will be the conditioning factor. But we may always wonder whether the line is an octosyllable because of the monosyllabicity of 'sort' or whether 'sort' is a monosyllable because of octosyllabicity. Either way, we must acknowledge that our ability to envisage alternatives is entirely dependent upon stipulations made by the line as it is already written and not by any codes borrowed from elsewhere; in other words, the poet alone has the power to suggest conditions and these conditions derive from principles invisible to us, because unverifiable; codes may be in operation, but we cannot consult them as motivators of choice, because they are beyond our scrutiny. Thus, in a sense, the poem can stipulate only what the poet has in fact chosen, and this is a crucial factor in the implicitation of the poet's authority, of which we shall have more to say in a moment; because the 'rules' governing the poet's choices cannot be penetrated, so those choices are absolutely arbitrary or absolutely necessary, but either way they are absolutely authoritative.

Where in free verse then does the reader have any opportunity to exercise his judgement in relation to choices made? The answer to this question will be 'nowhere', unless we feel that the one factor crucial to the poem's expressiveness and the one factor whose principle is apparently visible to the reader, is the principle of combination and division, namely lineation. While regular verse may make us wonder, given the codes, whether the individual words are the most appropriate, free verse asks us to accept the individual words – after all, what principles can we appeal to, if we are to wish to change them? – and allows us to wonder whether the line-divisions are the most appropriate to maximum expressiveness. But, of course, this proposal is inadequate. Where end-stopping functions as a presiding principle, as it does in 'Solo de lune', re-disposition of the lines is blocked, if the principle is not to be destroyed. And even where such an inhibition does not obtain, who is to say what kind of expressiveness a poem intends, or deserves? Since we as readers cannot hope to understand what motivated such and such a disposition, even though we may explain some of its effects, how can we justify tampering with it, other than as a desire to write a different poem (rather than a better version of the original)?

It is poetry's codes which confer authority upon it, and the extent of poetry's authority is proportional to the opacity of its codes; those codes are opaque in the sense that they are pure conventions and cannot be rationalised by reference to other processes; we may suspect that rhythm, rhyme and so on have their origins in certain physiological or organic principles, but no connections with such origins can be thoroughly demonstrated. And though any particular poem may be transparent in relation to its codes, the codes themselves remain obstinately impenetrable. This poses problems for the poet inasmuch as the codes constantly threaten to alienate his authority. He may, of course, appear in his own poem as a first person and assert himself through that persona; but this is authoriality rather than authority and is as subject to the codes of poetry as any other textual element. He can use figures, like apostrophe, to point to an authority beyond the poem, to the Muse herself, but in so doing he inevitably casts himself as mediator or medium, as the transmitter of an utterance which is not his own; furthermore, the poetic figure by which transcendence of the text is enterprised is itself assimilable by other codes. Laforgue's poetry, as we have seen, dramatises this particular predicament: on the one hand, he seeks through apostrophe to establish an authority for himself as poet, only to discover that this is no less a persona, and that apostrophe has a peculiar way of conniving with metricity; on the other, he invades his text, by means of exclamations which undermine the metrical code, only to find that authority is submerged in authoriality; the exclamation may disrupt certain codes, but it either establishes others or else circumscribes itself in its own contingency.

But fortunately there are solutions, solutions which, in regular verse, are paradoxically provided by the reader. For if the poem means, then its meaning can be seen to be meant; and poetic codes are merely the organisers and instruments of that meaning, meaning itself presupposing an author; and this may involve the reader's promoting authoriality to authority, by identifying poet with author, first person with a psychology behind the poem. If the poem, on the other hand, is 'difficult', is remarkable for its semantic polyvalence, and if, for this reason, an interpretative freedom and creative role are conferred on the reader, and poetic codes are seen as instigators of semantic productivity, then the reader will at least posit an author as authoriser of the ludic nature of reading, as maker of the structure which multiplies meaning, and as enigma at the centre of the poem's enigma; no poem, in regular verse, is uncontrolled. In free verse, the poet can establish his authority by the agency of those very codes, or by the agency of allusion to those very codes, which seem most to deny it, in the interests of their own authority. Laforgue again shows us how this works: while the reader seeks to explicitate authority in known codes or codes constructible from elements of the text, the poet encourages such explicitation only the better to compel the reader to re-implicitate authority; the sought-for codes do not sustain themselves, cannot, given the scrambling of numericity and free verse's unpredictability; the principles of rhythmicity and poetic organisation constitute a whole gamut of principles whose activity is recognised as significant, but beyond description, part of the poet's untransferable authority. Authority is no longer conferred upon the author by the reader, but wrenched back from the reader by the author. What we call irony is perhaps important not so much as a process of ambiguation, as a process of implicitation. When we speak of the modern ironist as an invisible or absent poet, we are speaking only of an invisibility, or absence, of the unequivocal; at the same time, however, we are signalling the *presence* of a poet who has made his authority implicit to his text.

APPENDIX

THE FUNDAMENTALS OF FRENCH VERSIFICATION

French versification is to be distinguished from English versification (syllable-stress metre) by the following broad principles: the integrity of the French line depends on the number of its syllables rather than on the number and nature of its rhythmic segments (French: *mesures*, English: 'feet'); the position of French 'accents' (equivalent of English stresses) is determined by the syntactic structure of the line rather than by the inherent stress patterns of individual words; the French accent falls on the last accentuable syllable of each syntactic unit in the line, and since these units naturally vary in length, French rhythmic measures obey no law of recurrence and no principle of regularity, and thus have no connection with the notion of beat; because French accents are linked with syntactic units (words or word-groups), they are linked also with pitch, and because the French line always ends with an accentuated syllable, there is a natural tendency in French verse for the end of the line to coincide with a syntactical break, that is, to be endstopped; it is for this reason that enjambement is potentially a greater transgression in French verse than in English. Individual lines of verse in French thus have a peculiar rhythmic autonomy and the rhythms of one line in no way predict the rhythms of the lines following.

Accent and alexandrine

The standard French line (equivalent in importance to the English iambic pentameter) is the *alexandrin*, a line of twelve syllables, with a caesura (point of structural division, often, but not necessarily, accompanied by punctuation and/or a pause) after the sixth syllable, dividing the line into two half-lines or *hémistiches*; there are fixed accents on the sixth and twelfth syllables. There are usually, but not always, two other, secondary, accents in the line, one in each hemistich, which is why the regular alexandrine is called the *alexandrin tétramètre*, e.g.:

Mais il faút | triomphér || du témps | et de l'espáce,
  1 2   3   45   6   7 8   9   1011 12

Arrivér | ou mourír. || Les marchánds | sont jalóux,
  1   23   4   5 6   7   8   9   10 11 12

L'or pleút | sous les charbóns || de la vapeúr | qui pásse,
  1   2   3   4   5 6   7 8 9 10   11 12

Le momént | et le bút || sont l'univérs | pour nóus.
  1   2 3   4 5 6   7   8 9 10   11   12

(Vigny: 'La Maison du berger')

We discover the rhythmic measures and the accents associated with them by identifying the principal syntactical units. To describe the rhythmic measures thus formed, we can mark up the number of syllables in each unit, putting a plus sign between them. So the rhythms of these lines from Vigny can be described as:

3+3+2+4
3+3+3+3
2+4+4+2
3+3+4+2

Coupe

The 'bar line' which marks off each measure within the line is the *coupe*, which falls directly after the accentuated syllable. The *coupe* normally has no significance for the enunciation of the line and does not imply a break or pause of any kind. It is a purely scansional mark. It does have some significance for enunciation, however, where the *e atone* (or e mute) is concerned.

e atone or e mute

Accent in French verse falls on the last accentuable syllable of the word or word-group. The qualification 'accentuable' is necessary because the word or word-group may end with an *e atone* which cannot, in any circumstances, be accentuated. An *e atone* at the end of the line is never counted as a syllable, but merely indicates that the rhyme of that line is feminine (lines that do not end with an *e atone* correspondingly have masculine rhymes). An *e atone* at the end of a word within the line is counted, and articulated, if it is followed by a consonant or aspirate h; it is elided (cancelled, not counted), if it is followed by a vowel or mute h. Thus:

Le navire roulait sous un ciel sans nuag(es)   feminine rhyme,
  1   2 34   5 6   7 8   9   10   11 12   e not counted

199

Commé un angé enivré d'un soleil radieux   masculine rhyme

1   2   3   4 5 6   7   8 9 10 1112

(Baudelaire: 'Un voyage à Cythère')

Coupe enjambante and coupe lyrique

Because the *coupe* falls immediately after the accentuated syllable and because an *e atone* cannot be accentuated, so, in the example above, the e of 'navire' becomes part of the measure following 'navire', thus:

Le naví: | re rouláit || sous un ciél | sans nuáges

$$3+3+3+3$$

similarly:

Je t'adóré | à l'égál || de la vóu: | te noctúrn(e) $3+3+3+3$

O vá: | se de tristéssé, || ô grán: | de tacitúrn(e) $2+4+2+4$

(Baudelaire: 'Je t'adore à l'égal . . .')

This kind of *coupe* is called the *coupe enjambante*, because the word – 'navire', 'voûte', 'vase', 'grande' – straddles the *coupe*, or is interrupted by the *coupe*. Some of the expressive effects of the articulated *e atone* and the *coupe enjambante* are discussed in Chapter 4.

In some circumstances, however, either for expressive reasons or because of the discontinuity of the syntax, the *coupe enjambante* may be an inappropriate way of dealing with the articulated e after an accentuated syllable. In Hermione's words to Oreste, Act V sc. iii of Racine's *Andromaque*, for example:

Barbare, qu'as-tu fait! Avec quelle furie . . .

'Barbare', syntactically, allows a *coupe enjambante*:

Barba: | re, qu'as-tu fait! || Avec que: | lle furie $2+4+3+3$

But expressively the line seems to demand the isolation of 'Barbare', to underline the stunned outrage of the epithet and the staccato nature of Hermione's thoughts as she struggles to collect them:

Barbare, | qu'as-tu fait! || Avec que: | lle furie $3+3+3+3$

Here the *coupe* does indicate a pause, a break; the *e atone* is not an agent of liaison and continuity, but a space of loss, of speech-lessness. This *coupe* is the *coupe lyrique* (sometimes called the *coupe féminine*), the *coupe* which falls after the *e atone*. And it may be necessitated by purely syntactic considerations; further on in Hermione's speech, we encounter the line:

> Mais parle: de son sort qui t'a rendu l'arbitre?

To practise a *coupe enjambante* on 'parle' would be to disfigure the syntax, destroy the inversion of 'de son sort':

> Mais par: | le: de son sort || qui t'a rendu l'arbitre?
>
> 2+4+4+2

Hence we need a *coupe lyrique* here too:

> Mais parle: | de son sort || qui t'a rendu l'arbitre?
>
> 3+3+4+2

Rhyme

In French, rhyme was considered an indispensable marker of verse until the advent of free verse in the late nineteenth century. Unlike English versification, French versification recognises different degrees of rhyme. These degrees, most commentators would agree, are as follows:

rime pauvre or *rime faible*: homophony of the final tonic vowel alone (eau/blaireau; bonté/aimé)

rime suffisante: homophony of final tonic vowel + one consonant, preceding or succeeding the tonic vowel (père/frère; assauts/vermisseaux)

rime riche: homophony of final tonic vowel + two or more consonants, preceding or succeeding the tonic vowel (arche/marche; rêve/trêve)

rime léonine: homophony of final tonic vowel + one or more preceding vowels (polysyllabic rhyme) (nacrés/sacrés; désir, Idées/des iridées)

Classical French versification demands an alternation of masculine and feminine rhyme-pairs. Many would argue that there is an expressive difference between masculine and feminine rhymes, that masculine rhymes are abrupt, unrelenting, circumscribed, and that feminine rhymes are evanescent, yielding, reverberant.

The French terms for the principal rhyme-schemes are as follows:

couplets (aabbcc etc.): *rimes plates*

alternating rhyme (abab): *rimes croisées*

enclosed rhyme (abba): *rimes embrassées*

Appendix

Other lines

The caesura is a feature of lines of nine syllables or more. In classical prosody, the *impair* (line with an odd number of syllables: 5, 7, 9, 11, 13) is uncommon, and of the lines with caesura, the decasyllable comes next to the alexandrine in order of significance. The caesura of the decasyllable usually falls after the fourth or sixth syllable, creating a three-accent-per-line norm:

Il est un air pour qui je donnerais	4‖2+4
Tout Rossini, tout Mozart et tout Weber, [pron. Wèbre]	4‖3+3
Un air très vieux, languissant et funèbre	4(2+2)‖3+3
Qui pour moi seul a des charmes secrets.	4‖3+3

(Nerval: 'Fantaisie')

Although less common, the 5‖5 decasyllable is by no means exceptional, and is rhythmically more volatile, varying between 2, 3 and 4 accents-per-line:

Il m'a répondu: ce n'est point assez,	5‖5
Ce n'est point assez de tant de tristesse;	5‖2+3
Et ne vois-tu pas que changer sans cesse	5‖3+2
Nous rend doux et chers les chagrins passés?	3+2‖3+2

(Musset: 'Chanson')

The octosyllable is the most popular of the lines without caesura; located between the three-accents-per-line decasyllabic norm on the one hand and the two-accents-per-line hexasyllabic norm on the other, it is always rhythmically mercurial, often rhythmically ambivalent:

Elle se répand dans ma vie	5+3
Comme un air imprégné de sel	3+5/3+3+2
Et dans mon âme inassouvie	4+4
Verse le goût de l'éternel.	4+4/1+3+4

(Baudelaire: 'Hymne')

For an exploration of the octosyllable, see Chapter 2.

Accent contre-tonique and **accent oratoire**

So far we have dealt with the prosodic accent, the *accent tonique*; and for scansional purposes, for the purposes of establishing the rhythm of the line, the *accent tonique* is the only kind of accent that matters. But in enunciating the line, we may introduce voice accents either as a support for the tonic accent, or as agents of emotional or rhetorical intensification. The *accent contre-tonique* (marked `) is a support-accent in syllabically extended measures, a point of relay for the voice, particularly in polysyllables; it falls two syllables before the tonic accent, that is to say, on the ante-penultimate syllable of an accentuated polysyllable without final *e atone*, e.g.:

> Et ne triòmphera ‖ que pour te còuronner 6+6
> (Corneille: *Cinna*, Act I, sc. 1)

> Porte le soleil noir ‖ de la Mélàncolie 1+5+6
> (Nerval: 'El Desdichado')

The *accent oratoire* (or *accent d'intensité*) is an expressive accent which encodes the voice's (poet's) emotional involvement in the word, usually adjective or adverb. This accent falls on the first consonant of the word and resonates through the following vowel, so that, to all intents and purposes, it is a syllabic accent, e.g.:

> *Ri*dicule pendu, tes douleurs sont les miennes! 3+3+3+3
> (Baudelaire: 'Un Voyage à Cythère')
> Ailleurs, bien loin d'ici! trop tard! *jamais* peut-être! 2+4+2+4
> (Baudelaire: 'A une passante')

In this latter example, Baudelaire's own italics indicate that we should read 'jamais' with an *accent oratoire*, thus '*ja*mais'.

The liberation of classical verse

Alexandrin trimètre

One of the features of the Romantic re-invigoration of French verse, apart from new departures in diction, was the exploitation of the *alexandrin trimètre*, sometimes referred to as the *alexandrin ternaire* or *alexandrin romantique*. The *alexandrin trimètre* is, as its name makes evident, a three-measure line, in which the medial caesura is superseded or cancelled by the demands of a tri-partite syntactic structure whose middle unit straddles the caesura:

> Le scarabée ami ‖ des feuilles, le lézard
> Les marronniers, la verte ‖ allée aux boutons d'or
> (Hugo: 'Ce qui se passait aux Feuillantines vers 1813')

The syntactic structures of these lines demand a three-unit rather than a four-unit reading, 4+4+4 rather than 4+2+2+4:

> Le scarabée | ami des feui: | lles, le lézard

> Les marronniers, | la verte allée | aux boutons d'or

The superseded caesura, it might be argued, has become a dis-placed caesura:

Le scarabée | ami des feui: || lles, le lézard (*césure enjambante*)

Les marronniers, || la verte allée | aux boutons d'or

But this argument should be treated with some caution: the caesura is a *structural* division rather than a break marking the principal syntactic division, and the hallmark of the caesura in the alexan-drine is precisely its mediality. In other words, in the *trimètre* the caesura can only be either spectral or effaced. In the Romantic *trimètre*, the caesura remains spectral; the Romantic poets still ensure that the sixth syllable is accentuable, even though, in the event, it is not accentuated. In the poetry of the later nineteenth century, the caesura is often totally eradicated by the *trimètre*; in a line from Verlaine's 'Dans la grotte', for instance, the sixth syllable falls in the middle of a word:

$$\text{Et la tigresse épouvantable d'Hyrcanie} \qquad 4+4+4$$

The *trimètre* most frequently creates a $4+4+4$ pattern, though a whole variety of divisions – $3+5+4$, $5+3+4$, $3+6+3$, etc. – is possible.

Vers libéré

The eradication of the caesura by the *trimètre* is one of the characteristics of *vers libéré*, a 'liberated' verse practised by poets such as Verlaine, Rimbaud, Mallarmé and their immediate succes-sors. Other prosodic features of *vers libéré* include: the use of imparisyllabic lines, bold enjambement, the polarisation of rhyme in the directions of the excessively rich or the excessively poor (assonance), a disregard for the rule of alternation of masculine and feminine rhymes, an intensification of line-internal music, thus reducing rhyme's privilege.

Vers libéré and vers libre

But however far *vers libéré* went along the road towards *vers libre*, it refused to sacrifice the two factors which are the very cornerstone of regular verse: the principle of syllabic regularity – which meant that the poets of *vers libéré* observed the conventions concerning the syllabic status of the *e atone* and were meticulous in maintaining a distinction between *synaeresis* and *diaeresis* (counting immediately adjacent vowels in a word as either one syllable or two e.g.: '*nuit*' (one syllable), '*délicieux*' (two syllables); and the principle of rhyming, where rhyme is seen as an indispensable marker of the line and thus of verse, and where rhyme-schemes are the sole source of stanzas.

Vers libre undermines syllabicity by casting doubt on the syllabic status of the *e atone*, allowing it to be counted in the normal way, but equally allowing its suppression, both at the end of words (*apocope*) and within words (*syncope*). *Vers libre* also confuses syllabic counting by its indeterminate practice in relation to synaeresis and diaeresis. (For some consideration of these issues, see Chapter 6). It feels free to use lines of any length (where length can no longer be reliably determined, other than by the number of measures, itself always open to doubt) and to use rhymes (with all the freedoms introduced by *vers libéré*), repetition or rhymelessness as the occasion demands. Jules Laforgue was the author of the first *vers libre* to be published in France, in 1886.

Vers libre and vers libres classiques

Modern *vers libre* should not be confused with *vers libres classiques*, a form of verse to be found in seventeenth- and eighteenth-century fables, madrigals, elegies, idylls, etc.

Vers libres classiques are heterosyllabic and free-rhyming, in the sense that they combine standard regular lines (including *vers impairs*) in an irregular way; but they observe all other rules of regular verse (proper placement of caesura, alternation of masculine and feminine rhyme-pairs and so on).

NOTES

Prefatory remarks

1 In *French Verse-Art* (p. xii), I was at pains to discourage the haphazard application of the word 'metre' to French verse. In this collection of essays, I flout my own advice, partly to bring my discourse into line with that of contemporary French commentators, partly because in this restricted usage – metre = the codified or rule-governed part of a poem's prosody – there is little room for dangerous misapprehensions.

1 Theme and syllabic position: Lamartine's *Méditations poétiques*

1 I think particularly of the work of Poulet (1961, 1968), of Gaudon (1969) and Manning (1969), of Richard (1970) and of Ireson (1980).

2 'L'Isolement', 'L'Homme', 'Le Soir', 'L'Immortalité', 'Le Vallon', 'Le Désespoir', 'La Providence à l'homme', 'Souvenir', 'L'Enthousiasme', 'Le Lac de B.', 'La Gloire', 'La Prière', 'Invocation', 'La Foi', 'Le Golfe de Baya ...', 'Le Temple', 'Chants lyriques de Saül', 'Hymne au Soleil', 'Adieu', 'La Semaine Sainte à la R.-G.', 'Le Chrétien mourant', 'Dieu', 'L'Automne', 'La Poésie sacrée'.

3 Roy Lewis (1982, p. 122) suggests that the sadness of these short last lines in Lamartine derives from two sources: the reader's sense of incompleteness and a deceleration of reading speed. It seems to me that these last lines in 'Le Lac' are as much extra hemistichs as short lines and should be read at the same pace (whatever that is) as the other hemistichs.

4 e.g. Letessier (1968, p. xxxii): '... mais il est bien difficile de dégager de l'ensemble une ligne directrice d'inspiration, de tracer la courbe de pensée d'un livre édifié à l'aide de morceaux disparates par leur date, leur origine, leur sujet, leur forme'.

5 Birkett (1982) has traced the 'demimeticising' of language in Lamartine's poetry, the absorption of the real landscape into a purely verbal meditation, and shown how Lamartine transforms poetic clichés into 'fruitful generators of poetry'.

2 The octosyllable, rhythmicity and syllabic position

1   There is, for example, no entry on the octosyllable in Henri Morier's otherwise fastidious *Dictionnaire de poétique et de rhétorique* (1975). A welcome and illuminating exception to this state of affairs is David Scott's 'Mallarmé and the Octosyllabic Sonnet' (1977).

2   e.g. Grammont (1965, p. 43): 'Vers de la poésie narrative, didactique, dramatique au Moyen Age, il devient essentiellement le vers lyrique au XVIe siècle, le vers de l'ode, et garde cette fonction aux XVIIe, XVIIIe et XIXe siècles, sans cesser pour cela de servir toujours pour la poésie légère.'

3   This refers to a problem more frequently encountered in the hemistich of an alexandrine, where two accents are to be distributed among three accentuable elements: *noun+adjective+et+adjective*. Should the rhythmic segmentation be (noun+adjective) (et+adjective) or (noun) (adjective+et+adjective)?

4   This is an extremer view than that to be found in *French Verse-Art*.

5   These complementary impulses are discussed by Driscoll (1973).

6   For an extended examination of this pattern of meaning in *Emaux et camées*, see Hunt (1980–1).

7   e.g. Claudine Gothot-Mersch (1981, p. 13): 'Peu de métaphores, les mots sont employés dans leur sens propre, ils sont précis, et souvent techniques'.

8   I borrow these terms from G. Rostrevor Hamilton's enduring *The Tell-Tale Article* (1949, p. 8).

9   See Hunt (1980–1).

10   Beside Taupin (1929), one might mention Warren Ramsey (1967) and Serge Fauchereau (1979).

11   See David Scott (1977, p. 152): 'Whereas in the dodecasyllabic sonnet, rhyme very often comes as a confirmation of the end of a statement, in the octosyllabic sonnet, it has a more important function: it confers autonomy or integrity on propositions syntactically incomplete.'

12   See Letessier (1968, pp. 499–500). Letessier quotes Lanson's description of these two poems as 'ces deux moments de la même rêverie' (p. 500).

3 Figure and syllabic position: simile in the poetry of Wilde and Baudelaire

1   And it is the intervention of the line-ending which defines and prolongs the suspended potentialities of the unqualified combination of hope and bat.

2   My figures are based on the poems which appear in *Complete Works of Oscar Wilde* (introduced by Vyvyan Holland, London, 1968).

3   Examined by Graham Chesters (1975, pp. 80–3).

4 A privileged syllable: the articulated e in *Les Fleurs du mal*

1 I take my cue from Baudelaire's remark in 'Fusées': 'Deux qualités littéraires fondamentales: surnaturalisme et ironie'.

2 I count the repeated line 'Un cœur tendre, qui hait le néant vaste et noir' of 'Harmonie du soir', and the similarly repeated 'La mer, la vaste mer, console nos labeurs' of 'Moesta et errabunda' as single occurrences. And I discount its single appearance in the rhyme-position ('Les Yeux de Berthe', line 9).

3 I again discount its appearance in the rhyme-position, in 'Le Voyage' (line 107).

4 That is, they borrow their initial consonant from the previous word.

5 Delas (1977) assigns to the *accent oratoire*, which he calls the *accent d'expression*, 'une place relativement libre: IN-CON-TES-TABLE, IN-contestable, in-CONtestable' (p. 60). He distinguishes between intellectual and affective expressive functions, as does Mazaleyrat (1974), who further proposes that while the affective accent strikes the first consonant and reverberates through the following vowel, the intellectual accent strikes the beginning of the word in question, usually the first vowel (pp. 112–13). It is the affective accent which particularly concerns me and which is peculiar to poetic utterance; and it is to this that my use of *accent oratoire* refers.

6 See my comments in *French Verse-Art*, pp. 48–9, 69–70.

7 Note again a purely negative 'vastes' and again supplied with an articulated e.

5 Rhythmicity and metricity: Hopkins's 'The Windhover' and Mallarmé's 'Le Tombeau de Charles Baudelaire'

1 For a discussion of the question of derivation and for a history of the pure-stress tradition in English verse, see Walter Ong (1949).

2 'Similitude entre les vers, et vieilles proportions, une régularité durera parce que l'acte poétique consiste à voir soudain qu'une idée se fractionne en un nombre de motifs égaux par valeur et à les grouper' ('Crise de vers').

3 'But he spake of the temple of his body' (John, 2:29); 'What? know ye not that your body is the temple of the Holy Ghost which is in you?' (I Corinthians, 6:19).

4 'Périssons' here refers to no death, I think, but has the sense of 'expirons' in 'Toute l'âme résumée': as a result of reading (inhaling) *Les Fleurs du Mal*, we exhale our whole souls; reading Baudelaire draws out the very quick of our being.

Conclusion: Choice and authority in verse

1 I do not use the term 'code', in the following discussion, in any semiological sense; my codes have nothing to do with those identified

by Roland Barthes in *S/Z* (1970) or Michael Riffaterre in *Semiotics of Poetry* (1978), to cite but two examples. I use 'code' to describe not what has been encoded, but what has been codified or is codifiable, as in the legal sense; 'code', in my usage, falls somewhere between 'rules' and 'conventions', and is preferable to both, because it includes both.

BIBLIOGRAPHICAL
REFERENCES

Austin, L. J., '"Le Tombeau de Charles Baudelaire" by Stéphane Mallarmé: Satire or Homage?', *Études baudelairiennes III: Hommage à W. T. Bandy*, Neuchâtel, 1973.

Barthes, Roland, *S/Z*, Paris, 1970.

Birkett, Mary Ellen, *Lamartine and the Poetics of Landscape*, Lexington (Kentucky), 1982.

Chesters, Graham, *Some Functions of Sound-Repetition in 'Les Fleurs du Mal'*, Hull, 1975.

Collie, Michael, *Jules Laforgue*, London, 1977.

Collie, Michael and L'Heureux, J. M. (eds.), *Jules Laforgue: Derniers Vers*, Toronto, 1965.

Cornulier, Benoît de, *Théorie du vers: Rimbaud, Verlaine, Mallarmé*, Paris, 1982.

Culler, Jonathan, *The Pursuit of Signs: Semiotics, Literature, Deconstruction*, London, 1981.

Davies, Gardner, *Les Tombeaux de Mallarmé: Essai d'exégèse raisonnée*, Paris, 1950.

Delas, Daniel, *Poétique/pratique*, Lyon, 1977.

Delas, Daniel and Filliolet, Jacques, *Linguistique et poétique*, Paris, 1973.

Driscoll, I. R., 'Visual Allusion in the Work of Théophile Gautier', *French Studies*, vol. 27, 1973.

Dujardin, Edouard, *Les Premiers Poètes du vers libre*, Paris, 1922.

Elwert, Theodor, *Traité de versification française des origines à nos jours*, Paris, 1965.

Fauchereau, Serge, 'Où Pound et Eliot recontrent Goumilev, Mandelstam et Akhmatova', *Europe*, vol. 57, no. 601, 1979.

Filliolet, Jacques, 'Problématique du vers libre', *Poétique du vers français*, ed. Henri Meschonnic, Paris, 1974.

Gardner, W. H. (ed.), *Poems of Gerard Manley Hopkins*, 3rd edn, London, 1948.

(ed.), *Poems and Prose of Gerard Manley Hopkins*, Harmondsworth, 1953.

Gardner, W. H. and Mackenzie, N. H. (eds.), *The Poems of Gerard Manley Hopkins*, 4th edn, London, 1967.

Gaudon, J., 'Esquisse d'un féminaire lamartinien', *Centenaire de la mort d'Alphonse de Lamartine: Actes du congrès III* (1969), Mâcon, n.d.

Bibliographical references

Gautier, Théophile, 'Paul Scarron', *Les Grotesques*, Paris, 1859 (1st edn 1844).

Gill, Austin, '"Le Tombeau de Charles Baudelaire" de Mallarmé', *Comparative Literature Studies*, vol. 4, 1967.

Gothot-Mersch, Claudine (ed.), *Gautier: Emaux et camées*, Paris, 1981.

Grammont, Maurice, *Petit Traité de versification française*, Paris, 1965 (1st edn 1908).

Guiraud, Pierre, *La Versification*, Paris, 1970.

Hamilton, G. Rostrevor, *The Tell-Tale Article*, London, 1949.

Hartman, Charles, *Free Verse: An Essay on Prosody*, Princeton (N.J.), 1980.

Hiddleston, J. A. (ed.), *Jules Laforgue: Poems*, Oxford, 1975.

Holland, Vyvyan (ed.), *Complete Works of Oscar Wilde*, London, 1968.

Holloway, Marcella Marie, *The Prosodic Theory of Gerard Manley Hopkins*, Washington, 1947.

Hunt, Tony, 'The Inspiration and Unity of *Emaux et camées* (1852)', *Durham University Journal*, vol. 73, 1980–1.

Ireson, J. C. 'Œil et vision chez Lamartine', *Mélanges de littérature française moderne offerts à Garnet Rees*, ed. C. E. Pickford, Paris, 1980.

Kahn, Gustave, 'Préface sur le vers libre', *Premiers Poèmes*, Paris, 1897.

King, Russell S., '*Emaux et camées*: sculpture et objets-paysages', *Europe*, vol. 57, no. 601, 1979.

Korg, Jacob, 'Hopkins' Linguistic Deviations', *Publications of the Modern Language Association of America*, vol. 92, 1977.

Kressler, Jane, 'Voices in Harmony: Gerard Manley Hopkins and Stéphane Mallarmé', unpublished Ph.D. thesis, University of Michigan, 1976.

Laforgue, Jules, *Mélanges posthumes*, Paris, 1903.

Leech, Geoffrey, *A Linguistic Guide to English Poetry*, London, 1969.

Letessier, F. (ed.), *Lamartine: Méditations*, Paris, 1968.

Lewis, Roy, *On Reading French Verse: A Study of Poetic Form*, Oxford, 1982.

Lodge, David, *The Modes of Modern Writing: Metaphor, Metonymy, and the Typology of Modern Literature*, London, 1977.

Lusson, Pierre and Roubaud, Jacques, 'Mètre et rythme de l'alexandrin ordinaire', *Poétique du vers français*, ed. Henri Meschonnic, Paris, 1974.

Malof, Joseph, *A Manual of English Meters*, Bloomington (Ind.), 1970.

Manning, J.-L., 'Les images aquatiques dans la poésie lyrique de Lamartine', *Centenaire de la mort d'Alphonse de Lamartine: Actes du congrès III* (1969), Macon, n.d.

Mazaleyrat, Jean, *Eléments de métrique française*, Paris, 1974.

Milner, Jean-Claude, 'Réflexions sur le fonctionnement du vers français', *Cahiers de poétique comparée*, vol. 1, no. 3, 1974.

Milroy, James, *The Language of Gerard Manley Hopkins*, London, 1977.

Bibliographical references

Molino, Jean and Tamine, Joëlle, *Introduction à l'analyse linguistique de la poésie*, Paris, 1982.

Mondor, Henri and Jean-Aubry, G. (eds.), *Mallarmé:Œuvres complètes*, Paris, 1945.

Morier, Henri, *Dictionnaire de poétique et de rhétorique*, 2nd edn, Paris, 1975.

Ong, Walter, 'Hopkins' Sprung Rhythm and the Life of English Poetry', *Immortal Diamond: Studies in Gerard Manley Hopkins*, ed. N. Weyand, London, 1949.

Perloff, Marjorie, 'The Linear Fallacy', *The Georgia Review*, vol. 35, 1980.

Pia, Pascal (ed.), *Jules Laforgue: Poésies complètes*, Paris, 1970.

Pichois, Claude (ed.), *Baudelaire: Œuvres complètes*, vol. 1, Paris, 1975.

Pommier, Jean and Matoré, Georges (eds.), *Théophile Gautier: Emaux et camées*, Lille/Geneva, 1947.

Poulet, Georges, 'Lamartine et le sentiment de l'espace', *Nouvelle Revue Française*, July–August, 1961.

'Lamartine', *Mesure de l'instant*, Paris, 1968.

Pound, Ezra, 'Irony, Laforgue, and some Satire', *Literary Essays of Ezra Pound*, ed. T. S. Eliot, London, 1954 (article 1st pub. in *Poetry*, vol. 11, November, 1917).

Ramsey, Warren, 'Uses of the Visible: American Imagism, French Symbolism', *Comparative Literature Studies*, vol. 4, 1967.

Richard, Jean-Pierre, *Poésie et profondeur*, Paris, 1955.

'Lamartine', *Etudes sur le romantisme*, Paris, 1970.

Riffaterre, Michael, *Semiotics of Poetry*, Bloomington (Ind.), 1978.

Roubaud, Jacques, *La Vieillesse d'Alexandre: Essai sur quelques états récents du vers français*, Paris, 1978.

Schulze, Joachim, 'Uberlegungen zur inhaltlichen Kommentierung dunkler Gedichte. An vier Beispielen', *Poetica*, vol. 8, 1976.

Scott, Clive, *French Verse-Art: A Study*, Cambridge, 1980.

Scott, David, 'Mallarmé and the Octosyllabic Sonnet', *French Studies*, vol. 31, 1977.

Sprinker, Michael, *'A Counterpoint of Dissonance': The Aesthetics and Poetry of Gerard Manley Hopkins*, Baltimore (Maryland), 1980.

Taupin, René, *L'Influence du symbolisme français sur la poésie américaine (1910–1920)*, Paris, 1929.

Taylor, S. W. et al. (Bristol Poetry Group), *Introduction to French Poetry*, Bristol, 1983.

INDEX

213

Index